I COULDN'T
Even Boil
AN EGG

A WESTERN WOMAN'S STORY OF
30 YEARS IN THE MIDDLE EAST

Elisabeth Lindesay

ELISABETH LINDESAY

I COULDN'T

Even Boil

AN EGG

A WESTERN WOMAN'S STORY OF
30 YEARS IN THE MIDDLE EAST

MEMOIRS

Cirencester

Published by Memoirs

MEMOIRS
PUBLISHING

25 Market Place, Cirencester, Gloucestershire, GL7 2NX
info@memoirsbooks.co.uk www.memoirspublishing.com

First published in England, December 2012

Book jacket design Ray Lipscombe

ISBN 978-1909304987

Printed in England

I dedicate this book to my late husband and to
my parents and mother-in-law, and to my children and
grandchildren, with all my love.

Contents

Foreword

Many years have passed since I decided to write this book for my grandchildren about the wonderful times we spent in the Middle East between 1950 and 1980, when my late husband John was working for an overseas bank. My life in some ways has straddled an extraordinary time of change in the world, which I hope is reflected in the pages that follow.

I regret not asking my parents and grandparents to tell me about their experiences. I was helped greatly by both my parents and my mother-in-law, who presented me with all the letters that I wrote home at the time. They helped to jog my memory from time to time about things I might not otherwise have remembered.

Chapter One

BEGINNINGS

In 1943 my parents took me to Rossall School, near Blackpool, to take my brother Stephen out on exeat. While we were there we met John Lindesay, who was in his final year. I was 14 years old.

Both our families lived near Dumfries in south west Scotland. Our mothers had met while doing Voluntary Service, packing prisoners' parcels to be sent to our prisoners of war in Germany. They also made bandages for the wounded at the front. These bandages contained sphagnum moss, rich in iodine, which grew abundantly on the banks of the nearby Lochar river. I helped to collect it.

John's parents lived on the other side of Dumfries from Glencaple, the village in which we lived. Col. Lindesay had a silver fox farm at Loch Arthur, a farm on the edge of Beeswing, a village on the Dalbeattie Road. Being too old to take part in the war on active service, he became Colonel in charge of the South of Scotland Home Guard. My father worked in Glasgow and was Area officer for the Ministry of Aircraft

Production. He too had served in the First World War and was deemed too old to see active service in World War II.

Col. Lindesay had to leave the school early and return to work, so my parents were asked if they would look after John for the last day of the exeat. So far as I recall John was of little interest to me as he was not in the least bit "horsey", in fact he could not even ride. Apparently, according to his mother, my behaviour was such that John decided that he would have to "tame" me. He would cheerfully say that he was still trying to do so right up to the day he died of cancer in 1995.

When he left school John was required to join up and go to war. He decided to join the Indian Army, as his ancestors had lived there and his father had been born in Mao. As it happens he caught an early train up to London to sign up and become an Indian Army Officer Cadet, so he had left before the post arrived. In that post was a letter informing him that his ID number had been drawn and he was selected to become a Bevin Boy and was to go to work down a coal mine. This caused dismay and confusion on his return. He contacted the Indian Army to tell them about the letter, and was sent a long telegram informing him that he was in the Army now and was not available to go down any mines. This was just as well as he was six feet three inches tall and not really the shape to be a successful miner. He began his initial army training at Maidstone in Kent and then sailed for India in January 1944.

He was on his way to Burma when the war ended in 1945, and he was diverted to the Occupation Force in Japan. He was demobbed in 1947 and planned to become a doctor. However there were so many men retuning from the war that places at university were hard to come by. He did get a place at St Andrews to be taken up in three years' time. What was he going to do in the meantime?

He saw an advertisement for ex army officers wanted for three-year tours in the Middle East, no previous experience required. John applied and got a job with the Imperial Bank of Persia, as the Bank was then known. In the meantime he had met me again. I was just 17 years old and the taming process was due to begin! He was not permitted to marry on his first contract, so he went overseas to Persia and was stationed in Kermanshah.

I filled the time by becoming a nursery nurse at Langside College in Glasgow, doing my practical training in the slums there, which greatly broadened my education. I decided to concentrate on child psychology. This was to stand me in good stead in my life to come.

We became engaged in 1948. John decided that he enjoyed banking and gave up his idea of becoming a doctor. He would have been 32 when he qualified and he felt that life was too short. I felt this was a shame, as he would have made a wonderful doctor. He had "kissed the Blarney Stone" like many Irishmen, and had a wonderful "bedside manner".

As the date for John's return drew near I became somewhat apprehensive about leaving home and moving so far away. I also was a little anxious about whether I still wanted to marry him. After all I had not seen him for three years. I wondered if John had the same misgivings, as he asked me if I would like to fly out to have a look at the Middle East and see if I could cope.

My godfather had left me a little money, so I decided to do just that. This was a very "avant garde" decision in those days, as I would be without a chaperone. I had never flown before, though I had been abroad to finishing school in Switzerland. I went out to Les Avants near Montreux on the first Golden Arrow train after the war in February 1946.

Wartime clothes rationing was still on, and my mother was fully occupied sewing and altering frocks which had been outgrown and passed down from older friends and cousins. This was an attempt to provide me with a wardrobe suitable for whatever would be required in Teheran, where John lived. I was in no way fashion conscious in those days, though I was very proud of my "new look" grey flannel suit with the nipped-in waist and long A line skirt. I knew what I liked and my mother did her best to provide me with as wide a variety of choice as she could. I think I had the original "mix and match" wardrobe.

The day came when I was to leave for Teheran. Mummy came with me to London by train. A friend of my father met us at Euston Station and we stayed the night with him. Next morning we drove out to London Airport, as it was then known. There were no smart terminals in those days. Nissen huts were ranged beside the mainly grass apron. My luggage was weighed and I said my farewells and walked out to the plane. My tummy was in a knot, partly with excitement and partly with apprehension. This was to be the first time I had flown. The roar of the engines seemed far louder than they are nowadays. It was so exciting looking down on the world beneath with people looking like ants, and vehicles which reminded me of my brother Stephen's model railway.

After five hours we landed at Rome Airport. I well remember the fearful clatter as our wheels touched down on my first landing. The other passengers and I all looked at each other with round eyes and mouths. We all thought that we must have crashed. As the din subsided, the stewardess apologised most profusely for not warning us that the runway at Rome was still a temporary wartime one, made of loose metal strips to prevent the planes' tyres from sinking into the soft sand. She would have to be more careful in future, as she might well have had to cope with heart attacks had we not been made of sterner stuff!

We disembarked and walked over the difficult, knobbly metal into the building and sat down to a three-course dinner. In-flight dinners were not served in 1950.

With the tanks refuelled we tottered out to the plane again and set off for Lydda in Palestine. We landed some five hours later. It was 5 am and the sun was shining on the barren desert. There were a few people sitting quaffing huge pints of beer, which made me feel vaguely queasy. This feeling was not improved by the offer of bacon and eggs in the airport building. I felt strangely disorientated and the hot air was stifling. I had not slept much during the flight, though I suspect one dozes rather more than one imagines.

This was my first taste of the Middle East and the first sight of the local people. Some wore curious unfamiliar long nightshirt garments and others were dressed in incongruous natty gents' suits, which did not look appropriate for either the climate or the time of day. I became very aware of entering a different world where I could not understand a word of what was being said. At least in France and Switzerland I understood French. The loud guttural voices were totally incomprehensible. I became slightly nervous.

Soon we were on our way again to Teheran. I was getting butterflies in my tummy. Would I even recognise John? What would I do if he were not there to meet me? Would he still like me, let alone still want to marry me? I began to feel weak at the knees. What had I done coming all this way just assuming that all would be as it was when we had last seen each-other?

I looked out of the window and the earth looked dry and barren with rocky mountains stretching all around. Next we were flying over what appeared to be a huge bomb site. Below lay rows of what looked like half-ruined, half-built, flat-roofed houses, with occasional imposing edifices in the middle of patches of walled desert, sparsely dotted by a few green trees. What a desolate place this looked from the air. How different from our own green and pleasant land. How could anyone live here? Well I had done it now, I would just have to wait and see.

We landed and taxied across the sand. The steps were wheeled up to the plane and the door was opened. A great whoosh of hot air rushed into the plane, accompanied by a man with a flit-gun, which he proceeded to pump up and down the plane. I had not been aware of any flies and could have done without the smell of the repellent. Then I was teetering down the steps and all panic disappeared as I saw my John peering upwards grinning broadly, arms outstretched. In those days visitors could be met at the foot of the plane's steps and accompanied into immigration to collect their baggage.

We both kept talking at once and giggling joyfully. Was it really three years since we had met? We had so much to talk about and were so happy to see each other.

John had arranged for me to stay with a lady called Connie, who was the secretary to the General Manager. She lived in a little house in Kutche Berlin (Berlin Street). She was a lovely person and made me very welcome. Everyone was very kind to me and I quickly learned my way about.

The town looked much better on the ground than it had appeared from the air. There were , modern dress shops, and some expert television salesman had managed to persuade an agent to display television sets for sale, though no television station existed to broadcast any pictures. There were very few sets even in the UK at that time.

Modern restaurants stood cheek by jowl with local emporiums stuffed with intricately-carved silver and brassware, and local Armenian artists displayed their pictures to ladies dressed in long flowing chadors, which totally enveloped them and were held in place by their teeth. Some women wore European dress and black see-through veils over their heads and faces. I suspect that this made them look more alluring, as their features were blurred and often pock-marked skins were disguised. Much was left to the imagination. The men, on the other hand appeared to go out in their pyjamas, which is the only way I can describe the striped garments that many non-clerical males wore. Others wore ordinary European dress.

Things seemed very expensive, but I could not really compare with anything, as much would not have been seen in post-war Britain, let alone Dumfries. This was all a new world to me. On looking back I was very young and naïve and must have seemed so to the sophisticated Bank wives who gave such glittering cocktail parties and smart dinner parties.

John worked hard training me to do what was expected of me. I learned to call on my seniors (which meant most people!) I learned to bend down the corner of my visiting card when I called personally. It was customary to give notice and then call in the early evening, stay for exactly twenty minutes, drink one drink, then leave. This entitled you to an invitation to their next cocktail party. This was a good system, if a bit nerve-racking, but it did enable a newcomer to become known and absorbed into the community. A list of who to call on could be obtained from anyone "in the know."

Sometimes someone would do me the honour of returning my call. This caused a panic, as I was staying in a spare flat in the Bank compound lent to me by the General Manager. It was supposed to be for visiting VIPs. This was good for me, but the flat was not really equipped for entertaining. However John's bearer, Saleh, sprang to my aid and laid on drinks and eats and waited on me in the appropriate manner. I was unable to speak Farsi and he was unable to speak English, so we developed a strange pantomime of gesticulations which generated a good deal of unseemly laughter. He even provided meals at my flat on occasion.

It was while I was staying in the flat that I saw my first hanging. I was awoken one morning very early by the noise of people shouting and wailing. On looking out of the window towards the main town square I saw a body swinging from a scaffold. I was amazed to see people jumping up and swinging on the man's feet. I talked about this later and was told that this was a compassionate concession. It ensured that the person died quickly, because in Iran the noose was put round the neck and then the body was hauled up and the poor person choked to death. In Britain, when murderers were hung, a trap was pulled and therefore the neck was broken and it was all over quickly.

John and I dared not stretch propriety, in as much as we did not actually sleep under the same roof! There were limits, especially in the rather stiff and formal Teheran ex-pat society. I was taken to task for wearing "pedal pusher" trousers in the Teheran Club by a formidable lady known as PS. She had been a nanny to the Shah's family and was feared and respected by many in authority in Teheran. It was not considered proper for ladies to wear trousers, though I tried to explain that I thought that trousers were more decent than summer frocks when I rode on the back of John's motor bike. Seeing me riding on the back of his bike was almost too much for them as it was.

John persevered with my "taming". I loved it all and somehow I managed to pass the inspection all potential Bank wives had to undergo before being deemed suitable to join the

"Club" of sophisticated Bank ladies.

We cabled home and let them know that the wedding was "on", then set about saying our goodbyes to all our friends before we returned home to the UK. We were married in Glencaple Church on May 26th 1950 and spent our honeymoon on the Norfolk Broads.

All too soon we were due to return to Iran. We packed all our wedding presents and boarded the train for Paris, where we transferred to the famous Blue Train for Marseilles. John decided that I was worth another bit of luxury, so he booked us a first-class sleeper. Actually it was two sleepers with inter-communicating doors. It was extremely comfortable and it seemed a waste to just sleep through it all.

We arrived in Marseilles and boarded the SS Champoleon for Beirut. We had four days at sea and the Captain decided to christen me Mademoiselle Madame, much to my embarrassment. I think he thought that I was too young to be a married lady!

One night we passed close to Mount Etna as the volcano was erupting. The red-hot fiery lava was leaping high into the sky like a giant firework display, reddening the sky for as far as we could see, with the reflection in the sea giving the appearance of molten rock floating towards us. I think it was the silence at our distance that made it all the more eerie.

We disembarked at Beirut and I developed a tummy bug. This was my first dose of this painful affliction. The way my compatriots dealt with it was to drink lots of neat whisky! This was my first introduction to spirits and so far as I remember I was not too impressed.

John decided that I was in no state to travel by road to Teheran, so he booked me by air. This was by Iran Air and, as European women were comparatively rare in those days, I was given special treatment when everyone else became airsick. The Captain came through the cabin, saw that I was not sick and invited me to come and sit in the cockpit with the crew. The plane was a bit bumpy at the time and I felt much better sitting in the co-pilot's seat, where I got a good view of Iran. He allowed me to stay there as we landed. It was quite terrifying watching the earth rushing up to meet us, not to mention illegal for me to be in the cockpit at that time.

John set off with our luggage in a large taxi to drive to Teheran via Damascus. It took two and a half days to drive all that way, so I was quite glad that I had been sent ahead by air.

John arrived in due course at Haftdaskah, which means Seven Houses. This constituted the compound where the Bank ex-pats lived. I was staying with Angus and Elizabeth Macqueen. They were very senior in head office, but nevertheless were very kind to me, the newest Bank wife and the youngest by far. I had met them when I was last in Teheran. There were six spacious villas where the senior British staff lived and a larger one known as "The Mess", containing the British Bachelor staff and where John lived when I first went out to Teheran. Each had its patch of garden, and there was a swimming pool in the centre.

At this time I was totally unaware of pecking orders, hierarchy and internal politics, which made for a complicated life for those at the top. I was at the bottom of the order so I had few problems. I remained oblivious to infighting throughout my Bank life, though I was aware that petty jealousies existed. I think these will always exist where people are thrust together in a foreign environment and feel the need to shine in some way.

I was fortunate in that I never had to live cheek by jowl in a compound where all the houses were deemed the same. I always lived in separate accommodation wherever we were posted. These varied greatly from place to place and were furnished to assorted standards. I found that I had to try to make the best of what was on offer. Some of our homes were palatial, while others were very sub standard. It all made for an interesting life and I am very happy to say that I did not feel the need to "keep up with the Joneses". I was very lucky.

Chapter Two

ISFAHAN

We were posted to Isfahan in central Persia, as Iran was then known. I was very excited at the prospect of setting up our first married home. We loaded our few possessions into and on to a large taxi and left Teheran early one morning. It is better to start really early when travelling across the desert, as it is cooler then. Added to our luggage were several cans of petrol, as there were no petrol stations along the way. In fact there was no proper road for most of the route, as we were to discover.

The first town we passed was Qum, a Holy City. I clearly remember the golden domes of the mosques standing high above the window-less walls of the town. These blank, faceless, mud coloured expanses, surrounded the gardens of the houses, were made of a mixture of mud and straw plaster, smoothed over sun-baked mud bricks, hiding colourful Persian gardens from prying eyes.

After Qum the road, such as it was, ran out and the track deteriorated into hard, ribbed sand alternating with pools of soft shingle. No sooner had our driver managed to get up enough speed, as urged by my husband to lessen the juddering of the "ribs" of hard sand on the wheels of the car than we ran into a pool of shingle that brought us nearly to a halt. After a few hours of this we felt it was time to stop and eat our picnic lunch.

We were crossing a huge dried-up salt lake. As far as the eye could see there was little other than sand, shale and stones. The scrubby vegetation was scanty and showed no sign of life. Not even a bird, let alone an animal, could be seen.

We sat down on a zeloo, as the woven cotton rug is called, with our driver who was a middle-aged Iranian with the scruffy dark five o'clock shadow sported by most men in Iran. He spoke a little English but I found it difficult to talk to him. John made polite conversation while we thankfully tucked into sandwiches and tea from a flask. This was before the days of cans of Coke and beer, cool bags and air-conditioned cars. Bottles of 7 Up and Pepsi Cola were available but, as today, they would have become very "lively" after being shaken by the ruggedness of the track. We were seated on a small hillock to get the benefit of what cooling breeze there was and could see for miles.

Imagine our surprise when a voice said, "Baksheesh Khanum!" ("Tips Madam!") A group of children had suddenly appeared, squatting in a semi-circle, just behind us. Where on earth had they come from, and what were they doing here in this vast wasteland?

They were all thin and scrawny, dressed more or less in

rags, with rags round their heads and no shoes on their feet. Their beady eyes were riveted on our sandwiches. So far as we could see the nearest civilisation was some two or three hours away by car. We all felt greedy as we munched our food. We gave them the remains of our meal and a bottle of drink, watching in amazement as they gobbled it up, stopping only momentarily to stare at the unfamiliar apples we had given them. Soon they were gone, blending into the desert as if they had never been. We looked for them as we continued along the bumpy track but no sign could be seen.

We still do not know what they were doing there in the middle of the Great Salt Lake, where nothing grew and the dried-up pools where water had been were white with salt. On making enquiries at a later date, we were told that the children might have been cleaners of the qanats. These were an ancient underground water system developed to bring water from the hills through a series of tunnels, often several kilometres long, to provide irrigation for the villages on the edge of the desert. Periodically there were airshafts and it is possible that these children had emerged from one of these.

The day was hot and the dust considerable and the juddering alternated with the patches of shale for the next few hours. There was still no sign of vegetation for miles, and no sign of life. Then we saw a car going in the other direction. As we passed there was much "tattooing" on the horn and yells of greeting by the drivers. We assumed they must be friends, but it seemed they did not know one another. The other driver was a stranger and was not wise to be setting out so late in the day, we were told, as it was hard to see the track by night.

"He'll learn," the driver said, nodding sagely.

On we went. Then, in the distance, we saw a distinct shadow of vegetation on the horizon. We kept our eyes fixed on it and saw it gradually become an avenue of tall eucalyptus trees. Soon we could see the peeling bark and the dusty leaves waving in a desultory fashion in the gentle breeze. The track miraculously became tarmac and a few shabby mud walls lined the road. We were at last on the outskirts of Isfahan. We had been driving for some nine hours and were very glad to have reached our destination.

We slowed to a walking pace, as our driver was forced to weave in and out of horse-drawn *droshkis*, which, I was to learn, were the main means of transport about town. The other appeared to be to sit, balanced precariously, side-saddle on the rump of a donkey. These poor beasts of burden sometimes carried enormous loads. On one occasion I was to incur the wrath of one donkey-man when I pushed an enormous bale of cotton off the back of his poor animal. I don't think he understood my point, as he was pretty cross. My action caused much amusement to the passers-by. But I digress.

Before long we arrived at the Bank, a splendid stone-built, single-storey building with deep-set windows and grand columns on either side of the imposing door. We were greeted by the manager, Henry Walton, a tall, florid-faced, man with, we were to discover, a great sense of humour, which was just as well as it helped one to survive in Isfahan in the 50s. The accountant John King, whom my John was to relieve, was a young and amusing bachelor with a relaxed view of life, and he had a very relaxed attitude to living in this very rural town.

On our way to our new home we turned off the main road and over the wooden planks which had been laid down over the deep ditches, or jubes, which bordered the main road and crossed the entrance to the sandy *kutche*, or side road, that led to our gates. These ditches were the town's irrigation and drainage system. Wooden planks had been laid across at the entrances to enable the wheels of the horse drawn droshkis and few cars to cross.

The entrance to our new home was anything but new. It was however, grand, by Isfahan standards. Great double doors set into walls about 20 feet high, were opened by two men in navy blue Bank uniforms, cheered on by a small black and white woolly dog with a "chrysanthemum" hair-do. Once inside the gate the world became a different place. The driveway was edged with periwinkles and marigolds and the lawns were lush and green. Round the walls, lilac trees and hibiscus bushes and bougainvillaea grew rampant. In the centre of the garden there was a round pool with a fountain playing in the middle. A row of very tall umbrella pine trees stood at the end of the garden, inhabited by some very noisy crows.

The house was very long and low with a flat roof; it was built of gatch, or mud and straw, as were most buildings in Isfahan. It reminded me of the old railway carriages, as all the rooms led from one to the other through double doors. If one stood on a chair at one end one could see through the fanlights above the doors from one end of the house to the other. The dining room led into the study, which in turn led into the 30-foot drawing room in the centre. There were several very large overstuffed easy chairs covered in puce linen, patterned with huge cornucopias of roses that matched the curtains all along the veranda windows. A fitted zelou covered the floor and double doors opened into a small sitting room, which in turn opened into the guest bedroom. Next came the bathroom and then, turning right, double doors led into the master bedroom. All the rooms had French windows leading on to the covered veranda which ran the length of the building and a working fireplace. In its heyday the house had been a harem adjoining a palace belonging to a member of the ruling family. The palace had long gone and the Bank had built a splendid modern house in its place for the manager.

The unbelievably primitive kitchen was next to the utility room, which led off the dining room. The sink was a concrete basin with a hole at the bottom and a tin basin was needed to hold water. As there was no running water all hot water had to be boiled on the charcoal cooker, which consisted of a concrete table with hollows in it, where hot charcoal provided heat with which to cook. The oven was a large Carr's biscuit tin on its side, with more hot charcoal on top to augment the base heat. I wondered how I was to turn this oven to 375 degrees, as my nice new cookbook suggested!

My "baptism of fire" was to be when the gate-man woke us up one morning bringing the news that Magaditch, the cook, had been knocked off his bicycle and was in hospital with cracked ribs. I quickly got up and went to the kitchen to try to prepare breakfast for John before he went to work. I did not know how to light the charcoal stove, but I noticed a bottle of kerosene on the shelf, so I poured a little on some pieces of charcoal and proceeded to fan the flames as I had seen the cook do. The smoke billowed and the sparks flew everywhere. I put my hand over my mouth and with streaming eyes continued to fan frantically. After a while the flames subsided and, joy, success, the wood began to glow hotly.

I put the kettle on and decided that the simplest thing to prepare was a couple of boiled eggs. The water boiled and I put in the eggs and marked the time for the usual four minutes. The local Naan was the slim flat unleavened bread, which was delicious when eaten really warm and fresh but became leathery when cold. Fortunately Magaditch had made a loaf of bread in the biscuit tin oven, so I was able to cut a couple of slices and attempt to toast it over the fire, which I had by this time divided into two. The toaster was a home-made contraption made with chicken wire. Very useful when barbecuing, I was to discover at a later date.

When the four minutes were up I took the breakfast into my John with great pride. To my horror the eggs were quite raw. I could not understand it. They had boiled for the correct time. John could not wait any longer, as he had to go to open the Bank. I was very upset that my first attempt to cook should end in such a failure. My husband could say with perfect truth that I could not even boil an egg when we got married. He was wont to remind me of this from time to time!

I was to discover that, as Isfahan is 5000 feet above sea level, water boils at a lower temperature and I should have cooked the eggs for a full eight minutes. Similarly I was to find that I required more flour in my cake mixtures. Oh yes, I did eventually learn to cope with my cooker. However our Armenian cook was able to turn out splendid meals at all times and I was very happy when he recovered and returned to work. I felt he was well worth the £9 per month we paid him. This was considered good pay in Isfahan, as the Persians paid much less. My husband's salary was about £700 pa at that time.

I found learning about my new home very daunting. I could speak very little Farsi and I had to make myself understood with the aid of a phrase book written by some farsighted Memsahib long ago. I remember the first phrase was to tell me how to request the servants to "put the beds in the garden" which made me pause to think. It vaguely reminded me a similar French phrase book that enabled me to say "My postillion has been struck by lightening" and "Où est la plume de ma tante?"

I was unaccustomed to having servants and was not sure I knew what I should tell them to do if I could speak to them. Fortunately John could speak Farsi fluently, so we had an "orders session" before he left for work and I just muddled on from there.

This inability to communicate and my reliance on the phrase book were to cause me much embarrassment. One morning I had reason to be angry with Magaditch because he had not cleaned the kitchen out as I had asked him several times to do. I had found it infested by cockroaches. I turned to my phrase book for what I took to be angry phrases. The more I berated him the more he laughed at me. By the time John came home at lunchtime I was in tears of rage.

"Sack him at once." I roared. "He's laughing at me when I tell him off."

My husband called the cook in and asked him to explain. The poor man tried hard to keep a straight face when he told how I had declared in angrier and angrier tones that I was a POMegranate. Then that I WAS a pomegranate. Somehow I had got my phrases mixed up and my furious declarations had been too much for him. We all had to laugh, and became friends again, but I always felt he was smiling at me. I can only hope it was with sympathy.

I decided that I would go to the Bazaar with Magaditch and try to learn the names and prices of things as I went along. The shops were quite unlike any I had seen before. They were set cheek by jowl in the dim bazaar, where the light was provided by shafts of dusty sunlight spearing from the roof. The ground was hard, dry sand which produced a light cloud of dust as people shuffled along. The smell of Gurgan Abi cigarettes mixed with opium smoked in the hookahs or hubble bubble pipes, and the strange smell of spices sold in open sacks on the ground, filled the air. The prices were difficult to relate to things at home, so I had to begin to learn values right from the beginning. In those days we were not highly paid, but fortunately the cost of living was not very high either. Mainly, I suppose, because choice was limited. There was a warm, thick, musty smell permeating the whole area. Meat hung from the roof of the "butcher's" and was crawling with flies. The cuts were totally unrecognisable. (Not that I was very clear myself about the various cuts of meat. I had grown up during the war and did not have the opportunity to learn about such things. The wartime meat ration did not lend itself to this.) Magaditch selected a piece and it was wrapped in a piece of newspaper. On we went to buy some sugar. This I did not recognise, as it was a solid hard cone about 12 inches high wrapped in blue paper. Later I was to find Magaditch breaking it up into manageable lumps with a hammer.

Tea, flour, spices, rice and so on were measured, somewhat haphazardly, by the handful and packaged in cones of newspaper. Fruit and vegetables looked very sad and my heart sank. I decided that in future, if this were how things were, I would leave the shopping to Magaditch and hope all would be well.

Slowly I learned the names and prices of things. I learned how to iron with an iron-shaped box with a handle and filled with hot embers, and I soon learned to hold it up to my cheek to "test" the heat, at the same time being careful not to tip hot embers on to the clothes. I learned how to clear out the Yakh-chal, the lead-lined box that served as a refrigerator, ready for the iceman to put in his large lump of ice early each morning. I learned too how to clean the pottery water filter, as every drop we used had to be filtered after it had first been boiled. I feel modern planners would be horrified by the fact that our water well was but a short distance from the soak-away cesspit.

The bathroom was relatively modern as the bath had three taps, one of which had to be turned on before water would run from any of the other taps in the basin as well as the bath. This water was supplied by a tank on the roof that had to be filled each morning with the aid of a pump. Each morning we could hear the clunk-clunk, clunk-clunk as Abdulla fulfilled the first duty of the day. The drain was functional, in that the water ran out on to the green tiled floor and then through a hole in the wall and out onto the garden. Needless to say various splendid creepy crawlies would crawl in to inspect us from time to time. If I spotted one, my "handsome white knight" was called to the rescue wearing his best hobnailed boots.

The loo had a chain flush and fortunately, drained down a pipe and out through the wall into a cesspit, or so I was assured. A wood stove was lit each morning before we got up to heat the water for the bath. This was an effective system as the chrome chimney was packed with sawdust into a doughnut. The fire was lit below and the flames heated the doughnut which, in turn, heated the water and created a nice warm bathroom in the winter.

John maintained that this was a great improvement on his bachelor home in Kermanshah. There he had had a tin bath which was filled by bucket and the loo was a "thunder box", reminiscent of the old privies down the garden in village cottages at home before the war. John recalled warnings about snakes which liked to wrap themselves round the warm bath while the bather, blissfully unaware, lay luxuriously soaking in the water. Although John always looked before getting out he never did see one. I am delighted to say that I did not see any snakes at all.

The walls were plastered on the inside with the same mud and straw as the outside and distempered a neutral cream, much as our houses at home were. One major difference was the way one had to secure curtain rods and pelmets. A six-inch nail was usually the most satisfactory method but one had to draw the curtains with care, as the whole curtain pole was easily detached. A two-inch nail was usually suitable for pictures as one could just push it in with the thumb, then if it was not quite right, it could be pulled out again, the hole gently rubbed over and the nail pushed in at a more suitable place.

The ceilings were also made of the same gatch, laid on wooden chundles, or poles of wood, covered with woven palm leaf matting, on which the mud and straw mixture was thickly laid. Although this was some two feet thick, it was quite possible to hear birds hopping on the flat roof as if they were wearing wooden clogs. When it snowed it was the duty of the gardener to roll the mud to ensure the roof remained waterproof. The first time I heard this I thought the house was falling down: the noise was like a tremendous roll of thunder.

CHAPTER TWO

One morning the British Consul's wife came to call. She brought with her a typewritten list of stores that could be ordered from Teheran. It seemed that orders could be sent every three months, as the powers that be at the Embassy were aware of the inadequacies of the local market and were kind enough to take orders from any ex-pats as well as the Consul. I was very pleased, as I had found my visit to the bazaar rather depressing. There were all sorts of familiar things on the list like baked beans, tins of fruit, tins of vegetables, Bisto, jam, tins of Kraft cheese, shampoo and toothpaste. My problem then was what to order and how much. Three months, I thought - that is ninety days. Say we had one tin of vegetables per day. That would be ninety tins of assorted vegetables. I made the same calculation for fruit. I had no idea how much dried milk we would use, so I think I decided on one tin a week and ordered accordingly, plus a few for luck! Then there were things like peppercorns. I had simply no idea how many peppercorns I would need. They were priced by the kilo. I supposed people bought them by the kilo, so I ordered a kilo.

As I had never kept house before and the manager's wife was home in the UK, and at that time I did not know anyone well enough to ask advice, I took the plunge and ordered a bit of everything. My poor husband had to ask for an overdraft to pay for it, and my order nearly required a special lorry. I was a bit horrified when it arrived and had to fend off remarks like "I see you don't intend to starve then". However I did note that, come the end of the three months, nearly everyone had called round to ask if I could possibly supply him or her with this or that. Anyway I didn't have to order anything next time. John's sigh of relief could be heard for miles. The same peppercorns were to last my mother about ten years when I took the "surplus" home to her some three years later.

In due course I became in need of a haircut. I had not seen a lady's hairdresser as I explored the town. Barbers sat in shops and cut men's hair quite openly. As most ladies wore the chador, which covered their heads, it was difficult to see if they had short or long hair. When I asked what people did, most Iranians replied that members of the family usually cut each others'. The few European ladies I knew wore their hair in a bun either at the back or on top of their heads. It simply was not the fashion to have short hair and I felt I was too young to wear my hair in a bun. My shoulder length tresses were becoming unmanageable and untidy. John very bravely offered to try to tame it with his Rolls razor! I hate having my hair, cut, even by a professional, and I was not enthusiastic about this plan.

The day dawned and we put a chair on the veranda. John stropped his razor and seized a hunk of my hair and stroked his razor downwards. I heard him gasp and then mutter that it cut so easily. I cringed. The blade felt as if my hair was being sandpapered and the slight sound was rasping. It seemed like forever, until John said he thought he was finished. Well... it was more manageable, I suppose.

As well as a cook, I had inherited a housemaid named Osnif. Actually "maid" was a misnomer as I suspect she was about 70. I found it very difficult to ask her to do things for me, partly because my upbringing made me feel awkward asking anyone old enough to be my grandmother to wait on me, and partly because she steadfastly refused to try to understand my efforts to speak to her. If I showed my exasperation she would burst into tears and rush from the room. However, on one occasion she forced me to sack her, grandmother's age or not. She had boiled my hand-knitted woollens. There were no phrases in my phrase book suitable to express my feelings on this subject, so she would have to go. I asked Magaditch to find me a replacement, not realising that this would not be easy. At that time there were few women servants willing to work for foreigners. After a period of time I still had not found a suitable replacement, so my "old maid" went to the Bank and asked if I would be prepared to take her back. No one else would employ her as she was too old and she had no money or home. I felt sorry for her and realised that probably she was unemployable by anyone else, so I took her back. She thanked me and promptly asked for an increase in salary. We were so dumbfounded we agreed!

The furnishings in our house were adequate but I suspect would not sell in a jumble sale today. The carpets were woven cotton and nailed down round the edges. I had noticed that clouds of dust rose as we walked across the room. Osnif had a broom much like the besom would use to sweep leaves at home. I had noticed that Henry's servant used an ancient vacuum cleaner in the modern Manager's house, so I arranged to borrow it. I was amazed at the amount of dust I was removing.

I was singing merrily and vacuuming away when I had a visitor. I had not met this lady before, but I quickly realised she was Persian. She opened the veranda door, walked in, and, without introducing herself, she said in good English "Have you looked under your carpets, my dear?" I was surprised and admitted that as the carpet was nailed down I had not liked to disturb it. She suggested that I did so. I pulled back a corner and discovered that the carpet was laid directly on the sand floor. The dust I had been getting out was being drawn through the carpet. Worse, the places where I had left the machine running when I moved the furniture had left holes in the floor, and the chairs had to be placed over the grooves, or they wobbled on the uneven ground.

My guest went to the kitchen and ordered coffee and, to my amazement, Magaditch came scuttling in, bowing to her at every step jabbering almost incoherently. He left the coffee and scuttled out again. I don't think I had ever seen him move so fast.

The lady introduced herself by name, but it meant nothing to me at that time. She explained that she had once lived in the house and that was how she knew about the sand below the carpet. We talked for a while and I found her very interesting. Later I found out that she was a sister of the local Prince, Saramen Doleh, and a relative of the Shah. She had lived in the house when it was a harem. In fact, the story has it that the prince, her brother, had murdered their mother in the mosque over the road because she had been unfaithful to her husband, their father. It was the custom for the eldest son in cases such as this to avenge his father. It was said that the woman crawled back to our garden to die and her ghost had been seen from time to time. One of our predecessors is reputed to have seen her disappearing into a wall by the gate. It is said that the skeletons of a woman and child were found in the wall when it was knocked down for alterations some time ago. We did not see any ghosts.

The reason Magaditch was so obsequious was that he knew who she was. Malakheh Khanoum was a lovely person and was very kind to me all the time we were in Isfahan.

My next ploy was to try to do something about the lumps in our hard cotton-filled mattresses. It seems one did not simply replace them, one sent for a pambezan. I was interested to know what was to happen. On the appointed day, which had to be dry, a man arrived carrying a long pole with a strong wire attached at the ends, rather like an archer's longbow. He also carried a heavy wooden mallet. Our lumpy mattresses were lugged out into a pre-swept corner of the garden against the wall, and the covers were removed, leaving the cotton filling in a heap on the ground. The pambezan then seated himself cross legged in front of the heap, the pole of his "bow" in his lap and the wire stretched over the cotton, held in place by one hand holding a sort of oven glove for protection. The wire was struck by the mallet. This caused it to vibrate and so fluff the cotton into the air and against the wall. This continued until there was a veritable mountain of fluffy cotton. I found it difficult to imagine such a mountain being replaced in the newly washed and ironed mattress covers. Somehow it was managed and our mattresses were suddenly 15 inches thick. The buttons were replaced and the mattresses returned to the beds. There was some difficulty in tucking in the sheets and blankets, and climbing into our bed that night caused much amusement. Certainly they were softer and more comfortable.

By this time I had got to know all the expatriates in the town. There were some 20 or so: British, American and a few French. I also met several Persian families and visited someone nearly every day or someone visited me. We, like most people, did not own a car and our method of transport was by horse-drawn droshki. If I wanted to go downtown, I would send the gateman to fetch me one. He would bring it to our gate, dust down the seat for me and stand by saluting while I climbed aboard. I felt rather as I imagine royalty must feel. All I had to do was give the name of the person I wished to visit and, as all the drivers knew where everyone lived, I was taken at once.

Our house was in the red light district of the town. It was all very discreet behind high blank walls. The drivers were always very protective of me when I was being driven down the kutche. In fact I found everyone to be very good to me. There was one occasion when a wheel came off a droshki and I was unceremoniously dumped on the road. I was not hurt, but the poor driver was nearly lynched for not looking after me properly.

I found that as a newcomer to the community everyone was eager to show me their pet places of interest.

As Isfahan was the ancient capital of Persia, there was

much of interest to see. Opposite the Bank there was a summer garden palace built some 360 years ago in the time of Shah Abbas, the time when most worthwhile things in Isfahan appear to have been created. The building in this garden was known as the Chehel-Satoon, which means 40 pillars. Actually there were 20 pillars along the veranda, but there was a pool immediately below them. The reflection doubled their number, hence the name.

Beyond the Bank there was the main square. At one end rose the great blue tiled domes of the "Masjed Shah" Mosque with its twin minarets, from which the calls to prayer could be heard all over town. The entrance to the mosque was decorated with thousands of little blue mosaic tiles, forming niches like honeycombs high up to the roof. The inside of the hall and the dome were also decorated with coloured tiles and inscriptions from the Koran. There was a double echo below the main dome so if one clapped one's hands the sound could be heard reverberating on and on.

The Maidan or Open Square had a series of flowerbeds in the centre with seats where one could rest, and lawns where children could play. The road ran round the outside of the gardens. On one side sat the pretty little Mosque Lutfulla. Its dome was lower and wider than most and was a particularly attractive turquoise and yellow. Opposite the Lutfulla stood the Ali Kapoo. This was the Gatehouse for the Palace of Shah Abbas when he ruled Persia. It was small and had a remarkable music room, the acoustics of which were still in order. There was also a veranda from which the Imperial Family could watch the polo matches played in the square below. The stone goalposts still remained.

At the other end of the square was the entrance to the main bazaar. This was a fascinating warren of some five miles of undercover streets, lanes and alleys. I loved to wander in the bazaar and came to know some of the artists and craftsmen. There were silversmiths who chased intricate patterns on all manner of surfaces. Persian silver is not sterling silver but is about 84 per cent.

There were printers who sat on the ground and stretched lengths of cloth over a low table. Next they dabbed an intricately-carved block of wood on to a pad of ink and, colour by colour, created tablecloths and bedspreads. Some were small fleur-de-lis designs and others were stylised pictures of people, animals and flowers. There were also stalls where men with sewing machines decorated waistcoats and hats for the local market. Tin Pan Alley rang with the noise of sheets of tin being fashioned into cooking pots and trays. These activities might be next to a spice seller who had sacks of his wares set in rows along the path.

As many visitors came to see Isfahan, I became the unofficial guide to those who called at the Bank. There was the Iran Tour Hotel run by an Armenian and his French wife. The foreign community used it as a meeting place and several British engineers building the power station lived there. As the hotel was small there were times when I was called upon to provide a bed for the night for passing friends. I enjoyed showing people round the town and was able to make many friends in the places of interest.

One of my favourite places to take visitors was the old Olive Oil Press. It was reputed to have been working for some 360 years since the time of Shah Abbas, and it was a contraption of which Emmet or Heath Robinson would have been justly proud. What is more, it was a genuine working press. On entering the dark cavern all one could see at first was a huge stone wheel to which was attached a blindfolded camel. The press chamber was dimly lit by a shaft of light from a hole near the roof, which shone down on to the centrepiece, like a searchlight beam filled with motes of dust. As one's eyes became accustomed to the gloom one could dimly see the olives being placed below the wheel and the camel plodding round and round turning the grinding stone and producing a messy, oily pulp, which was formed into flat cakes. These cakes were then placed below a wooden press formed by a tree trunk, some three feet in diameter, which in turn was attached to a series of pulleys. The ropes on these pulleys were wound round a horizontal capstan which had huge poles sticking out from it. A man then climbed up to the roof and leaped, rather like a monkey, and clung to the pole, forcing it, by his weight, to turn the capstan, and work the press. This way the oil was squeezed from the pulp and was collected in a tank. A man below pushed another pole into the next hole in the capstan in preparation for the next leap.

Another of my favourite stops was to climb a rickety staircase up to a room where I could visit a local artist called Imami, who loved to paint typical whimsical Persian figures of turbanned men and huge-hipped women, wearing garments decorated with delicately-sketched gazelles and flowers, sitting in gardens through which rivers flowed. Probably he had verses from Omar Khayyam running through his head. He drew, in the main, with a very fine brush and ink. He also liked to decorate verses from the Koran, much like illuminated manuscripts. I think it was the attention he paid to the minute detail which fascinated me.

Then there were the carpet factories with their rows of looms hanging from the ceiling and the children, some as young as five, sitting cross-legged in rows, knotting the silks and wools to the rhythm of a chant. The best silk rugs were made by children this young, as their little fingers were better suited to the finer knots. Their fingers flew along, twiddling like lightning. By the age of seven or eight their fingers were considered too big, and they progressed to the heavier wools with a small picture of the pattern they were making, threaded through the strands above their work. I must say I was appalled to think of children so young actually working, but I suppose, if they did not know anything else, they did not mind. There were few schools for them to go to and the work gave them something to do. They earned money to help feed their numerous brothers and sisters. Certainly they looked cheerful enough when I visited them, and my presence in European dress evoked much amusement.

Walking through the bazaar had its hazards. I was often pursued by the clanking of the bells hanging round the necks of the camels as the camel trains made their way along the lanes, laden with incoming bales of cotton or outgoing bundles of pans, carpets or boxes of foodstuffs, flour or leather goods. Several times I was pulled from the path of a camel whose padding steps I had not heard in the cacophony of banging and clanking which added to the picture of daily life. The smell of the spices and the dust sometimes blended with the smell of opium smoked in chai khanehs, or teahouses. Often one was offered a glass of the strong sweet tea and sat in companionable silence just enjoying the scene and thinking private thoughts, leaving when one had rested enough.

John and I were invited to try opium once just to see what it was like. Our host was a real addict and we were provided with the whole paraphernalia, consisting of a wooden pipe the shape of a flute. On the end there was a pottery globe with a hole in it. Then a piece of opium, which looked much like sealing wax, was heated on a charcoal brazier and applied to the hole in the pot. One then had to suck on the pipe and thereby draw in the fumes. I am sad to relate that I did not experience any wild dreams or have any fantasies at all. The taste was rather like burned potatoes and I found the whole thing rather disappointing. Perhaps if we had persisted we might have understood the addiction of so many Iranians.

Opium could be smoked by means of the hubble-bubble pipes, or hookahs as they were also known, as seen being smoked in the cafés and, indeed, by the shopkeepers sitting in their shops gossiping or just quietly waiting for custom. Taken by and large, the Iranians of those days seemed to have plenty of time to spend sitting around.

There was little or no "canned" entertainment in Isfahan in 1951. There was however, a cinema showing second-rate films. This was before the days when films were dubbed into the language of the country (later on we could marvel at the accent of Perry Mason as he exposed each murderer speaking in perfect Farsi). Instead the film was cut, indiscriminately, and a written explanation was shown. The cinema buzzed as those that could read enlightened those who could not, then the film started again.

The "best" seats were hard kitchen chairs set on a slightly raised platform at the back of the hall. The "one and nines" consisted of school benches set in rows in front of the screen. The scraping of chairs and benches often drowned the words and the cuts spoiled the suspense.

There was no television or theatre, so we all had to make our own entertainment. I was persuaded to learn how to play bridge, as three men in the Bank compound required a fourth. I had to learn fast too. I can still hear Henry exhorting me to "be aggressive". Now whenever I play bridge, I'm not sure my present partners are as enthusiastic when we go down on our contract.

We whiled away the evenings by giving dinner parties, usually playing a game of some sort. I developed a reputation for organising rather mad games parties where we raced peanuts along the floor propelled by our noses. We played an early form of the modern Pictionary game called "Clumps".

We organised "beetle drives" and a hilarious fancy dress and Halloween party. The house was decorated with various skulls gleaned from walks in the desert. The food was served on banana leaves and the punch from a cauldron bought in the bazaar. After dinner we had arranged for a well-known storyteller to tell the story of our resident ghost. The lights were dimmed and a few skulls lit by candles gave a guttering light. In case the ghost did not appear, we had decided to illustrate the story with a few sound effects. The glass in the French windows was held in by nails, with the result that they tinkled eerily in the gentle breeze. They were also very draughty. John and I planned to "waft" through the room dressed in a long sheet. I was to ride on his shoulders and make ghostly whispering noises. Unfortunately my husband trod on the sheet as we "wafted" through the doorway, I hitched it up too far and his legs were in full view. I was still shrouded and making ghostly noises, much to the astonishment and ribald laughter of the gathered guests.

We had a small swimming pool in the Manager's garden and there was a tennis court made of the same mud and straw gatch as the plaster on the houses. Rain turned it into a sea of mud and we had to wait for the sun to dry it off again. However, as it rained very little in the summer, this was not a problem.

Henry liked his garden and took a pride in growing vegetables. One year he tried to grow Brussels sprouts. They were doing very well and the gardener was encouraged to pay particular attention to them. One morning Henry went to inspect their progress and the gardener explained with great pride that they were doing much better since he had removed all the 'growths' off the stalks. Poor Henry was most upset, but supposed that as Brussels sprouts had never been seen in Isfahan, the gardener could not be blamed.

All the while we were in Isfahan the political rumblings ebbed and flowed. The government was short of money and was trying to nationalise the oil company. Britain was pretty unpopular with the Iranian Government, so the mullahs would rail against the British from the Minarets and pulpits.

The Government issued 20 year bonds called Gharz-e-Melli. One Isfahan industrialist who bought bonds, thereby proclaiming himself a great patriot, started a scam. He used them to pay his factory workers their wages. While these bonds were good value, they were of little use to the worker who wanted to buy food for his family, so he was forced to sell them to the brokers in the town at a 50% discount. The industrialist then bought them back at 60% of their value and paid them out again to the workers the next month. This situation caused justifiable discontent and trouble brewed.

At times foreigners were advised, mainly by word of mouth, to keep off the streets in case of trouble. I remember one day I was downtown and heard the roar of a mob nearby, and so I went to the safety of the Bank without delay. We watched the shouting, waving, mob, surging along the street outside. There was a body lying on a stretcher being carried shoulder high, while the leaders exhorted the mob, through loudhailers, to shout louder.

"Down with the British, scorpions of the earth. The dirty British killed this man." Before long the local riot squad arrived and proceeded to lay about the rioters and they all ran away - including the "dead body". All that was left was the stretcher and the winding sheet!

There was an excellent maternity unit in the British Church Missionary Society Hospital in the town, and they took very good care of me when I went there to have our baby. Our daughter Patricia arrived at 7.30 am on 18 February, 1952. A messenger was sent to John and he rushed to see our baby, having borrowed the cook's bicycle, arriving before I left the labour ward and carried her to my room. When he left us and called a droshki to take him to the Bank, the driver congratulated him on her birth. She was barely an hour old, but the news had travelled fast and all the Bank clerks were waiting to congratulate him.

There had been a lot of interest in our baby as she was the first European baby to be born in Isfahan for nine years. (Patricia, incidentally, was the last British Bank baby to be born in Iran before the Bank closed in 1952.) I recall that I was called from my bed to admire the moon, which was covered in a blue haze. I don't think I realised that there really was a blue moon once in a while!

The private rooms at the hospital were in a row across the middle of the Mission compound, with somewhat primitive ensuite facilities. They did have fireplaces, and the roaring fire ensured that the room was always warm. It was the custom in Iranian hospitals for patients to bring in their families or servants to wait on them and, in some cases, cook the food. I had to bring in my "maid" as someone had to make my bed and do my laundry (there were no disposable nappies in those days), also to fetch my food, which was very kindly supplied by Mary Wild, wife of Peter Wild FRCS, the Mission doctor who delivered Patricia. One snag about this arrangement was that Osnif had to sleep in my room in case I had any reason to call the night nurse, and she SNORED!

I was annoyed by the way the doctors would congregate in my room, warming their backsides at my fire while discussing various cases, then leave on their rounds without so much as a glance at me or my lovely baby. I would not let them leave until I felt that due homage had been paid!

On one occasion a mob outside the hospital decided to vent their anger with the Oil Company and the British government on the Mission. The rabble shouted and yelled and hurled abuse and stones over the hospital wall. Several times when the stones rebounded and a rioter was hurt, they banged on the gates and asked the doctors to patch up their wounds. This was done and the victims put outside the walls to continue throwing stones. Strangely, no one thought this was at all odd. The next day the town would be quiet and people would carry on their lives as usual, visiting the clinics and their relatives in hospital as before.

Our baby daughter caused a lot of interest and many people came to call bearing gifts of all kinds. Malekhe

Khanoum's eight-year-old granddaughter Firouze came to visit me - and burst into tears. She was so sorry my baby was not a boy and was amazed that I was delighted with my baby girl. Firouze was due to go to school in England, so she came to visit me at home to practise her English. Iranians, like many Moslems, prefer to have boys rather than girls. However Firouze brought me the most enormous box of chocolates I have ever seen. I suspect it had been waiting a very long time for an occasion such as this!

One of the main frustrations of being a doctor in Iran was that they were not allowed to operate on women, however serious the reason, until the husband or father had given his permission. Often he would not do so until he had consulted the mullah, and asked him to consult the Koran to discover if indeed it was a favourable day for the operation to take place. It could take ten days for permission to be obtained. Then if he said "yes" and the patient recovered, the mullah got the credit. However if the patient died, the doctor got the blame.

The hospital was attached to the church, where Bishop Thompson of Isfahan held Sunday Services when he was at home. His see included Teheran as well as Shiraz and other towns in Iran and he had business to attend to all over the country. We managed to arrange for the Bishop to christen Patricia when she was six weeks old.

There was also a Blind School run by the Missionaries. I spent time making stuffed animal toys for the children and for the orphans in the residential part of the compound. All the children were so pleased to know Patricia and she became known as Khanum Kucheek, or little madam.

Banking in Iran in those days was a pretty difficult business, as communications were slow and unreliable. I remember once our servant brought us a cable early one morning and at the same time, told us that we had a visitor at the door. We read the cable and then hurried to meet the visitor. Poor Peter Mason had to make his own way to our house unheralded. It seems the message had come by the same plane as he had. This was a common problem. There was no national telephone system at that time.

John came home one day to tell me that he had received a cable from head office instructing him that in future, all transfers of cash to or from the National Bank Melli should be under armed guard. He had looked out of the window to see one of his messengers passing along the street with a tea tray piled high with bundles of 1000 toman notes on his head, as had been the custom for many years. Times were changing. The new instruction was caused by an incident at our Ahwaz office. The custom there had been for the cashier to take a cheque to the Bank Melli, draw the cash and count it, then telephone to the office for a taxi and escort to come and collect him. The inevitable had happened. One day no call came for a car. No sign was ever found of the cash but the cashier's clothes were found plastered into the inside wall of a well in a village between Ahwaz and Teheran. The mystery of what happened to the cashier and the money remains.

I used to walk with my baby along to the bridge over the river Zaindeh, to watch the new carpets being washed. This was a colourful sight as the carpets were laid flat in the water running over steps under the bridge, the patterns glowing like jewels. Then they were hauled out of the water and spread out on the roadway in the sun for the passing traffic to "age" and squeeze them dry. This bridge had been built in the days of Shah Abbas early in the 17th Century, to provide a link between Isfahan and the town of Julfa. The latter town had been specially built for the protection of the Christian Armenians that Shah Abbas had brought from Georgia in the north of Iran, because they were very artistic craftsmen and especially good workers. No moslems were allowed into Julfa and the gates used to be closed at night. It was not until about 1945 that the town was opened up and people could pass freely. Julfa Cathedral was a grand building, but inside there were very gruesome murals of Christians being tortured on racks and in vats of boiling oil which sent shivers down the spine. There were also more conventional holy pictures of saints with benign smiles. Somehow the savage torture left a more lasting impression.

One holiday Henry took us out into the desert on a picnic. This required a certain amount of preparation as we were obliged, as foreigners, to obtain passes to travel more than five miles from the town. Henry's lodger came with us and we had packed shish kabab and pieces of naan, the flat, unleavened local bread. We also had the makings for a charcoal fire and, of course, bottles of Ahbjo, the local beer. We also had a pack of cards as Henry could not survive for long without his "fix" of bridge.

The reason for the holiday was a day of mourning for Hussein, an assassinated grandson of the Prophet and first leader of the Shi'ite Moslems. The zealots beat themselves on their backs with chains and sometimes drew blood. Muharram, as this period of mourning is called, is a very serious occasion and it behoved infidels like us to keep out of sight. Unfortunately the shady copse we had chosen for our picnic was too near a village and we were spotted. Angry villagers came out and threatened us so we were about to beat a hasty retreat when the headman appeared and said we must finish our meal and then go. He was very polite and calmly handed back the hubcaps which had been stolen from our car when we were not looking.

We ate our kababs and decided that we would play our game of bridge at home. When we got back to the car we found to our horror that it was locked and the keys were hanging in the ignition. What would we have done if we had had to make a strategic withdrawal? John managed to "burgle" the boot with a kebab skewer and then push up the squab enough to be able to unlock the back door. We were happy to get home.

Eventually the political situation deteriorated to the point where the British Consulate closed. As the Bank was due to close too, John constructed two incinerators in the compound behind the bank and, over the next two months, proceeded to burn all the Bank's accumulation of sixty years' records. The vouchers and hand-written ledgers were all sent to head office in Teheran to be stored.

The Bank Manager was considered the senior British resident now the Consul had gone, and so the senior local Iranians came to call on him to pay their respects when King George VI died.

About two months later we were informed that we were to leave Isfahan and go to Amman in Jordan. John was to go on the Arabic course in preparation for Arab country postings.

I was sad to say farewell to all our friends but finally we packed up our belongings, loaded most of them on a lorry and sent them all to Teheran ready to be transported to Amman. Included in these cases were the remnants of my initial food-shopping spree when I first arrived in Isfahan.

John and I put our baby in her carrycot into the back of a taxi and began the long drive back to Teheran. The route had much improved since our last journey. The patches of shingle had been filled in and a steady pace could be maintained. However when we reached the mountains near Qum there was a cloudburst, which caused a landslide to block the road. There was a bus full of Iranians following our car, so my husband got them to manhandle the worst of the large stones off the track until there was a gap wide enough for us to get by. As we drove down the pass we came upon people moving small stones from the other side. We suggested that they save their energies for the larger boulders on the road behind us.

When we arrived back in Teheran we arranged to make a

radio phone call to our families at home, who were anxious about us. In those days we had to go to the main cable office downtown. We were seated in a small room with a desk microphone in front of us. My parents had been contacted and warned to expect a call.

The moment arrived and we found ourselves talking to them. It was quite an emotional occasion and we all talked at once, as one is apt to do. We were supposed to say "over" when we had finished, but we always forgot. Never mind- I had heard my parents' voices and they knew that all was well with us.

We had to wait in Teheran to get our visas and inoculations for Amman. I had a lovely time showing off my baby and doing some shopping in shops that supplied European clothes, and even some baby equipment. John spent a lot of time being debriefed on the closure of the Branch in Isfahan.

One morning I was walking downtown to do some more shopping when a mob emerged from a side road. They were shouting and throwing stones. When they caught sight of me, a European, they started to chase me and throw stones at me. I was really scared and ran as fast as I could along the road. The shopkeepers ahead of me pulled down their metal shutters to save their shops from damage. There was nowhere for me to go. Suddenly a car drew up beside me and a voice said,

"Get in. Lie on the floor" I scrambled in and the car took off. I had no idea who my rescuer was, and frankly did not care at that stage. After a while the car stopped and the driver said, "You can get up now, Khanoum" I got up and looked about me. I was in a taxi outside my own front door at Haftdaskah.

"How do you know where I live?" I asked, as I thanked him for his help.

"I took you home yesterday, Khanoum, with Khanoum Kucheek. I am sorry my people behave like that to you. Government problems are not your fault. I am glad I was there to help you." So was I. To my great shame I did not think to take his name so that my husband could thank him in the time-honoured way, but somehow, I don't think he would have expected or appreciated a reward. I still shiver when I think of that occasion, but it is always good to remember that there are many kind people in the world.

We were dreading going through customs as we had heard that they were giving the British a hard time at the airport. However we need not have worried. Our little Khanoum Kucheek drew a large admiring audience and the fact that she had been born in Isfahan was an extra bonus. It seems that the Chief of Customs was an Isfahooni like our daughter, and his brother was buying the Bank house in Isfahan. This made us VIPs in his book, so we were shown every courtesy and ushered aboard the Swedish SAS plane for Baghdad as if we were royalty.

When we became airborne the stewardess brought a tray of all sorts of baby milk powders, apologising for not having asked what brand of milk I required for the baby. I felt almost guilty when I told her that Patricia was breast-fed. How lucky I was that I was able to feed her myself. It was so much easier and safer in those days.

We arrived in Baghdad in a sandstorm and were transferred to the Sinbad Hotel. The next day we set off by taxi on the five-hour journey to Amman.

Chapter Three

AMMAN

The five hour journey from Bagdad proved long but uneventful, so we drove directly to our new home on Jebel Amman. The town, like Rome, is built on seven hills, the business and market area being in the valley and the residential areas spread over the steep slopes around the central basin. Our house was near the top of Jebel Amman. It was a smallish modern villa with three bedrooms, a dining hall and sitting room. There was a lovely view over the town and the sunken rose garden proved a lovely place to sit and read.

We were to share the villa with Jill and Tony Panter and their three- year- old daughter Pru. They were already there and had organized themselves into the two back bedrooms, leaving the larger front room for us. I was relieved to note that the kitchen was very modern in comparison with my rather "Harry Tate" arrangements in Isfahan. The sink was moulded concrete with a proper drain and running cold water with an electric hot water tank. The cooker was a civilized smart Calor gas stove. We had a Moslem Arab cook named Mahommed and a Christian Arab maid whose name was Mary.

John was to attend the Bank's Arabic school in Amman. There were three other students on the course. Tony and Greta Miller lived in a flat downtown with Col Kelly, a bachelor, living with them. Then there were some newlyweds, Jean and Mac Mcleay, who lived in a small villa further up the hill, where the course lessons were to be held. The men went to "school" six mornings a week and spent the afternoons doing their "homework". The wives had to occupy themselves as best they could. I was kept pretty busy looking after Patricia and helping Jill amuse her daughter Pru. We had to keep the children out of the way of the men as they learned their vocabulary. Arabic is a complicated language to master and all the men had difficulty in settling down to learn it. It was difficult for us to help as the words were written in Arabic script. John spent a lot of time transcribing them into phonetics so I was able to ask him his vocabulary at least. I remember that the first word I learned was "huot", which means whale. Such a useful word, one uses it in every conversation!

Shopping in Amman was such a pleasure after Isfahan. Most people spoke good English and the shops stocked many familiar items. The main problem was the steepness of the hill leading to the shopping centre. Letting the pram pull me downhill was fine, but coming home in the heat was an exhausting business. Sometimes we clubbed together and paid for a taxi. According to my letters home at the time we were nearly always broke. Certainly Amman was more expensive than Isfahan, but as we were sharing the expenses of the servants we should have been all right. Jill and I shared the catering three days on, three days off and on Friday, (our holiday) we usually went out.

It was the end of April when we arrived and it was beginning to feel hot and sticky. There were ceiling fans in the bedrooms but I was worried that the draught would not be good for Patricia. Sometimes we had difficulty in sleeping at night, with the result that tempers were frayed. Sharing a house is never very easy but I think we managed pretty well on the whole. As a nursery teacher I was able to think up amusements for Pru and she enjoyed helping me with Patricia.

We were not really interested in clubbing every night at the Amman club as we could not afford it, but Tony and Jill went from time to time. Not that they could really afford it either, but they were older than we were and the strain was telling on Tony. I remember Tony bought the cheapest bottle of whisky he could find, as funds were so low one month. I can see him now putting it on the table and pouring himself a measure. He sipped it and his face was a study of disbelief. He had another sip, then quietly put the cork back on the bottle and put it in the sideboard.

"That stuff is dreadful" he said. "This will be my next drink if I am sufficiently desperate." From time to time the bottle was brought out and put on the table, studied thoroughly and quietly replaced in the sideboard. We had several laughs about it.

Much to our surprise one morning, Mahommed, our cook, announced he was getting married the next day, so he asked if he could be have the day off and would we please come to the wedding. He explained that his first wife was a German lady, but she was ill and unable to manage on her own so he was going to marry this young Arab girl as well, to look after her. I asked if she knew that that was why she was being married. Oh yes, he had arranged for her to be sent to visit his first wife as she was the person she had to please. It seemed that the girl had met with approval so the wedding was "on."

I then asked what he thought of her. Was she pretty? Could she cook? Mahommed had not seen her but he had been told she was satisfactory! I asked why couldn't he just employ a nurse to help, but it seems it would be cheaper to take a wife. As a Muslim in Amman he was allowed up to four wives.

We went to the wedding, which was a somewhat confusing affair, as both sides, as it were, had their own tents. The women crammed into one tent, where the poor bride was set upon. Her hair was dressed and tied up in little knobs and the palms of her hands and the soles of her feet were painted with henna. Her nails and her face were made up and her eyebrows were plucked to a very thin line, which gave her a rather surprised look. Then finally she was dressed in a brightly-coloured skirt and blouse and all sorts of jewellery, bangles, belts, necklaces and rings. All the time this was going on a musician was playing on a single stringed fiddle, and every now and then someone would shriek the traditional high-pitched "loolooloo". The girl, who looked very young and frightened, sat wide-eyed and expressionless like a rather limp doll.

We went to find Mahommed in his tent, where he was sitting with his male friends. They were drinking tea and eating a variety of sweet cakes and biscuits. I asked if he had seen his bride yet, but he shook his head and said he would see her when he took her to his home later. Finally a taxi arrived and the bride was ushered into it. Mahommed came and found us, asked if we had enjoyed ourselves, thanked us for coming and told us that he would be there in the morning to make our breakfast. Then he got into the front seat of the car and away they went to Nablus, the village where Mahommed and his German No. 1 wife lived.

We could not stop thinking about that poor little girl. She was married at a very young age to an elderly man who worked all week in Amman and returned home to his invalid wife only on Fridays. What kind of life would she have?

The course was a strain on us all. Jean found it hard having the school in her house every day as she could not call her home her own. Greta was lonely in her flat, as she did not have a child to keep her occupied. We did not have much of a social life, not being in a position to meet anyone through our husbands' work.

When the men had a day off we hired a taxi and visited a place of interest. There was the castle high on the hill opposite and the Roman amphitheatre on the other side of the town. It was in good repair but it was very hot in the sun. How we longed for a swimming pool. There weren't very many in Amman as water was a precious commodity. However there was a large pool downtown which was opened for Europeans one afternoon a week. Women were of course not allowed to go at the same time as Arab men, as this was not considered decent. However we did enjoy such time as we were permitted. Some weekends the men were invited to play cricket at Zerka with the Arab Legion, so this made a pleasant change of scene for us all.

One evening a group of us hired a couple of taxis and went for a swim in the Dead Sea. We had been warned that we should carry containers of sweet water as we would need to rinse off after swimming, as the water was so salty. We arrived at the beach and turned the cars so their lights shone towards the water, then we ran into the sea. It was very warm. I waded out to nearly waist level when my feet left the ground and I was walking in the water. I stretched out to swim breaststroke but my body just rested on the water and I couldn't get deep enough to swim. It was very difficult to stand up again, and then I couldn't touch the ground. John had discovered that he could just sit in the water and float his half drunk glass of beer beside him. I "walked" over to him and sat behind him, hooking my feet round his tummy. It was like sitting in a boat. The others came and joined us and we had a great time paddling ourselves about and racing our "boats". When it was time for us to go, we poured the sweet water over each other to wash off the salt and drove home.

At last our heavy luggage arrived. It had taken nearly two months to come overland from Teheran. I was looking forward to having some different clothes as I was tired of the ones I had brought with us. The boxes were put on the veranda outside our bedroom so I could open them at leisure. I did not have the space to unpack everything, but I wanted to have a look at our things.

It is just as well I did, as I was appalled to find that the customs in Teheran had searched our luggage thoroughly. I had packed some tins of grapefruit marmalade left over from my shopping spree in Isfahan. It seems the customs did not believe that the tins did indeed contain marmalade and so had opened them to see. Having done so, they then repacked the opened tins in the case which contained our blankets and sheets. The mess was indescribable, to say nothing of the smell. Washing machines were not on the inventory in those days, so all the blankets and sheets had to be washed by hand, in the bath. Drying was not a problem once we had hung everything on the line.

Certainly the searchers had been very thorough, as I had packed our eight table mats inside the sewing machine case. When I came to unpack there was a mat in each of the seven cases and two in one. Most of our breakable wedding presents were broken, but nothing was missing so far as I could see. I repacked the remains and put the trunks in the empty garage to await our next posting in four months' time. Provided of course, John had passed his Arabic exam. We could not claim on insurance as breakable objects were not covered unless they had been professionally packed, which was inconceivable in Isfahan in the 1950s.

One morning I came home from shopping and went into our bedroom to change Patricia and there, marching in through the open window, was an army of large black ants. They were streaming down the wall, along the floor, up the corner of the bedspread, across the bed, down on to the floor again, out of the door, down the corridor, through the hall, and out of the kitchen door. I ran outside to see where they were coming from and found them marching up the garden path from the road. There were thousands of them just marching through our bedroom. Thank goodness we were not in bed.

There was no one in the house at the time and I did not know what to do. I tried to stop them with boiling water, but nothing would divert them from following their leader. The water caused them to scatter for a while, but they quickly returned to the same track, as if they were following a specific trail. There being nothing I could do, I sat at the dining room table and watched the ants march relentlessly on through the house. Eventually the flow decreased and the last remaining stragglers found their way out of the back door and were gone. I still wonder where they were going and why.

One holiday we left Patricia with Jill and drove to Jerusalem. The journey took us past the Allenby Bridge, which was mentioned on the news on the radio during the war, and down to Jericho, which is below sea level. We passed the Dead Sea, where we had gone swimming that night. My goodness it was hot down there. The shore did not look very inviting.

We drove on to Jerusalem, stopping to visit the Dome of the Rock Mosque where King Abdullah had been murdered some weeks before. The next call was at the Via Dolorosa and the Holy Sepulchre. I recall being rather shocked by the commercialization of everything in Jerusalem. Everywhere we went there was someone with his hand out for payment of some sort. We found our enjoyment and concentration disturbed by a constant stream of beggars or pedlars selling tatty souvenirs.

The Basilica of the Garden of Gethsemane towered over the building housing the Stone of Agony, tiny chips of which were on sale with a sliver of olive tree purporting to come from the olive tree which had been grown from the seed of the olive tree, grown from the seed of the olive tree from under which Christ was taken all those years ago. We bought a Bible with a beautiful polished olive wood cover.

Our next port of call was to drive over the long winding road to Bethlehem. I'm not sure what I expected to see there, but I was not prepared for the walk down into the deep cave with a star-shaped plaque set in the floor proclaiming that Christ had been born here. The church in Bethlehem was small and pretty and the bells had a clear ring. It was dark and late when we got home. Patricia was asleep and did not seem to have missed me. That was the first time we had left her for more than an hour or two.

We would have liked to visit the Rose Red City of Petra, but in those days it was a long drive and then a long horse ride to get there, and we felt it was too hot for Patricia, as it could not be done in under three days.

At last the six-month course was over and we packed up our belongings and travelled to Beirut, where the men were to take their examination. It was a relief to have it all over and to know that our men had all passed. Apart from still having jobs, it meant they got a bonus of £75 at once and an increase of £100 pa, which was very welcome. We spent a few days celebrating in Beirut and then we all went our separate ways to our new postings. We were to go to Aleppo in northern Syria.

Chapter Four

ALEPPO - 1953

We flew to Aleppo by Air Liban in an old and draughty Dakota plane. It was a short flight and we were about to land when the stewardess gave Patricia a chocolate biscuit! Needless to say she managed to spread it all over herself and much of me too. I left John to cope with passports while I headed for the ladies to try to clean up before meeting our new manager, another Henry. I was nearly there when a voice said, "Mrs Lindesay I presume". I was caught, chocolate and all. How dare he presume who we were, I fumed inwardly!

Henry took us to our new home. It was a first-floor flat in a large triangular block set on an island surrounded by roads. It had two bedrooms and a sitting room with double doors opening into a dining area, which had a window opening into the well down the centre of the building. There was a third room that could be a guest room or study. The kitchen was pretty basic but still better than our Isfahan home. The three-burner kerosene stove was one up on my charcoal burner, and the shallow terrazza sink was an improvement on the tin bowl

I had become accustomed to. Later I was given a brand new Calor gas stove.

The bathroom was adequate, with water heated by a kerosene drip boiler. The whole floor was laid with terrazzo tiles, easy to keep clean and cool in summer, if a bit chilly in winter. On two sides of the flat we had a three-foot wide veranda overlooking a large area of open ground which was to provide a lot of interest throughout the year.

There was a very strong French influence in Aleppo, due to the old French mandate for Syria. The buildings lining the wide streets had little wrought iron verandas, with shutters at the windows of the flats above the shops. The souk or local market was very extensive, with cobbled streets which were mostly under cover, a contrast to the dirt roads of Iran. As in Isfahan there were streets of shops all selling the same things. The extensive fresh produce market, where the country people sold their goods, was much like the country towns of France. Most people in Syria, including the shopkeepers, spoke French. There were several good shops and a supermarket. The usual taxis abounded, together with horse-drawn droshkis, only here they were called gharries. The donkey with his perilously perched rider was also much in evidence.

Dress was mainly European for the townspeople, while the country people wore tribal costume. The women had long full skirts with tight long-sleeved blouses and long scarf headdresses wound round the head. These country women walked beautifully, holding themselves straight, moving along with a loping stride carrying bundles of produce or hand-woven rugs on their heads, while driving a laden donkey. Often one would carry a child in the shawl on her back. These women were usually tall and strong and offered themselves for all kinds of work in the market. They could be seen heaving heavy bricks on building sites or washing laundry while their menfolk sat in the market place chatting and perhaps selling the goods their wives had carried into town.

The countrymen wore black baggy trousers, very full between the legs. These trousers were nicknamed "catch Mohammeds." The saying was that the next Mohammed would be born of man and these trousers were to ensure that He had a safe arrival!

Aleppo's geographical position put it at the gateway to the East from Europe, as it was on the old trade route and that of the Orient Express. It is one of the oldest continuously-inhabited towns in the world and has a magnificent citadel dating from pre-Crusader times. The entrance was through an arched gateway and across a causeway over the moat. Then came a series of double corners designed to foil the use of battering rams. The Citadel had been almost entirely self-contained, with a huge granary and a deep well and space to house livestock. There was a secret tunnel, which ran from the centre out to a cave in the hills. It was besieged many times, but fell only once, when the defendants thought the siege had been lifted and got drunk. The town was so old that one of the most vivid impressions was of gravestones. No road could be made without cutting through a graveyard dating from some period in the city's past. We visited the graveyard of the East India Company's agents outside the town and read the inscriptions on the stones.

When we first arrived we were invited to parties given by the foreign community to welcome us. There were few Europeans, so newcomers were quite a novelty. Soon I was going to coffee mornings and playing bridge, though Patricia proved to be a major distraction, as I had to take her with me.

It was September when we arrived in Aleppo and the temperature was going down. I spent a lot of time walking with Patricia, exploring the town. We still could not afford a car, but sometimes the Manager lent me the Bank car. Margo, the Manager's wife, showed me the best places to fulfil such needs as I had. George, a red-haired Armenian, was the Bank driver and was a fund of knowledge as to where things could be found and who could do what. He was a character and well known in the town.

I remember being terrified one day as he reversed at speed up a one way street, because he considered it took too long to go round the correct way. On another occasion I was sitting in the car waiting for George to collect my order from the butcher, when suddenly the butcher started to shout at George and thump his cleaver on the block to emphasise a point. I was afraid that he was going to murder George, so I leaped out of the car to try to mediate. Both men stopped and looked at me in amazement. It seems they were asking after each other's family. I was to learn that Syrians rarely talk quietly.

Patricia, who was a very small dainty baby, walked at ten

months and, although she still fitted in her carrycot, it was no longer safe at night. So we had to buy a cot. George helped us find a large chromium one with string netting which could be let right down on both sides. Patricia loved it as it was like being in a proper bed and the mosquito net lay over it giving her plenty of room.

I decided that I must at least learn to speak "kitchen Arabic," so I selected a shop where I could do most of my shopping and where the owner spoke no English or French. This was quite unusual, as most people in Aleppo were multilingual. We became great friends and I learned to ask for a kilo of carrots, potatoes, onions or whatever and to pass the time of day. The shopkeeper however, was quickly able to greet me, ask after my family and discuss the news of the day in perfect English.

My Armenian maid Mary, who was quite a linguist, also spoke Turkish (all Armenians in the North of Syria spoke Turkish), English, French and German (having worked for many foreign families) and of course Arabic because it was the language of the country. I suppose that because everybody could speak to me in either English or French, which I already spoke reasonably well, I had no need to speak Arabic and people were not prepared to listen to me struggling, feeling it kinder to "help me out". Arabs are notoriously bad at understanding foreigners' Arabic as the mispronunciation of a vowel can make nonsense of the whole sentence.

Christmas was coming and there were sufficient Christian

Armenians in the town for the shops to provide a few tree decorations and streamers as well as other festive items. We bought an artificial Christmas tree and started our collection of glass baubles, of which, fragile though they are, I still have a few left. I had just been provided with a Calor gas cooker with an oven I could control. I decided to celebrate by making my first Christmas cake.

I remember Margo asking whether the flour I was using had weevils in it. Actually I had found the weevils and was about to return the packet to the shop. Margo told me that this flour was the best imported kind, and that the local brand, without weevils, was too coarse for cake making. All I had to do was sieve the creatures out.

I had to de-stone the raisins and sultanas as in those days, there were no stoneless ones. I also had to candy the fruits and blanche the nuts, as ready prepared ones were unavailable. The preparation of my ingredients took hours.

At last I was ready to pop it into my new oven. I set the timer to remind me to turn the oven down and went to rest from my labours in the sitting room with John. Suddenly there was a wonderful smell of Christmas cake. I was surprised that it smelled so good so soon as it had a couple of hours or so to go. I went to have a look and burst into tears. My cake was a black charred lump in the middle of the tin in the oven. It turned out that the thermostat on the oven had not been set, so the gas had been burning full on and the whole oven was red hot. I was not happy.

We were invited to the Manager's house for Christmas lunch, which was a splendid traditional feast during which Patricia sat in her high chair gnawing on a huge turkey leg. It was a lovely family occasion. There were several other parties to go to, but we still felt a bit homesick and would have liked to introduce the first grandchild on both sides to our parents.

Harold Adkins, a travelling vicar, came up from Beirut to take the Christmas service in the room in the hospital especially set aside for the purpose. The doyen of the community took the collection in his battered old trilby hat, as he did each month when services were held, and it was traditional that one might take change if required.

An Armenian family, the Altounians, whose general attitude was very British, owned the hospital. They had a home in the Lake District and Arthur Ransome, who used to stay with them, based his Swallows and Amazons stories on the family. Their names were Mavis, Bridget and Roger. Ransome added John to balance the family in the book.

The bar in the Hotel Baron was the meeting place for the community and was owned by an Armenian with an English wife. At one time it was the only hotel in the town of any consequence. Less affluent travellers usually stayed at the local caravanserais, where they did their own cooking and washed in the courtyard; they were much cheaper than the splendid panelled walls and leather sofas of the Baron. The guest book had many exciting names in it: Max Mallowan, archaeologist husband of Agatha Christie (who also often stayed there on her way to join her husband in Baghdad); Jim Mollison and Amy Johnson, the famous aviators; and even Lady Edwina Mountbatten. There was a framed bill run up by TE Lawrence hanging on the wall of the bar. Signatures of many British soldiers staying for a bit of R&R during the war filled several pages. Koko, the owner, was an amusing host and ran a very comfortable oasis for land travellers on their way to India. In those days Aleppo was the gateway to Europe - nowadays of course air travel has caused it to be bypassed.

People making their way to India or beyond in a variety of ways often came to us for help or advice as to the cheapest place to buy stores for the next leg of their journeys. There were four people driving a London taxi, with its flag still lit, to Australia. They told us that while they were resting by the side of the road in Yugoslavia they could see in the distance a cyclist pedalling towards them. He was the only moving object to be seen on the horizon. As he drew level, much to their surprise, he said, "God, aren't these roads terrible." in English and pedalled on. They passed him later and learned that he was an Englishman bicycling to India, so we should expect him in due course.

These travellers used to call in at the Bank for their money and John used to pass them on to me for advice. They would come to the flat and I would light our Mazout fired water heater, so they could all enjoy nice hot baths. Then after a good meal, I would take them to the souk to do their shopping at the cheapest places I knew. After they had eaten all my home-made cakes and biscuits they would wave goodbye and promise to send me a card when they reached their destination. Sometimes afterwards, we read articles by people who said that they had travelled from London to Bombay on £5. No mention of other peoples' money! I did not receive one promised postcard from any of the dozens I helped.

This cyclist eventually arrived and stayed in town for a while, painting pictures and murals to earn enough money to enable him to move on.

There was an American Mission College on the outskirts of town where we often went to square dance in the evenings. One of the professors was a real square dance caller, having worked as a caller in his student days. I can visualise him now, wearing his cowboy hat and the longest, thinnest, most pointed boots I have ever seen. He had us all "digging for the oyster" and "diving for the clam".

There was a swimming pool at the college and we were lucky enough to be invited to swim quite often. I remember one holiday we played scrabble round the pool and got really badly sunburned. I had to go to the Bank and put soothing pads on John's shoulders for days afterwards.

We also went to the British Council, where we had play readings and tried our hands at Scottish dancing. Most of these dances we learned book in hand, as we went along. Some evenings we gave English conversation classes to mature students. I felt very strange teaching middle-aged bald men how to pronounce words properly and failing to satisfactorily explain why cough, though and plough are pronounced as they are. I witnessed 'also' spelt with two ls so many times that I had to check in the dictionary to ensure that I had the correct spelling. I enjoyed teaching, as we made a variety of friends.

The time passed and I became pregnant again. I was pleased, as this would provide Patricia with a playmate. The new baby was due in June or early July. My mother decided that she would come out to be with me so plans had to be made.

Henry and his wife Margot went home on leave at Easter and Jimmy came to take over as manager. It was now my turn to show someone the ropes. Not having his family with him, Jimmy was very generous with the use of the Bank car, so we were able to go out on picnics at weekends to watering places where there was a bit of greenery. There was also the ruin where the remains of the Pillar of St. Simeon Stylites could be seen. History tells us that several thousands of years ago, the pagans of North Syria would have priests perched at the tops of pillars for seven days at a time. In the 5th Century AD St Simeon was the first Christian monk to practice this form of asceticism. At first he was satisfied with a column a mere ten feet high, but after seven years the famous saint moved to a tremendous 60ft one with a platform on top 12 ft square, where he stayed for 30 years. I find it hard to imagine how anyone could spend thirty years in so draughty a place. There was very little left of the pillar now, as earthquakes and pilgrims had chipped it away over the years.

On our drives out into the desert we came upon masses of wild anemones growing amid the olive trees. There were also wild tortoises wandering about. We thought we would take some home as pets for some of the children. We put them on the floor in the back of the car and were amazed when they began to fight, bumping each other quite viciously. We decided that perhaps we wouldn't take them home after all.

In the spring, the open ground across from our flat was ploughed up using a hand-guided plough pulled by two mules. When the earth was turned and ready for planting, the farmer, wearing the traditional baggy trousers and scarf wound round his head, walked up and down, casting the seed from side to side from a bag round his waist. He looked very biblical. It was strange to see the wheat growing lush and green in the middle of the town. I was interested to note that when the time came to reap his harvest the farmer cut it with a scythe, tied it into sheaves and set it into stooks as we used to do in Scotland.

After the farmer had removed his crop, some circus vans arrived. They put up their tent and fairground rides and the crowds came. The noise, the mess and litter were considerable, right outside our windows. The daytime was not too bad, but about teatime the jangling of Arabic music began and blared on until midnight. There was one small advantage in that we got a grandstand view, free, of the lady on the high wire and of the trapeze artists. We also got far more than our share of flies. The electric light flex hanging from the ceiling, was black and thick as a rope with them every evening. The difficulty was that, if we sprayed them with our flit gun they lay in rafts on the floor fizzing and dying. If we ignored them they flew about the flat and we flapped at them with fly swats. Whatever we did they were a great inconvenience, and we were not sorry when the tent was folded and moved on.

The time was coming for my mother to arrive. She was sailing on a Swedish cargo ship, which was due to call at Limassol in Cyprus at the time of her silver wedding anniversary: we contacted the Cypriot National Bank manager there and asked him to send flowers on board. He replied that unfortunately the ship had already left, but had he known she was there he would have been only too delighted to take her out to dinner. He returned the money we had sent for the flowers, saying it was far too much anyway - he could have filled the ship for that amount

Mum was to disembark in Beirut, so we had asked that the Bank Manager there should meet her and put her on the train for Aleppo. As it happened they managed to find someone who was driving up and was prepared to give her a lift.

Chapter Five

VISIT FROM MUM

At last the day arrived when my mother arrived at our front door, brought by the Beirut manager's driver. She arrived about teatime, just as we all got up from our afternoon rest.

I well remember her remark on climbing the stairs: "My, what a long way away you do live." She must have been travelling for weeks. I was so happy to see her and she was so delighted to meet her first grandchild. We had explained to Trisha at great length exactly who Granjo (as she became known) was, so she was very excited by the time she arrived.

Aleppo was very hot in summer, and I was beginning to feel the heat, as I had about one month to go before the birth of my second baby. It was a real tonic to have my mother there to help me and to introduce her to our life in the Middle East. Mum protested that we had said Aleppo was practically European, which it was to us after Isfahan, whereas to her it was anything but, and very new and different.

Granddaughter and grandmother getting to know each other took up the first few days. This was no problem, as they took to each other at once. We gave a party to introduce my mother to our friends, and she was immediately caught up in the farewell parties given by people going to cooler climes for the summer. The grandest was that given by the British Consul, to celebrate the coronation of Queen Elizabeth II. We had listened to the BBC giving us a detailed description of the ceremony on the radio and enjoyed the excuse to dress up and celebrate.

Granjo enjoyed finding out the different ways we did things in Aleppo. One thing in particular that interested her was the way I sat on my front doorstep when the eggman called, and solemnly floated eggs in a saucepan of water to choose the freshest ones. The best eggs were those that lay flattest. If they floated or stood on end they were considered to be stale.

Eggman Mohammed invited us all to visit him at his village. A date was agreed and we drove out into the desert, turned left at a bush (this was simpler than it seems!), followed a track over a rise and there was the village. The collection of beehive-shaped huts was clustered beside a vineyard of the most luscious grapes. In the centre of the village a man was sitting on the seat of a roller, which was being pulled by a donkey round and round over a pile of straw. This was their method of threshing. A little distance away a woman was tossing the wheat grains in the air, allowing the chaff to blow away in the wind. The winnowed grain was then swept up and put in sacks. Later we were to see the grain being ground between two round slabs of stone. This was probably why the local flour was too coarse for my Christmas cake.

The insides of the conical-roofed huts were scrupulously clean with a striped cotton mat on the floor and huge, fat cushions with woven covers to sit on. There were round, brightly-coloured, woven rush mats hanging on the walls above narrow decorative stucco shelves holding rows of tin plates. A mirror and an oil lamp stood beside a stucco spoon rack holding a row of teaspoons. A roll of bedding lay on a shelf. That was all the furniture, apart from twists of coloured toffee papers and coloured feathers dotted around the walls as decoration.

We were given tiny cups of Turkish coffee while Granjo was squeezed into a tribal wedding dress. We tried not to laugh and Mum tried not to breathe, as she was afraid she might split the prized garment. The village brides were much smaller than she was, it seems.

We returned home with some fresh eggs and several bunches of delicious grapes. John had taken some photographs of the village and the eggman's wife, son and mother. They were good pictures and he was able to enlarge them and present Mohammed with copies when next he called. Mohammed was absolutely delighted. We also took a picture of Granjo dressed in a tribal wedding dress.

Patricia enjoyed the extra attention Granjo gave her and the walks in the park. These outings were quite a pantomime at times, as Patricia was very small and dainty. Her blonde hair and blue eyes were much admired by the Aleppan ladies. It was the custom to kiss Patricia to show appreciation and to ward off the "evil eye". Patricia hated this adulation and would run away shaking her head, waving her arms and shouting "gi wai," her best effort at saying "go away." This caused much amusement to all and sundry.

As far as I was concerned time was dragging and the heat was beginning to get me down. My time came and went, and I was accused of having my dates wrong. Jimmy was very good, leaving the car outside the flat every night "just in case".

John was having some printing done for the Bank by some Franciscan Brothers and they gave him a "candle" to burn when the baby arrived. One evening Jimmy said that he was going out to dinner that evening and was it all right to take the car. Of course, at three in the morning I awoke, aware that I was beginning to have contractions. There were no gharries at that time in the morning, so I had to walk to the hospital. John did offer to carry me but I took pity on him! We staggered the half-mile to the hospital and had great difficulty in stirring the watchman who couldn't think what I wanted at that time of night! We persuaded him to let me in. The doctor was called and my room prepared - then I went "off the boil".

At six in the evening it was suggested I should go home again for the night. In fact Christopher was born two hours later at 8 pm, but not before John had raced through the streets to recall the obstetrician. We named the baby Christopher because we were so happy that he had arrived before Christmas. This was 30 July 1953.

Christopher was a lovely, big, bouncing baby with that special look of being overdue. His skin was peeling, his nails were long and he was quite jaundiced. Shortly after he was born we had a cable to say our friends Ian and Scilla Dobie had a baby daughter, Amanda, born three days earlier in Scotland. Scilla had won the race.

Later I was unwrapping Christopher from his shawl to let John take a good picture of him, as instructed by the great-grandmothers: "We don't want a bundle of shawl with a nose sticking out," we had been told. Suddenly, I noticed that he had six toes on one foot. John clicked the camera just as I was yelling "He's a freak!"

John always joked that like a good banker's son, Christopher was paying past due interest for arriving late! We were to learn that there was a saying that the next reincarnation of Alexander the Great would have eleven toes. Well, Christopher hasn't been crowned yet! The day he was born, the headlines in the papers proclaimed that the first man on the moon had just been born. They were a bit out in their calculations, as Christopher was not yet 16 when men did land on the moon in 1969. It seems they could not wait.

The ship on which Granjo was to sail home was due in Mersin in Turkey in five days' time. She had delayed her departure as long as she could. Jimmy very nobly gave her the Bank car and George to drive her to the ship. When they got to the Turkish border, George discovered that he was not permitted to take the car into Turkey as he was not the owner. Never at a loss, he hitched a lift for himself and Granjo on a lorry and got her to Mersin. The ship was not yet there, as it had secretly gone to Israel for a day and was delayed.

George put Granjo in a hotel for the night. She was taken

out to dinner by a Turkish doctor, much to George's dismay. He could not find her when he returned to check that she was all right before he turned in. The following evening the ship arrived and Granjo was safely put aboard. Much to George's relief, he was free to return home. We were pleased to see him and to hear all that had happened.

Margo and Henry went home on leave and kindly lent me their Persian nanny, Katy, while they were away. She was a great help to me when I came out of hospital. This was especially fortunate, as one morning Patricia did not come to wake us up as usual. John went to the nursery and picked her up only to find she was quite limp and unconscious. She was white and seemed very hot and her breathing was very shallow. He ran with her to the hospital and she was admitted at once. She was plunged into a bath of iced water to try to bring her temperature down. Eventually she came round, to our great relief, but the reason for her collapse is to this day a mystery.

The system throughout the Middle East was that mothers nursed their own children when they were admitted to hospital, so I was permitted to stay with Patricia. I had to take her temperature every hour and plunge her into the iced water if it went up to 104°. Katy looked after 10-day-old Christopher and brought him to the hospital for his feeds during the day. Each time feeding time came around I had to take a shower and dress in a sterile gown to try to safeguard Christopher, in case he caught whatever Patricia had contracted.

We worked out a system to cope with our babies. John came home from work at about 2 pm, had lunch and then went to bed and came to the hospital to relieve me in time for me to return home for Christopher's 10 pm feed. I then slept at home, gave Christopher his night and 6 am feeds, and returned to the hospital to relieve John. This went on for some five days until Patricia's fever left her and we were allowed to bring her home. She quickly regained her strength and was very happy to be with her baby brother. Katy was a great help and I was very lucky to have her.

Katy loved to drink stewed tea, collected from the remains of our tea left in the teapot. This she boiled and drank, sucked through lumps of sugar. She also liked the hottest chilli peppers I could find, which she ate like sweets. I was instructed to choose the small green ones with the sharpest points, as these were the hottest.

Some time before, John had taken up photography as a hobby. We would spend happy hours in our kitchen developing and printing our own films. Then he found a second-hand enlarger and progressed to producing some very good pictures. We glazed them by sticking them, when wet, on to the shiny chromium tank of the water heater in the bathroom. This worked a treat. They were of course black and white, but have become very good reminders of our time in Aleppo.

During the cricket season I had to keep an ear to the radio and be ready with the score from time to time. I also had instructions to keep the Bank informed if anyone was called out and tell them the bowler who was responsible. It appeared that all the staff were serious followers of cricket.

We had an ongoing chess game laid out on the sideboard

in the dining room. John would make his move before he went to work and I had until he returned at lunchtime to make my move. Woe betide Marie if she disturbed the pieces. Sometimes the game lasted for weeks.

Sadly, the man who lived across the landing died, and there were three days of mourning when a stream of callers came and went. The women in the household kept up a chorus of loud "Loolooloos" in the traditional manner. When the time came to actually take the body for burial, the coffin was carried down the steep staircase, held vertically to negotiate the corners, and we were surprised to see it loaded on to the roof rack of a car, which sped off to the cemetery. It was not long before the car returned and the empty box was propped up against the wall, presumably to be re-used at a later date. There were no flowers or wreaths: in fact it was a rather sad farewell.

Then I developed a very painful leg and I found it difficult to walk. The doctor decided that it was phlebitis and it was necessary to put my leg in plaster of Paris. This was extremely heavy. On one occasion I turned over in bed and my leg fell on the floor, and of course I fell after it. One of the worst things about wearing a plaster in the heat was that I developed prickly heat. I had to carry a knitting needle to enable me to scratch.

One evening just after I had had a new heel fitted and it was not quite dry, we decided to go to the cinema. I had to hop of course, so John went out to fetch a gharry while I hopped out to the street. At the cinema there was a long flight of stairs. Going up, John walked behind me carrying my leg as I hopped. We earned some very funny looks. The film I remember was "Streetcar Named Desire", in English but partially obliterated by French and Arabic sub-titles.

Coming down the stairs afterwards was really awkward. At first John tried to carry my leg behind me, but that necessitated him walking downstairs, bent double, which was nearly impossible. Then he walked in front of me, carrying my leg under his arm. We were laughing so much we felt quite weak when coming out of the cinema. Then he had to hail a gharry, which is not so easy, as when you have caught one, people tend to climb in on the other side and sit on the seat, thus claiming possession if you are not nippy. John made several abortive attempts, but it is difficult to defend your carriage on your own. Finally he got into a gharry and drove off, yelling for me to RUN!. I was helpless with laughter and couldn't run anyway. Eventually he persuaded the driver to turn round and come back for me. I don't think we have ever laughed so much.

The time was coming near when we were due to take home leave, so I began to pack our belongings into boxes and to store them under beds and on top of wardrobes. We had decided that I should go home a little early to settle the children in UK wherever we were to stay. That meant that John would be able to pack up our trunks ready for our next posting.

The time came for me to leave, and John was to take me to Beirut, where we would spend a night before we left for the UK by BOAC, as the airline was known then. We were to take off at about midnight, so I put the children to bed and we sat down to have dinner at the club with friends. Then the telephone rang. "Would Mrs Lindesay and family come at once to the airport as the plane is to leave early."

I hastily grabbed the sleepy children, dressed them, piled the luggage into a taxi and headed to the airport. We said our farewells to Daddy and went through immigration. As I was now in "the system" there was no reason for John to stay, so he returned to the club and then on to Aleppo the next day.

I settled down to await the call to board the plane. After about an hour I was told that there was an hour delay, then another hour delay. By this time Christopher was asleep in my arms and Patricia was running about the departure lounge. Passengers for a plane to Moscow were called and a crowd passed through the gate. When they had all gone I looked for Patricia, but there was no sign of her. Panic. I called ground staff and eventually a stewardess could be seen in the distance on the tarmac, holding a diminutive figure by the hand. The little madam had seated herself on the plane quite calmly and everybody thought she belonged to somebody else. It was only because the plane was full and the staff discovered they had a passenger too many that they realised Patricia should not be there. When that excitement had died down, I was told that I was being taken to a hotel in town, as they did not know when we would take off.

We got to our room and I got the children settled down and off to sleep. I had just put my head on the pillow when the phone rang and I was told, "Time to get up Mrs Lindesay, your plane leaves in one hour." By this time I was in a muddle with Christopher's feeds. I had prepared bottles suitable for a night flight and was running short of feeds for him.

At last we were seated on the plane and had taken off.

Christopher was screaming for his breakfast. I rang for the stewardess and asked for his bottle to be warmed, but was told that the breakfast for the passengers had to be done first. I was angry and said I imagined that the passengers would prefer that the baby stopped screaming and would be prepared to wait for their breakfast. The bottle was taken away and brought back too hot to hold. I was cross again and the bottle was snatched away and put to cool on a block of ice in the cool box. It burst. By now the other passengers were nearly as frantic as we were. I found a dirty bottle and the milk powder and took over the kitchen while passengers tried to pacify a near hysterical baby. Patricia had her arm round him, saying "Never mind Pissipa, I here".

Eventually peace reigned and we landed at Rome, where I got off and went to the airline desk to tell them that I was not going any further on that plane. They should find me another airline. However I was persuaded that the crew were changing in Rome and that I would be given every assistance by the incoming crew. I think I was so tired I couldn't argue.

The flight to London was much better and when we landed, a private bus was awaiting me and we were ushered straight through immigration to be greeted by Granny Lindesay. I was so happy to see her and to introduce her to her grandchildren.

Chapter Six

HOME ON LEAVE, 1954

It was late in the evening by the time we got home to Romsey. I'm afraid I don't remember much about the children's first night in the UK. Granny L. had found a cot for Christopher and had made up a camp bed in my room for Patricia. I expect I bathed the children and tried to keep to their routine. According to a letter John received from Granny, Trish was not at her best. All things considered, I am not in the least surprised. The flight left a lot to be desired.

As the great grandmothers, who both lived in Bournemouth, were clamouring to see the children, we all moved to 27 Alyth Road, the home of Frances L Dickson, or GG, as we all called Great Granny Dickson. The house was a mother's nightmare. There were glass-fronted cabinets full of antique china against every wall in every room. The polished parquet floors had beautiful antique rugs scattered about. Patricia, like all children, always ran and never walked, which made me very nervous. Christopher had not yet learned to crawl, so he was not a problem.

GG was a well-known antique ceramics and glass collector and was honorary curator of the Ceramic Department of the Fitzwilliam Museum in Cambridge, where the Glaisher Collection was her main interest. Dr James Glaisher had been a Don at Cambridge University, the son of James Glaisher, a scientist whose record balloon ascent of 25,400 ft in 1862 was not surpassed until 1894 and is mentioned in the Guinness Book of Records. Dr Glaisher was somewhat eccentric in that he had had rooms in the town, as well as his rooms in the college, full of his vast collection of ceramics of every variety. When he died in 1928 he left all his treasures to the Fitzwilliam Museum with the proviso that Mrs Dickson could have anything she wanted. They had been very good friends over the years and shared a great interest in all things antique. At the entrance to the Glaisher Gallery today, an enormous Martinware owl sleepily stands guard. He was made to the order of some businessmen in San Francisco, but was rejected as imperfect. A replacement was made and shipped out to the East Coast of America, only to be destroyed in the big earthquake.

GG was a great character, born in Kinsale, Southern Ireland, on August 4th. No one knows exactly what year as she could not, or would not remember. Birth records of the approximate time were destroyed in the "troubles" in Eire. She died in Bournemouth in 1967. She had two daughters, the elder of whom became Granny Lindesay.

GG was well known for, among other things, always

wearing a red hat: a felt one in winter and a straw one in summer, which she repainted herself every spring. She put one on when she got up in the morning and wore it until she went to bed at night. GG lived with a housekeeper and her dachshund Puck, who was incredibly spoilt and very much adored by his owner. She drove a huge Daimler car, slowly, down the middle of the road, much to the consternation of other road users and the embarrassment of her passengers. It seems GG was under the impression that to drive in the middle of the road was better for the springs of the car! Actually, she was so small that she could not be seen through the rear window by anyone driving behind, which gave the impression that the driver's seat was empty. On one occasion, much to the horror of her garage mechanic, she tried to stop a leak in the water system by pouring porridge oats into the radiator.

"Porridge in the radiator of a Daimler!" wept the garage man, who was appalled at the idea of clearing out the fine tubes that made up the Daimler cooling system.

Going to the cinema with GG was another embarrassment. She hated to climb stairs and always insisted on sitting downstairs, in the back row of the one and nines, where the lovers preferred to sit. She usually fell asleep and, on waking up, would demand, in a loud Irish voice, an explanation of the film so far, because she couldn't understand it.

On other occasions I can remember being told to stand outside the gents and "keep them out" while she went in, because the ladies was upstairs. None of the family really minded her idiosyncrasies and loved her dearly. She was generous to a fault and so one hesitated to mention the need of anything. When I introduced Patricia and Christopher to her, the first thing she did was to take us down to Edwin Jones, her favourite shop, and kit them out with warmer clothes which were better suited to an English summer than those they wore in Aleppo.

I took them to see Great Grandmother Hill, who lived in Boscombe with their Great Aunt Joy. They too were thrilled to meet the first of the next generation of the family. Granny Hill lived in a flat above a railway line, which was a great fascination for the children, who were not at all familiar with steam trains.

My brother, Stephen, who was stationed at Larkhill, came to Abbotswood to meet his nephew and niece in his 1929 Morris Cowley Tourer, which he had purchased for four pounds ten shillings. Patricia called it his "broker car" because it had no roof. One morning he took Patricia downtown and bought her an ice-cream in a cone. She had not had ice cream before and complained bitterly that it was too cold. Uncle Stephen was a bit nonplussed by this, but offered to warm it up beside the engine of his car. She loved to ride in the "broker car," especially in the back where she could see the road rushing by through the hole in the floor.

Naturally Granjo and Gramps were eagerly waiting their turn to meet Patricia and Christopher, so we decided that I would take them up to Scotland by train. I was a little nervous embarking on any journey alone after the experience of the flight home from Beirut, so it was decided that I would travel by night and have a sleeper. The children were very excited at the prospect of going in a train, at least Patricia was, and Christopher was excited at anything we did.

Granny L escorted me to London and helped me on to the train. I remember we were able to get on at least half an hour early, so I was able to put the children to bed, toe to toe at each end on the bottom bunk. We arrived in Dumfries very early in the morning and there was Gramps to meet us. I think the grandchildren and grandparents became friends at once. Gramps had a wonderful way with the young and was easily able to capture their interest. Granjo was happy to meet Patricia again and to have a good look at Christopher, as she had to leave Aleppo so soon after his arrival.

Glencaple was paradise for Patricia. The shore of the River Nith was a wonderful place to run and my father, known as Gampy, was always prepared to take her for a walk with Christopher in his pram. Glen, Stephen's collie/labrador cross, ran alongside playing his interminable game of dropping stones, to be kicked along the road for him to fetch and drop to be kicked again.

Old Glen took his duties of guarding the children very seriously. If Christopher was asleep in his pram out in the front of the house, no one was permitted to even peer at him. Even people he knew were warned off. It was wonderful the way he allowed the children to maul him about, considering he was not really used to children about the house.

Granjo had gone to a lot of trouble preparing a toy box for the children. It had once been full of baby bathing equipment that was used for my brother Stephen and me, when we were infants. Now it was filled with all sorts of interesting playthings. The box itself was on casters and could be pushed along making a lovely rattling noise, so it became nicknamed "Noisy."

Not long after we arrived in Glencaple, Patricia ran one of her temperatures. I thought that she was having another attack of tonsillitis, but Granjo wanted the doctor to see her. He diagnosed scarlatina and advised isolation and bed rest. This was a bit sad, as we had invited one or two friends, to celebrate Christopher's first birthday, including Amanda Dobie, who had beat him into this world by three days. Patricia's quarantine forced us to delay the celebrations.

The doctor arranged for Patricia to see an ENT specialist about her frequent attacks of tonsillitis. It was decided that, even though she was only two and three quarters, her tonsils were so enlarged and unhealthy that they were obviously holding her back and she would be better if they were taken out. I took her to Dumfries Infirmary, where I had to leave her. In the Middle East mothers were expected to be with their children while they were in hospital, so I felt awful leaving my little girl alone in such a place.

The operation went well and I collected her the next day. I swear she ate more for her first meal on her return home to Glencaple than she had eaten in a week before she had her tonsils out. She ate and grew so much it was a real relief to see her thriving so well. The doctors were absolutely right to risk operating, although she was so young.

It was time for John to come home at last. The children and I caught a sleeper to London and I managed to get them and the luggage to Winchester, where Granny L met us and took us back to Abbotswood. The next day we all drove up to London Airport to meet John. The children were so pleased to see Daddy and I suspect, judging by the enthusiastic greetings, that he was pleased to see them too.

At this time we decided that something had to be done about the sixth toe on Christopher's left foot. We thought about the extra pocket money he could perhaps earn, letting other children see it. Then we remembered the problems we would encounter providing odd shoes all his life. The problems prevailed, and we took him up to Great Ormond Street Hospital and sat in a waiting room while they snipped the outside toe off. I think it would have been a neater job if the inside one had been removed, regardless of the metatarsal which showed up on the X-ray. However we were glad to have had it done before he learned to walk. Now we were able to buy his first shoes.

Granjo and Gramps had managed to borrow a holiday cottage in the village for us to live in on our own, which was clever of them. However much I loved my family and they loved us, it was a strain on all concerned when we stayed in other people's homes. We went up to Scotland again and moved into Cot House. All went well for the first week and then I fell ill and the doctor diagnosed viral pneumonia. Granjo and Gramps were very busy, as the wildfowling season had begun. They had so many wildfowling guests staying that they were unable to help John look after the children.

John managed on his own for the first week, but we then learned that I could be ill for some time. A week later Granny L came up to help. Mrs O'Reilly, a friend of long standing, took me into her cottage, as it was difficult to keep the children away from me in Cot House and we did not want the children to catch the virus. The doctor visited me every day and once a week I was taken by ambulance to the infirmary for an X-ray. During this period Christopher took his first steps and he was quite good at it by the time I saw him again. It was difficult to stay out of their sight and John and the grandmothers did well to cope so well for so long. What a sad waste of our first leave.

Finally after eight weeks I recovered and was considered fit enough to travel south by train, which I did with the children. We had arranged for a Universal Aunt to meet me and to assist me transfer to Waterloo to catch the train for Winchester. Unfortunately she was an elderly lady and not up to carrying the cases and doing the things we had hoped she would. However, I managed and we caught the train and moved back to Romsey.

John drove our car, Penny, down south and we started to prepare for Christmas and for our departure for the Middle East again in late January.

On Dec 23rd Granjo and Gramps arrived to stay with us

all for Christmas in Romsey. The children were getting very excited as the shops were much more Christmassy than in the Middle East. We all went to Alyth Road in Bournemouth for a wonderful Christmas dinner and lots of lovely presents. We returned to Romsey in the evening. On Boxing Day Reverend Sam Boothman christened Christopher at Braishfield Church. It was a real family affair and a great many of the family came to the service. A family tea party was held in the afternoon and Christopher and Patricia were introduced to a great many of the family.

After Christmas Granjo and Gramps went back to Scotland. John's sister Mary and Aunt Joy, my mother's sister, accompanied us on a visit to the Isle of Wight. The children enjoyed the trip on the ferry and clambering over the grounds of Carisbrook Castle

Then the time came for us to pack our bags and take leave of the family and board a plane for Beirut again, for our next three year tour. We were on our way to Jeddah in Saudi Arabia.

Chapter Seven

JEDDAH 1954-1956

We arrived in Beirut, where our heavy luggage was held in transit. There were many forbidden imports to Saudi Arabia contained in our trunks, dolls and teddies for example, or anything that could be taken for a "graven image." We were anxious about Christopher, as he was at a very amusing stage: perhaps the Saudis might think he was a caricature? All alcohol was strictly forbidden, which was a pity as we had a large collection of miniature bottles packed in our trunks. We were not permitted to take a bible or any religious artefact.

Jeddah was the main port of Saudi Arabia, situated on the Red Sea. It was the gateway for all pilgrims on their way to Mecca, which was some 80 miles inland. Mecca is a Holy City and it is the hope of every true Muslim that he or she will kiss the black stone at the Kabbah and perform the rite of the Haj (pilgrimage) at least once in their lives. As keepers of the Holy Shrines, the Saudis feel that strict adherence to the Koran is essential.

We left the children with friends and set off to unpack all our forbidden bottles, bibles and bears in the customs shed.

As we would be charged duty on our miniatures if we took them into Beirut, we decided to have a party on the spot. We did not have any mixers for our drinks so there were a few very jolly Lebanese customs men by the time we had finished!

Before we left for Jeddah we had to try to think of ways to smuggle in at least "Favourite Dolly" and one bear, if not the huge "Teddy Ah". I must say the thought of not having some of their favourite toys was a bit distressing. I searched the shops in sophisticated Beirut for patterns to sew dolls and things, as a last resort. In the end I unpicked the lining of the sleeves in our jackets and pushed a doll in one and a teddy in the other. We practised walking nonchalantly with our jackets carelessly thrown over our shoulders. We did not tell the children, as we were convinced that they would be bound to give the game away. Actually, when we arrived in Jeddah Airport no one took any notice of our luggage. I think they were all so fascinated by our two very blonde children that they forgot to look in our cases. This was more annoying than if they had searched them, as I kept thinking of all the things I might have smuggled in.

John King, who my John was to relieve again, and Dave Morgan, the assistant accountant, met us at the airport. As it was early February the temperature was quite pleasant. The airport was not bustling or noisy - in fact we were nearly the only passengers getting off there, which might have warned us!

We were taken by taxi to our new home in a modern block of flats on the waterfront. There were four rooms, plus a kitchen and bathroom. There was a small veranda off one of the rooms so I decided to make that over to the children. The ceilings were very low so that the wall-mounted air-conditioners could cool the rooms more economically than the high-ceilinged traditional houses in which the local people lived. As in Aleppo, we had no space for the children to run. In fact we were worse off, as there was not even a park nearby.

Unpacking looked as if it would be a major problem, as we had no cupboards of any kind. There were two chests of drawers, a sideboard, a bookcase, one small wardrobe and some shelving in the kitchen. This was our total storage space and we were not to have any more furniture it seemed, as the manager, a bachelor, did not want to waste money on such luxuries! We put our packing cases on the kitchen veranda and made ourselves some shelving out of the lids. Actually we did not require any storage space for some months, as our heavy luggage was to take a very long time to clear customs. We understood that our books were the main problem, as each and every one had to be inspected, and it took many visits to clear it in the end.

The Bank was in a very old building a short distance from the flat, so John could walk to work. Lawrence of Arabia had used it as his headquarters when he had distributed largesse during the 1914-18 war. The walls were thick with high chundle and barasti ceilings similar to those in our house in Isfahan. It was too high to be suitable for air-conditioning, but ceiling fans slowly disturbed the air. If the speed was increased the draught tended to blow papers about and to redistribute the dust. Periodically huge cockroaches would fall from the ceiling on to the desks below. There was no counter in this bank, as the work was done at desks, and the counting of the money, which was all coin at that time, was done by a cashier, who sat on the floor beside large wooden trays that held rows of piles of ten coins. There were, of course, no computers in those days. All records were kept by hand in huge ledgers written mostly by clerks from Aden, in their old-fashioned copperplate writing learned from the British. At that time there were very few Saudi clerks, as their standard of education was insufficient.

The doors to the bank were about twelve feet high and made of solid wood, quite decoratively carved, with huge wooden bars to slide across on the inside to secure them at night and during the Haj or Pilgrim season. At the rear of the building were storerooms and the strongroom, where the bags of rial coins were kept, behind some rather rickety bars locked with a padlock and chain. These bags, each containing 1,000 rials, were very heavy, and they periodically caused the floor of the strongroom to sink slowly into the cesspit below! When this happened more concrete was poured on to the floor to make it level again. The rial and fil coins were the only currency of Saudi Arabia at that time. I remember being told by the Manager that if I could carry off a bag, I could have it. Sadly, as 1,000 rials was not to be sniffed at, I could not even lift it.

When cash was transferred to the National Bank, a donkey cart was used. This was considered quite safe as the poor little donkey could hardly drag the load along, let alone run off with it.

It was found that the price of silver had risen in Mexico, where the coins were minted. Old coins would be shipped to Mexico, melted down and re-minted into rials at a ten per cent profit. It was then deemed more economical to produce paper money.

One day the Chief Cashier of the National Bank changed the number of the combination lock of their posh strongroom door. Then they tried shooting the bolts with the door open. Unfortunately he had made a mistake in setting the combination and could not unlock it. It so happened that John had had some experience with this problem in Bahrain, and was asked if he would try to repair the damage, as the National Bank's safe was now locked open. He set out to try his luck with the aid of a doctor's stethoscope. Eventually he disassembled the tumblers of the locks and reset them. He could claim to be chief safe-cracker to King Ibn Saud, as it seemed that no-one else in Jedda had seen a combination safe before.

When, during the Haj, Persian women came into the Bank to change their money, John sent for me to come and help him. I found him surrounded by women dressed in their chadors clamouring for their money. The problem was they were supposed to be identified by their passport photographs and, as they could not write their names, they had to "sign" with a fingerprint. As a male, John was not permitted to touch these women, and they were having difficulty in selecting which finger they wished to put on the inkpad. My job was to decide for them and get the job done more quickly. I had to laugh as

John looked at the pictures in the passports of one eye peering out of a chador, then he looked at the woman in question and noted that the eye probably looked the same but the chador was different. I then took a hand and firmly pressed a thumb on to the inkpad and then on to the document. The lady was then given her money and off she went. We sat there and did this all day and it was a great relief when the last chador swished out of the back door.

That year the Turks did not come on the Haj, as the Turkish Government was short of foreign exchange. Rumour had it that the Hajis got on the boat and then were told that they could consider themselves Hajis, as the fact that they had started on the journey to Mecca was just as good as actually getting there, so now they could go home. The following year we were still in Jeddah and the Turks came by the boatload, and were either very old or very noisy and belligerent. It seemed that they were convinced that the money would run out, so they besieged the Bank. John arranged for a chain to be put on the door to prevent it from opening too wide. A few Turks were allowed to get in, then the clerks put their shoulders to the door, kicking back the arms and legs struggling to squeeze in, then pushing home the wooden bar. Those inside were then dealt with as fast as possible and sent out of the back door before they wrecked the place or dropped dead. There was a huge notice on the door, in Turkish, saying there was plenty of money and begging them to be patient. Poor John - that turned out to be a very long day.

At first I would visit John with the children every day, as there were very few places for me to go. Walking in the street was quite nerve-racking as there were very few European women or children in Jeddah, and we were considered oddities to be stared at. In the case of Patricia, her blonde hair and blue eyes inspired people to touch her hair or pinch her cheeks. She would get very angry and would protest loudly, but it was difficult to protect her. The local women wore long black garments covering them from head to toe, with a lace insert across the eyes to enable them to see. I was surprised at the way they appeared to recognise each other, as they all looked the same to me.

As a woman, I was not permitted to go in a taxi on my own, as all women had to be escorted by a male. We had a Yemeni male servant called Saif, who had been trained in Aden so spoke reasonable English, and he would escort me on shopping trips. This was just as well as no shopkeepers spoke English, and such Arabic as I had learned in Aleppo was of little use. I learned that there is no universal Arabic, as each country had its own dialects. The Newspaper Arabic that John had learned was not the spoken Arabic of the people, and a slight nuance could alter the meaning totally. The shops were, at first, of the "hole in the wall" variety, but the choice of goods was much wider than in Isfahan. There were tins from all over the world and cereal packets from America. I remember some packets of Corn Pops with chips of Marshmallow in them. They contained little plastic toys, which were joyfully received by the children. I suspect that they were very old and stale by the time we bought them. Certainly the Corn Flakes tasted very stale and were not improved by the powdered milk we had to use. However, there was one Cold Store where I could buy meat and sometimes-fresh vegetables if I got there on the right day.

We suspected that the meat had arrived in Jeddah on the hoof from a long way away, as it was invariably tough. The best meat was imported from the Lebanon and we bought it by the inch as it was frozen lengths of fillet steak. I used this meat for everything as it was, at least, edible. Pork was, of course, a forbidden commodity, but some manufacturers, or perhaps importers, would get round this, for example by inking out any mention of pork on the label of a tin of baked beans and sausages. I used to ask for black marked tins and feel very smug that we were eating forbidden pork sausages, which somehow tasted all the better. By the time we left, nearly two years later, there were a few glass-fronted shops and several supermarkets had been built.

There were no automatic telephones, as it was feared that men would talk to other men's women. The telephone system worked by calling the exchange on an archaic machine with a handle, rather like an old coffee grinder, which rang a bell in the exchange. If and when the exchange responded you asked to be connected to the number required. The operator listened to your conversation and if he did not approve of your call or could not understand what was being said, you were disconnected. If one tried to make a call at prayer time, one found the exchange was not manned. We did not have a telephone, as there was little point.

Keeping myself, and the children occupied was a time-consuming business in itself. I spent a lot of time brewing wine and beer, which, of course was forbidden. The children would help me weigh out the rice and raisins and count the grains of yeast, then carefully measure the correct amount of water. I remember trying to make sherry with tinned grape juice, honey and icing sugar, in a pail with some yeast spread on a piece of bread floating on the top. This was not a success, as it tasted much like vinegar when I had finished. I bottled it, but told Saif to pour it down the drain. He misunderstood me and stored it high on a shelf in the kitchen. We discovered it months later and found it to be a passable sherry, or perhaps our palates had, by then, become blunted.

Saif used to "moonlight" by running the local "off licence". He took us to see his shop once and it was stocked to the roof with a variety of eau de colognes. It seemed the locals would drink these "nice smells" in lieu of real alcohol.

We had not been in Jeddah long before we decided that we really could not do without a car. As we had just returned from leave we were not flush with cash, so John took out a loan and bought a Volkswagen Beetle. This enabled us to get out of town whenever John was not working in the late afternoon, and on Fridays (his day off). Women were not permitted to drive in Saudi Arabia, possibly because there was no knowing where they might go.

After a period of time Saif thought he would like to learn

to drive so that he could drive me to various coffee mornings and tea parties. There were no formal driving schools in Saudi Arabia. Men learned to steer, more or less, and then just drove. The rule of the road was supposed to be to keep right, but I think the one that really prevailed was "after me," especially if one was a sheikh or a member of the Royal Families. We tried to teach Saif the rudiments of safe driving, but unfortunately he did have an accident and was put into jail.

We went to visit him and tried to give him a good character reference. It was very interesting to see the inside of a Saudi prison. We were given the VIP treatment, especially as I was there, because women did not usually appear in such places. We were ushered into the Commandant's office and given tea and treated very courteously. After a short wait Saif was brought in and we asked if he needed anything. I think there was some question of a fine, which we paid, and Saif said he would work it off. He was soon back at work.

On Fridays most of the European community would drive some thirty miles down the coast to the creek, where there was a good beach, shallow water for the children, and a coral reef that dropped down to a great depth. At midday, when the sun was overhead, really large fish could be seen sluggishly milling about some 200 feet below. Floating on the surface, wearing mask and snorkel, made us feel quite dizzy, as if we were leaning over a precipice: the feeling that if we did not hold on we would fall was very strong.

It was fascinating to watch fish of every colour, darting in and out of the coral. Amazingly they did not appear to be in the least concerned that we were there, as they nibbled their way in and out of the coral trees and gently wafting seaweed. The cuttlefish darted away and squirted ink when disturbed. The children loved to collect hermit crabs and build sandcastles for them, or secrete the poor things in the car ready to take home. On one occasion they succeeded. During the night, the crabs escaped from the bucket and crawled all over the flat, hiding under beds and behind chairs where they died and, in due course, starting to smell.

One of the Dutch Bank bachelors caught a fish and gave it to Patricia, who brought it home. She was caught tucking it up in her bed. When John suggested that perhaps we might cook it for the cat, which Christopher had been given some time before, the idea met with very stiff opposition as "Fishy" was declared the love of Patricia's life. Eventually we managed to persuade her that really it would prefer to be wrapped in silver paper and live in the fridge, where it remained for many days, being paid regular visits.

There was no shade at the beach, apart from that under the three-foot high cliff where the desert met the beach, so we found a tarpaulin in the souk and took it along with us, tied on the top of the car. When we arrived we laid it out on the ground, above the cliff edge, and then parked the cars so the front wheels anchored it. Next the spare wheels were attached to the guy ropes on poles at the front, as the sand was too soft to hold pegs. This gave us an area of about 250 square ft of shade. This was much appreciated as the sun was very hot and the sun creams of those days did not really protect us.

On one occasion we were returning from the beach when suddenly a swarm of locusts appeared. They looked like huge grasshoppers, about four or five inches long. We hastily wound up the windows of the car, but not before one or two had got in, much to the horror of the children. They landed on the car and the desert all round us was heaving with them. John wondered if our windscreen wipers would work and move enough of them to enable him to see to move on. We had not required the wipers before, as we had not seen rain for many months. With a mighty effort the wipers managed to clear a space to enable John to catch a glimpse of the track before more locusts landed and they had to clear the space all over again. They were thinning out by the time we reached the road, and we were able to get up some speed and blow the remaining locusts off and then open the windows again. Whew, it was hot with them closed.

There was a period of about four and a half months when the water to the town was cut off completely. This was when King Ibn Saud had built his new Palace in Jeddah, and had ordered a rose garden. Roses need water, so the entire supply for the town was diverted. Our daily supply was brought by donkey cart, carried up the stairs and stored in the bath, using all our saucepans, jugs and any other containers we could find. I filled the toilet cistern and flushed once and then filled it cistern again. There had to be a large jug set aside to clean the bath in preparation for the next day's supply. We all had to bath in the same water, cleanest first. I managed to get some salt-water soap from the ships so we were able to bathe in the sea, though this necessitated a 30-mile drive down the coast.

Laundry was a problem, especially as Christopher was still in nappies and this was long before the days of disposable ones. Fortunately, as it was so hot, the children and I lived in bathing suits most of the time, so I had only John's shirts and undies to cope with and such clothes as we wore when in public. One of my main difficulties was getting clothes dry. The climate was so humid I found I had to iron Christopher's towelling nappies dry and check they did not steam by holding them against the mirror.

Friday was the day convicted thieves had their hands cut off and murderers lost their heads. This was done as a public spectacle in the square outside our flat; the hands and heads would be hung on posts along the roadside, so we had to distract the attention of the children as we drove past on our way home. Usually, I would drop some sweets on the floor of the car and ask them to pick them up.

One Friday we came home from the beach to be greeted by a stream of water running down the stairs. Opening the flat door sent a wave rippling down the hall and into all the rooms. The carpets were afloat, as there was about three inches of water all over the floor. We were in a panic as a new boutique had just opened downstairs and I was convinced that the water was cascading all over the racks of very expensive frocks.

The water had stopped running but it was evident that the water supply had come on while we were out, and a tap in the basin had been left turned on. A face flannel had blocked the plughole, with the result that the water had overflowed on to the bathroom floor. The drain in the floor was at the highest point, so the water had flowed into the flat.

I tried to sweep the water out with a broom, but it made little impression. In the end John and I took a side of a carpet each and scooped the water through the door and down the stairs. Eventually we drove it all out and then tried to peer into the boutique to see what damage there was. We could not see any and were very pleased and relieved to learn the next day no harm had been done whatsoever.

We hung the carpets over the veranda, where they dripped on people walking below. I think we probably had the cleanest floors in Jeddah, and spent the most humid night. We regretted the waste of water as we could have put it to good use had we been at home.

To help entertain the children and keep them cool, we had built a sand pit and paddling pool on the small veranda off their room. One morning they were playing out there and I was ironing when Patricia called for me to go and see what Christopher had done. I said I would come when I had finished Daddy's shirt. I put the ironing board away and went to admire, as I thought, Christopher's sand castle. Imagine my horror when I saw Patricia leaning over the balcony holding onto her brother's feet while he hung upside down over the path below. I think I nearly died when I remembered I had insisted on finishing the ironing. We put up fly screens to keep the children in and the flies out after that.

On another occasion I put the children to play for a while on our flat roof. There was a three-foot wall round it and nothing to climb on, so I thought they were quite safe. I was busy in the house when an Arab woman came to the door and kept pointing upstairs. I did not understand what she wanted but thought I should go up and see. As I walked out onto the roof, there was my son and heir walking along the wall on the far side of the patio, with the wobbly gait of a 16-month baby.

I was petrified. How I managed to walk calmly across the 15 yards to get to him I'll never know. I remember I whistled a tune and took huge strides. When I got to him I opened my arms wide, conscious of the danger of knocking him off the wall, or causing him to overbalance and fall the 40 ft to the ground. When I grabbed him my legs gave way and, much to his amazement, I burst into tears.

Not long afterwards, the town's electricity supply gave up trying to cope with the influx of air conditioners and went off during the day. In the evenings, we put the children into the back of the car and drove round with the windows open, keeping cool until about 11 pm when the electricity came on and we could switch on the air conditioners. In retrospect, I was kept so busy trying to cope with problems of ordinary living that I suppose I didn't have time to miss the luxuries of life.

The staff of the British Embassy were a great source of help and entertainment. They had a motor launch, and we were lucky enough often to be invited out on it for picnics. Usually we went out to Baatchy Island, a real desert island in the Red Sea. There were some wonderful shells to be found, some of which were really large. The north side was covered in round flat nacre or mother-of-pearl shells, often used to make expensive lampshades. The water was so cool and clear it was a treat to swim in it and the children enjoyed playing with the bachelors, who were so good with them.

Once a week the Embassy showed British films on their roof. The whole English-speaking community was invited and sat in rows with their legs in pillow cases and with arms, legs and necks smothered in Vick vapour rub to ward off the mosquitoes. Usually the films were old and scratched and kept breaking down, but they were greatly enjoyed by everyone.

One evening we were invited to dinner with the British Ambassador and left Saif baby-sitting. Half way through the soup a message came that Patricia was screaming and would one of us go home quickly. John got home to find Patricia very upset as she had managed to pull the head off her doll and the rubber chip stuffing was pouring out. In fact she was "bleeding" to death. John managed to get most of the stuffing back into the doll and Patricia settled down. He returned to the dinner table just in time for coffee.

Chapter Eight

HOLIDAY IN KHARTOUM

The summer became hotter and more humid and there seemed no end to the water shortage. I was invited to stay with some friends in Khartoum in Sudan, so John said I should go and have a break. Though I hated leaving him behind, we agreed that it might be easier on us all if I took the children to a civilised place for a spell, as he would find it less traumatic if he did not have us to worry about.

We flew to Khartoum on the day the first Juba uprising in the southern province of Sudan began. Juba was a town in the south of the country and was predominantly Christian. There were undercurrents of religious fervour and tribal infighting was fermenting all the time. It was discussed as sketchy details came over the BBC World service. The newspapers we received were at least a week old and we were quite unaware of any local home news.

The aeroplane had 12 seats and the pilot could be seen through the open door to the cockpit. As there were very few passengers on the plane we became friends with Captain Joe and he told us a little about Khartoum. He said it was a far more sophisticated place than Jeddah. There was a large department store named Morhigs, where all manner of luxuries could be found, like children's shoes, ladies' undies and cosmetics, and there was a coffee shop on the roof where the most delicious ice creams were served. I hoped the finances would stretch far enough.

We were met by our host and hostess and driven at once to their house in Garden City on the outskirts of town. It was a pleasant house with large airy rooms. Fans high in the ceiling gently moved the hot and dry air, which was a contrast to the hot humid atmosphere of Jeddah. The children and I were thrilled to see green grass and bushes bearing the pink and red trumpets of hibiscus flowers and the cascades of purple and scarlet bougainvillaea hanging from the walls and trellises round the garden.

The first thing we all did was to have a shower and luxuriate in the rich, soapy lather. The salt-water soap we scrounged from the ships in Jeddah had never really given us a satisfactory wash in the sea.

In Khartoum there was no water supply problem, but there was a drainage difficulty. The Nile flows through the town, but the land on either side of the river lies below water level, with the result that at that time, there was no drainage system. The bath water flowed on to specially planted Canna lily beds. These Cannas looked a little like gladioli and were well suited to soaking up waste water as they required a great deal of moisture to survive. The loos were outdoor privies, or thunder boxes, built into the garden wall along the road. This enabled the buckets to be emptied early each morning by lorries known as lavender wagons. I was a little nervous visiting this place, especially at night, as there were scorpions lurking in the corners, and snakes in the grass and flowerbeds. There were also spiders hanging from the ceiling in the loo, and from branches overhanging the path. As I had to escort the children, I had to run the gauntlet fairly often.

It was customary in Khartoum in the height of summer to sleep in a fly-netted cage on the roof, where the gentle breeze helped to cool the night air. Certainly we slept better up there, but it felt strange waking up in the morning in the same cage as our host and hostess and in full view of the neighbours sleeping in their similar cages.

After our arrival my host took me to the British Club and made me a temporary member. As both my host and hostess worked during the day, I had to find my own way about and to find friends with whom to pass the day. Like everywhere in the Middle East, the working day began early. The shops were open and the town bustling by 8 am, as if everybody wanted to get their business over before the wilting heat of the day. I had taken both the children's tricycles with me, which was just as well, as I found that I could save money by walking to the club, towing Christopher on his trike while Patricia pedalled hers. The walk took about half an hour, and even in the early morning it was quite hot work, so we were all ready for a swim when we arrived at the Club. The gardens were extensive and there were plenty of tarmac paths for the children to ride along, and bushes to hide in. I was always uneasy in case there were snakes or other horrors lurking ready to pounce, but really my fears were quite unfounded.

The swimming pool was a very grand affair with Grecian pillars round the tiled surround and sweeping steps leading up to the edge of the pool and then down into the water. There was no shallow end and it was quite deep all over, so I had to watch the children like a hawk, as they had no fear of the water and were not really accustomed to swimming in a pool.

I well remember on one occasion Christopher leaped into the water yelling that he could swim. He sank to the bottom and just lay there with his eyes open. I was paralysed for a second, then a woman dived in and brought him to the surface, whereupon he sproggled for a second then, very annoyed at being pulled out of the water, yelled very loudly.

One morning we arrived at the Club walking or pedalling as usual. Outside the gate was a magnificent red Rolls Royce with what looked like a rajah in full fig. He wore a long brocade gown and matching turban with a white fluffy cockade. He was dusting and polishing the already glistening car. We walked to the pool and there, sitting on the edge, was Christopher's rescuer and another young woman. I ran up to them, very excited to know what important visitor had arrived.

"Please tell me, who owns that magnificent car with the gorgeous flunky dusting it?" There was a silence for a minute. Then I learned that I was talking to the wife of the British

Governor of the Sudan, and the car was hers. It appeared that Christopher had been rescued by the Governor's wife, no less. I was to meet her again.

One evening, Joe, the captain of the plane from Jeddah, came to ask me out to dinner. He wanted to show me some of the nightlife of Khartoum. We had dinner in a nice little restaurant and then he took me to a nightclub. It was a very seedy place, although it was supposed to be the best in town. I was unimpressed by the dancers with holes in their fishnet tights and the juggler kept dropping his Indian clubs. The music appeared to be a little flat, so we did not stay long. I wanted to get home as I did not want to disturb my host and hostess when I crawled into bed in the cage.

The way home during the day was along the waterfront and through the Governor's front gate, past the front door of the Residence and out the other gate and on along the road. We swept through the first gate and, just as we went through, it shut behind us. On we went to the next gate, only to find it already shut and locked. No one came when we shouted, so we had to go up to the front door of the Residence and ring the bell. The Governor and his wife came to the door and I explained what had happened. He told me that he had just arrived home himself, and as the gates were usually locked at 10 pm every night, he imagined that the gateman had supposed that we were guests and had let us through. He arranged for the gates to be opened for us, and Joe got me home somewhat later than intended.

The time came for us to return to Jeddah. I went to the

Sudan Air Office to book my flight, only to discover that, as my residence permit for Jeddah had expired, I could not fly until it was renewed. I cabled to John to send the requisite documents.

The days turned into weeks and still the permit did not come. It seemed that all residence permits had to be sanctioned by the King himself and he simply had not got round to doing so. At last I received a cable to say that John had my permit and I could catch the first plane home. I went to the airport with my luggage and the tricycles and two very excited children. But the Sudan Air ticket desk would not accept my cable as evidence that I had a permit awaiting me in Jeddah, and refused to let me fly. No matter how I pleaded, they were adamant. They would be fined a lot of money if they allowed me to fly to Jeddah.

I was desperate. I couldn't go back to my hostess as she really thought she had seen the last of us. I do not blame her, we had been invited for a fortnight and we were now into our ninth week. I had to go somewhere. Where was the next plane out going? Asmara in Eritrea. I knew the British Consul there, as we had been in Aleppo together, so I would cable him and ask him to meet me. I would cable John to let him know where I was and then leave Khartoum. It was 9.30 am and the temperature was 109 degrees. I found my way to the Eritrean Consulate and persuaded them that I really required a visa to enable me to visit Asmara right away. The Consul was not accustomed to strange European women having such an urgent need to visit his country in this way, but having agreed to inform the British Consul in Asmara that I was coming he provided me with the necessary papers.

We landed in Asmara and a very puzzled Consul was there to meet me. I explained what had happened and that Asmara was my refuge. He could not put me up at the Consulate because he had a trade mission staying with him, but he had booked me into a hotel. He was sorry his wife, Sheila, was in England but he would do what he could to help me.

Asmara was the capital of Eritrea, on a plateau 3,000 ft above sea level. On a clear day we could see the world spread out below like a map. The gardens and parks were green and lush. The children were fascinated by the hairstyles of the local women; it had been plaited and fixed in neat lines like a ploughed field on their heads. It must have taken hours to create. When we arrived in Asmara the temperature was 70 degrees and we all felt cold. It was 109 degrees in Khartoum when we left. We did not have any warm clothing or any money to buy anything, so I dressed the children in several layers to try to keep them warm and I wore three frocks myself. The hotel was Italian and no one spoke English, so I was back to miming again. No word from John yet.

I discovered that there was hot water in the bathroom on Wednesdays and Saturdays only. It was Monday, and the children were in need of at least a good wash. With difficulty I managed to make my request for some hot water understood and after a long wait, a very small saucepan of hot water arrived. I put the plug in the basin and proceeded to undress the cleaner child. By the time I turned back to the basin all the water had gone. The plug did not fit properly and the precious hot water had leaked away.

The following morning, on my way to the dining room, I overheard an Englishman struggling to make himself understood at the reception desk. To my joy, he turned out to be a pilot on his way to Jeddah. I asked him to go to see John and ask him to send me some clothes as soon as possible. Meeting this pilot was a real piece of luck, as when he went to the Bank and spoke to John, it was the first news my husband had heard of us. He had not received any of my messages and did not even know that we were in Asmara.

Meanwhile, I asked for more hot water the following evening. This time I got a larger saucepan of water. I had found a better plug in another basin. I washed Patricia first, as she was the cleaner of the two, and was about to wash Christopher when I heard the gurgle of the last of the water going down the drain. Patricia helpfully had let the water out for me. Oh well, I had one clean child and the next night was bath night.

An Italian who came to stay at the hotel spoke good English, which was a great help. It turned out that he had been a prisoner of war in England during the last war, and had worked on the land. He told me tales of how the Italians had sabotaged their own tanks by putting water in the petrol cans shipped to North Africa from Italy. He also described how he had searched for the British lines as soon as he landed in North

Africa, as he did not want to fight. He was a nice man and he made life a lot easier for the next few days. The pilot came back with a suitcase of clothes and the news that my husband would join us very soon.

We were very pleased to see John when he arrived. It was fun exploring Asmara with him. He too, found the climate difficult. We felt warm in the sun, but if we crossed the road to the shaded side we felt the need of a jacket or cardigan.

After prohibition in Saudi Arabia we were amazed at the number of bars in Asmara. All shops had a bar at one end where one could have a whisky and soda or a coffee while choosing shoes or shirts. This was very helpful, as the hotel did not have anywhere for us to sit, and the bed was very uncomfortable for two as it sagged in the middle.

After one week we had had enough and the money had run out so we returned to Saudi Arabia.

Chapter Nine

A BRUSH WITH THE LAW

After we had been in Jedda for about nine months the Manager changed. The new Manager, Eric Jenkins, took pity on us living in the flat and gave us permission to move. We now had to find somewhere to move to.

We heard of a ground floor flat in a villa five kilometres out of town on the Mecca road. We went to look at it and it looked like heaven after the flat. It had two good-sized bedrooms, a large sitting room with a similar sized dining room off it. The kitchen was adequate and so was the bathroom. There was a room in the compound for Saif and, above all, there was a garden, or at least a patch of desert with two thorn bushes in it. There were two other families in the compound and a tennis court. What was more, we had our own electricity generator, which could be used when the town electricity supply broke down.

The Dutch Bank flats in the town also had their own generator, which could be used when the public supplies failed. I recall one occasion when their generator cut in and a whole street in the souk lit up as well. It seemed the Dutch Bank's private supply was not so private.

Our new manager, Eric, had a wife, Wyn, who came out to Jedda in the winter months, so I had a happy time introducing her to the community and showing her the best places to shop. This also meant that we were able to make use of the Bank car and driver.

The patch of desert round our house was unfenced so, as we felt it necessary to keep the children from straying too far, we built a fence to keep them in and marauding pariah dogs out. I also marked out what we hoped would eventually be flowerbeds. The ground was so hard that we had to use a pickaxe to make any impression. I found this to be very heavy going and used to wear shorts to try to keep cool. Imagine my surprise when one day, a messenger arrived at my door asking me not to wear shorts when I was in the garden, as some people found it offensive - when looking through their binoculars!

I looked round for the nearest house. Apart from those in the compound which contained Europeans, there was a palace about 500 yards away and a few villas beyond. As I did not know anybody living there I was unable to protest, so I decided that I had better do as I was asked, though I disliked the idea of being watched through binoculars.

I awoke one morning with the most terrible toothache. I tried all the usual remedies, oil of cloves, chewing an aspirin, but nothing would help. I asked around my friends to see if anyone knew of a dentist, but no one did. I was in such discomfort that I decided to go to the Bank to see what the Saudis did in such a case. One of the messengers knew of someone in the souk. I was such a coward that the very idea of visiting a dentist of any sort made me panic.

However the pain was sufficient to drive me to follow the messenger into the souk, into an old building and up a flight of dark stairs. I wondered where I was being taken, as I had visions of white slave markets and never seeing my family again. On the second floor we went into a darkish room with no furniture other than a bicycle fixed to the floor and a plain, high-backed wooden chair which stood beside a table with some instruments on it. A bearded Arab came into the room and my escort burst into what appeared to be a dramatic description of the trouble I was in. I could only grin fearfully and point into my mouth.

The dentist pointed to the wooden chair and I sat down, resting my head on the high back. I was petrified, as I did not understand a word of what was being said, and had great difficulty in opening my mouth without my lips quivering. I fully expected the dentist to take a pair of pliers and yank the offending tooth out. But no, after prodding about in my mouth and making what I took to be reassuring noises, he hopped onto his bicycle and proceeded to pedal like mad to operate the drill on my tooth!

I did not dare move as I was convinced that I would make his hand slip and he would cut me up. I need not have worried. He was most efficient and did a splendid job in filling my tooth; I still have the filling to this day. When I returned to the UK and visited my own dentist, I learned that the drill powered by a bicycle was like those used in Victorian times in the UK before electricity was universally available. As the dentist spoke no English he had probably trained in Egypt. Wherever he learned, I was very grateful, as he was able to solve my problem and save my tooth.

Sometimes, for a change, we took a picnic and drove inland to a wadi, or riverbed, about five kilometres up the Mecca road. There we found trees surrounding a garden and a cafe where we could buy cold Coca Cola and sit at tables in the shade. Mecca was some miles further up the road and we had to be careful not to even see the Holy City, as this was strictly forbidden to all 'infidels'.

Occasionally pilgrims would make their pilgrimage in some spectacular way, believing that they would earn extra credit for so doing. I remember one man, a Turk I believe, passing our house by falling full length on the ground, crawling a few feet forward, standing up then falling again full length. His progress was slow, and I imagine rather painful.

Water holes were scarce and shade was essential, but to sit under an umbrella in the middle of nowhere lacked interest. There was one place, however, where we found some weaverbirds' nests hanging like miniature cradles from the branches of some tall thorn trees. There were very few places to go for a picnic in those days in Saudi. The hot desert lacked any appeal. I remember someone asking what there was to see in and around Jeddah and getting the answer that if you drive 30 miles up the coast the sand changes colour.

We were certainly taxed to find amusement for the children, especially in winter. Sometimes we drove into the desert and let them drive the car. They had to sit on John's knee as they were too small to reach the pedals, but they enjoyed wig wagging the winkers and zig zagging to match!

We lived in Jeddah for twenty-one months, which included one Christmas. It was quite difficult to inspire the Christmas spirit, but we had a party on Christmas Eve at our house. We invited the entire English-speaking community, including the Desert Locust Force. This was a group of men who spent most of their time searching for locust swarms in the desert. When they found them they tried to destroy them while they were at the hopper stage. This was to try to prevent them descending on such green pastures as there were, in Saudi and countries further afield. Poor chaps, they were very pleased to have a few home comforts and to have the opportunity to play with the children.

We had nothing to offer our guests by way of Christmas spirit, other than home brew and a traditional turkey with most of the trimmings and mince pies with home brewed "brandy sauce." I also made a Christmas pudding and poured some "sediqui juice" over the pudding and set it alight. You had to be looking to see the flames, as it went up with a whoosh and clouds of black smoke. The pudding became a bit sooty but I think it tasted pretty good. "Sediqui juice" was the name given to the distilled "gin" bought from the American Airline pilots, who had homemade stills built from pressure cookers and copper piping. I would not try to do this as it was, potentially, very dangerous. The airline pilots at least were able to take samples of their "brew" to Beirut to have it tested for lethal wood alcohol

We spent the rest of the evening playing games of various sorts until everyone went home about three in the morning. The last car had just gone when there was a crash of thunder, the heavens opened and we had a tropical rainstorm. We were horrified to discover that our veranda sloped inwards, with the result that the rain poured into the living room under the French windows and the carpet was afloat. We hastily lifted as much furniture as we could up off the floor and piled it on the table and the sideboard. It was fortunate that the floor was terrazzo tiled and would come to no harm. We tried to sweep the water out of the door, but it was a losing battle.

Luckily we were to have Christmas lunch with the Manager, so we were all able to have a lie in. It was still raining when we awoke in the morning and the desert around us was a lake as far as we could see. It was evident that the Mecca road had been constructed along an old riverbed, as it had become a raging torrent and parts of the tarmac had been swept away in the night. Jeddah was in no way equipped for rain, as there were no drains or ditches.

The time came for us to go to lunch, and much to our surprise the car started. With the aid of nearly everyone in the compound we were pushed through the mud, out on to what was left of the road. We inched our way to the Manager's house and found that they were above water, but that their roof was leaking. The result of this was that we had a splendid Christmas lunch to a chorus of plink, plonk, plunk as water dripped through their ceiling. The drips were caught in a series of vessels dotted around the carpet.

On the way home John wanted to go past the Bank to see how it had fared. There was a lake outside the building about two feet deep, but the water had not reached the top of the steps leading into the Bank, so we imagined all would be well inside, though we did wonder about the strongroom over the cess pit!

The next day the rain stopped and the sun came out as usual. The desert was still a vast lake, looking strangely like a mirage, though we knew that the water was all too real. Gradually the water subsided from the roads and groups of men began to repair the damage. We dragged our carpets outside and hung them on the veranda wall to dry. It took a great deal of mopping and sweeping to dry our floor sufficiently to take the furniture down off the dining table. By the time John came home we were able to sit at table again.

Two days later we got up in the morning to find the desert green. If we looked along the ground it was as if a lawn had appeared. However, looking downwards the blades of grass appeared very sparse. Tiny flowers sprang up amid the grass and insects appeared from nowhere. They seemed to be having a feast as if they had never seen the like before. It seemed they were right, as the last time it had rained in Jeddah was some ten years earlier. The greenery lasted two more days and then the winter sun dried it all up again and the dry dusty desert returned. It was surprising to think that seeds lie dormant in the ground so long just waiting for water to appear.

It was not long after this that I heard the awful rumour that three American children had been kidnapped and ransoms had been asked. It was said that one child had been returned, one had been found dead and the third had not been found. I was horrified, and convinced that our children would be obvious targets, being Bank children. Saif was very sweet, and tried to calm me down by telling me not to worry, as if our children were stolen, they would be sure to be taken to Mecca, where he could go and get them back!

For weeks I would not let the children out of my sight. I insisted that they were watched even while playing in the garden. Other mothers were equally nervous and we kept a close eye on each other's children. Actually we did not hear of any further cases, but the fear remained with me always. I did tend to be a little over protective of the children, and latterly I had to make a conscious effort to let them go anywhere without supervision. I ought to say here that at no time did our children receive anything but kindness at the hands of people in the Arab world.

One afternoon, the children were invited to a birthday party in the American Embassy. John was driving us there and we were about to overtake a cyclist, who was riding along the desert beside the road carrying a large block of ice wrapped in a sack, on his shoulder. Suddenly he turned left across the road. He hit the side of the car, and incidentally my arm which was resting on the open window, fell off his bicycle and lay in the road.

The police arrived and we were all taken off to the police station for questioning. An English speaking officer was sent for and we gave our statements, while sipping tea and the children drank Coca Cola.

Progress seemed very slow, and the children were getting restless, so we decided that I should walk, with the children, to the Embassy to inform the British Consul of the situation. When I returned with him to the police station, we found that John had been told to drive himself to the hospital to see if he was too drunk to drive! We waited for him to return. Eventually John asked if he might take me and the children home. I could not go by taxi, as I did not have a male escort. We climbed into our little Volkswagen, the children and me in the back, as we had to take an armed guard with us, presumably to ensure that John did indeed return.

It was difficult sitting and waiting and not knowing what was happening. I bathed the children and got them ready for bed. They were too young to understand the situation and it was difficult to explain why Daddy was not there to read their story.

At about 9 pm John arrived home and announced that he had to go to prison for the night. Saif, very upset, declared that prison was no place for Sahib, and offered to go instead. In the meantime John ate a rather over-cooked dinner and I found the Lilo, a torch, and a book for him to read. The police guard was sitting with Saif in the kitchen when suddenly the dining room door was thrown open and Saif rushed in, grabbed a bright red tablecloth from the sideboard drawer and rushed out again. I was later to discover that he had thrown it over the large glass container in which our next brew of wine was fermenting, in full view of the policeman. Fortunately the policeman either turned a blind eye or did not recognise an illegal brew. However, nothing further was heard about it.

John washed and cleaned his teeth. Clutching a sheet as well as his torch and air bed, he set off with his armed guard to drive himself to the prison. When he got to the police station he found that it was closed. A message had been left there that his guard should take him to the main prison. However, the Consul had extracted a promise from the Governor of Jeddah that afternoon that John would not have to go to prison while further inquiries were being made. John told his guards, (two now that the messenger had joined the party) that they would go to the central police station and see what could be done.

When they arrived at the area police station, the guard was half asleep and simply did not want to know about John's problem. John says that he made himself as unpleasant as possible to the duty officer, but he was not in the least impressed by any threats of dismissal with ignominy that were flung at his head. By now John was very angry and sent one of his guards to try to raise the consul while he drove round and round with the other. The guard came back after a suitable interval, saying he could get no reply to his attacks on the embassy doors. Whether he actually tried we shall never know, but he was very apologetic about it. It was then decided, as the guards were past due to go off duty, that it would be helpful if John would actually let them deliver him to the prison.

Jeddah prison is not the place for a rest cure. When John arrived he peered through the barred gate into the central courtyard. He decided that it looked like Dante's Inferno, with bodies lying about all over the ground, and was no place for him to venture in the dark. So he stalked on into the Commandant's office, remembered from the time we had visited Saif, and told the guards that he would sleep there. He blew up the Lilo, lay down and composed himself for sleep. Unfortunately the floor sloped and he had put the Lilo down with the head at the lower end. He did not dare get up and turn it round as the guards were standing round gazing at him and to move might have broken the spell.

In the morning a deputation of guards came to say that the Commandant was about to arrive, and it would be much appreciated if John would go inside the prison so that they would not get into trouble. They had even brought out an English-speaking prisoner, an Adeni serving a six-month sentence, he said, on suspicion of having liquor in his house, to help to persuade him. John decided that honour had been temporarily satisfied, so he accompanied his guide, who led him to a room about fifteen feet square. About twelve individuals of various nationalities, Saudi, Adeni, Sudanese, Somali and Egyptian but no Europeans, occupied it. They appeared to be serving sentences for anything from adultery to murder. All had their possessions piled in their own bit of space where they could sit and guard them. There were two Primus stoves for cooking, in the middle of the room.

For the next five hours John walked round the prison, stumbling over prostrate bodies and holding his breath at the more fearsome smells. His Arabic was sufficient to enable him to have a good chat with his roommates, none of whom were guilty of any of the crimes of which they were accused, of course. They were very ready to sympathise with another sufferer and plied him with tea. Outside the room was the courtyard, with a large concrete pool about two feet deep, half full of water. This was the province of the Palestinians, who had strung up tarpaulins, blankets or just sheets of cloth over ropes to give them some shade.

At the back of the courtyard was a large airy room with very few occupants. This was the preserve of the long-distance truck drivers, who seemed to be an élite. Beyond them and through a tunnel were some of the smelliest lavatories John had ever had the misfortune to come across. Beyond these were some sinister tunnel-like catacombs, pitch dark to the unaccustomed eye, where, it seemed, the long-term prisoners gravitated, away from the constant coming and going of those who were only in for a few months. There were no internal partitions and once inside the gates everyone was "free" to wander wherever they chose. There were armed guards stationed on the walls surrounding the complex, but they seemed to have little say in what went on inside. John learned that the prisoners were given a small allowance in prison, with which to buy food or stationery from a few hawkers who had the concessions to sell inside. Food was provided, but it was very basic.

I arranged for friends to take the children for the day and persuaded one of the bachelors upstairs to drive me to the prison with a thermos of hot water, some clean clothes and breakfast. First we went to the police station where John had said he would be. He was not there, so we went to the main police station, only to find that he wasn't there either. Eventually we arrived at the prison and the guards on the gate were reluctant to let me in. As they could not speak English and my Arabic was certainly not equal to what was required, I had to resort to firm action, so I pushed them aside and marched into the Commandant's office, carrying clothes, food and shaving kit, and demanded to see my husband. I suspect they were not sure how to cope with me, so John was sent for. We discussed our next course of action and John took the clothes and food and set off to wash and change in the slightly more salubrious Commandant's private washroom.

I left him and set off to find the Consul and to inform the Bank Manager that he was short of an accountant that day.

When the Consul heard that John had been found literally

behind bars, he practically exploded. The whole Embassy sprang into action. The Consul went to see the Governor, the Vice-Consul went to the hospital to check up on the boy who had been knocked down, and the third secretary went to the police. The Ambassador was informed and told to stand by with the heavy artillery in case the lighter stuff made no impression. The result of it all was that after John had shaved and changed his clothes, he was asked to sit in the Commandant's office while things were sorted out.

The Consul discovered that, though the governor admitted that he had promised that John should stay the night at the Police HQ, he had omitted to give the necessary instructions to the police. However, would John please be so good as to accept the hospitality of the police HQ until he was released?

The instruction for John to move came at an opportune moment for the Commandant. While they were sitting in the office one of his ex-room mates was brought in wrapped in a blanket and huddled in a corner until an ambulance came to take him away to hospital. It seemed that he had been in an argument with another prisoner and had been badly burned when they had managed to upset one of the Primus stoves. Shortly afterwards a large and obviously influential Saudi came storming into the office, pulled the Commandant out from behind his desk and demanded to see his son. The son, it appeared, had been caught *in flagrante delicto* with either a woman or a bottle and had been jailed at his father's insistence.

Father was the head of the Haj Committee, and a man of some considerable consequence. It transpired that his son had been in the fight. When the son arrived the Commandant grabbed him by the scruff of his neck and thrust him at his father, urging him to kiss and make up. The father would not agree. He just wanted his son to be properly dealt with. A Court of Enquiry was in full swing, and the Commandant seemed to be getting the worst of it, when the telephone rang and the Commandant, after listening for five seconds, sighed with relief and said, "Come on Mr John, we are going to the police HQ."

John gathered up his belongings and gave them to one of the guards to take to the car, which had remained parked outside the prison. John had not let anyone take it away or relinquished the keys, as it was just about the only thing of value we owned at the time. The policeman climbed into the back and the Commandant got in the passenger seat, when they found that the damp had got at the plugs overnight; the car refused to start. The Commandant leaped out of the car and called the guards down off the prison walls, telling them to give them a push, and so they set off.

The main police station was a rather more salubrious place than the prison. It was opposite the British Embassy, which was convenient, as they said they would take over the job of feeding John. It was difficult for me to do so when our house was so far out of town and I lacked transport, so I was very grateful. The community was very kind and went in to visit him whenever they had a spare moment. I took our typewriter in so he could get on with letters.

I went to see the Ambassador to ask what he was doing to

help. Poor man, he had only just arrived, and was not officially there until he had presented his credentials to the King, who was on a hunting trip somewhere in the desert. It was the same inability to locate the King that was delaying John's release. In those days no one could do anything without the King's express permission, and the penalty for mistakes was too dire to contemplate. Anyway, I was sure that the Ambassador was not doing enough to secure John's release, so I picked up a large book from his desk and threw it at him. Some nine or ten years later I noticed someone ducking his head behind his arm at an Embassy function in Teheran, and there he was, pretending to be afraid of me. Very embarrassing!

John arrived at the police HQ at about 7 pm and was duly signed for. He was put in the orderly room, where he had to sit and await developments. Orderly room life was quite entertaining, as the policemen were the scruffiest lot of individuals he had seen for a long time. They came in with the usual lot of army gripes: "Someone has pinched my shirt", "I want a day's leave to bury my grandmother" etc. At one time the office was filled up with recruits who were made to stand under a mark on the wall to be tested for size, the only standard required it seemed. The two policemen who were peering at the candidate's heads and standing on their ankles to keep their heels on the floor would hardly have reached the mark if one had climbed on the other's shoulders! However, having chosen one man a good six inches under the standard and another who would have looked at home in a lunatic asylum, they disbanded the parade.

The next day life became duller, as the Chief of Police had tired of climbing six floors to reach his office and had decided to exchange it with the orderly room. Both rooms had to be redecorated, so John was moved up to a room two storeys higher. As it took them about five minutes to get their breath back, his visitors were subdued at first. However it was peaceful. But he did not have the antics of the would-be recruits to watch. He was in a private room shared by a huge Sudanese, whom John had previously taken for a night watchman. However it turned out that he was much more important than John, as he was the head of an area of Jeddah, and was being held to ensure the good behaviour of its population!

In the afternoon I found John had moved out on to the veranda which overlooked the British Embassy, but the Inspector objected to him waving to the Embassy people in case he was arranging his escape! Eventually word came that John could be released on the guarantee of a reputable Saudi. A customer was found and John came home, after ten wasted days.

Shortly after his release I injured my back and was sent to the hospital for some heat treatment. My appointment was for 11 am and I was there a little early. I sat in the waiting room reading my book when a cloaked lady came in and started shouting in Arabic to the doctor, then came and sat down. The Egyptian doctor turned to me and said in English that this lady was one of the King's court and she insisted on having her treatment ahead of me. Then we exchanged remarks about how rude and inconsiderate the Royal family were at times. I said that I didn't mind waiting as I had a good book and quite appreciated the doctor's difficulty.

"What part of England are you from?" asked the lady, throwing back her cloak. I was quite taken aback to hear her speaking English, and her accent was very good. It turned out that she was the Turkish sister of a wife of one of the princes. She had been to Oxford University and was in Jeddah on holiday. I asked her what it was like being an educated woman living in a harem. She told me that it was an extraordinary life and the women lacked for nothing. Only that week a great trunk of haute couture garments had arrived from Paris, and they had had a wonderful time trying them on. Anything they saw in a magazine they could ask for and it would be ordered. When they were tired of living in Jeddah they asked to go abroad, and the world was their oyster.

When she went in for the treatment the doctor was in a panic. He did not realise that she spoke English, or he would not have spoken his mind about the Royal Family. He was afraid he would lose his job, or worse, be sent to prison.

The next time I went to the hospital, the same lady came in and bowed to me, saying, "You are first today Mrs Lindesay." She asked me where my husband worked. I did not want to tell her the truth, as we had seen enough of prison to last a while, so I told her he worked in a garage as a mechanic. I thought it would take her a while to find out the truth. Actually neither the doctor nor I heard any more. The authorities there were so unpredictable, especially towards the

Palestinians and Egyptians who did most of the work. I mention this as it illustrates the strain of living in Saudi Arabia at that time, and how we appreciated having freedom of speech at home.

The Bank had tired of the ancient building it had occupied since it had opened in Jeddah, and had been actively seeking new premises in the modern buildings which were beginning to appear on the Port Road. Negotiations came to a head during Ramadan, the Moslem month of fasting, when office hours were from 2 pm to 5 pm and then from 8 pm to midnight. The manager and John would then go to call on one of the merchants who was building a new block and sit for one or two hours sipping tea, trying to persuade him to allow the Bank to have the ground floor of his building, even though he really wanted to have a car showroom there. The next night they would return, only to find themselves back on the first floor again and forced to talk their way down, step by step, to the ground floor. After a month of this, they gave up and settled for a building to be built by one of their other customers, on a rather awkwardly-shaped plot quite close to the old office.

The building was nearly finished when the strong-room door arrived. John took the keys down to the site, as they had to be kept under his control. Unfortunately these keys would have to be replaced, as the "sardine" can in which they had been sent direct to the Bank from UK had been opened by customs, so they were compromised. When John arrived on the site he found that the contractor had decided that the aperture he had been instructed to leave was too small to take the door. He was starting to enlarge the opening when John arrived and quickly pointed out that the flanges at the back of the door were supposed to be taken off and replaced when the door had been fitted, so that the door frame held on to the back of the wall. If he had enlarged the opening as he planned, the door would have been balanced in the hole and it would have fallen on top of the first person trying to open it, probably John!

It was at this point, in 1956, that the Egyptians decided they wanted to nationalize the Suez Canal and life became a little more difficult for the British in the area. The Embassy was asked to repatriate all British women with children. I believe there was a gunboat sitting over the horizon ready to repatriate British citizens if necessary, but they did not want to have to cope with children. As John had been posted to Beirut and was due to go in about six weeks' time I was sent there to await his arrival.

When he joined me in Beirut we had served nearly two years in Jedda and were the first married couple to survive the posting with our marriage intact without resigning from the Bank. All our married predecessors had either divorced or left the Bank. From then on our postings were measured using Jeddah as a yardstick. I think we can safely say that Saudi Arabia in the 1950s was our worst experience, and we reckoned that if we could survive that we could survive anything. Everywhere else was paradise in comparison.

Chapter Ten

BEIRUT

The children and I were very sad to leave John in Jeddah, and I was a bit apprehensive about setting off again without him for an unknown destination. We were met at Beirut Airport by the accountant and taken to La Residence Hotel. We had been allocated a suite of three rooms with a little kitchenette and bathroom. The Bank was to pay for my accommodation and I had to provide my own food. There was a restaurant on the top floor but the menu was not suitable for the children and was rather more than I could afford, so I cooked on the electric ring in the kitchenette and sometimes made up a picnic lunch for us all.

There were no Bank wives in Beirut at that time, apart from the Manager's wife, and she left soon after we arrived. The Bank bachelors were very helpful while I got myself organised. I was made a member of the St George's Club, which was a very short walk from the hotel. I could take the children there to swim and have lunch for a reasonable price. We developed a routine of making our own breakfast at the hotel, shopping or walking and exploring in the morning, then on to the club for lunch. Back to the hotel for a rest in the afternoon, and then we returned to the club for tea and a swim until the children's supper and bedtime.

Most evenings the Bank bachelors would take turns to come and babysit for me while I either went to the club for dinner or was invited out to a new-found friend's house. People were very kind to me and made a great effort to see that I was not too lonely and did not miss John too much. Even so, I must say I looked forward to his arrival.

The American Navy was paying a courtesy visit to the Lebanon, showing the American flag. One afternoon an American sailor made friends with the children while they were swimming at the Club. We started chatting and he told me that he had two children the same ages as my two, and that he missed them very much. He enjoyed playing with Patricia and Christopher and was impressed by how well they could swim and dive. He invited me to dinner on board his ship, the aircraft carrier *US Forrestal*, that evening at 6.30 pm. I explained that I was living in a hotel and had to put the children to bed, and would not be able to get a baby sitter so early at such short notice. He replied that he meant that the children should come too and said a Jeep would come to collect us at shortly after 6 pm. Christopher was not yet two and a half years old and Patricia about four, so I was not sure how they would cope.

At 6 pm sharp a Jeep drew up at the hotel entrance - with two motorbike outriders! We climbed in with great excitement, and off we went. The aircraft carrier towered above us from the dock as the Jeep bumped up a ramp and into an opening in the side of the ship. The children were lifted out of the jeep and I stepped out as elegantly as I could.

We were led into the middle of a great platform which rose steadily until we were level with the flight deck, where our friend awaited us. Then we were piped aboard, feeling very important. It was then that I learned that our sailor was none other than "Jimmy the One", second in command of the Forrestal. We were to have dinner at the Captain's table in the wardroom!

I was horrified, as I did not think that the children were really up to a formal dinner like this. I was quite wrong. They sat on either side of me and a sailor stood behind each child, helped them cut their food and even spooned some into them. I must say the children made me proud as they behaved so beautifully.

The meal over, they were taken away and entertained for about an hour, while I finished my coffee and chatted to the officers. Many of them were family men and I think genuinely enjoyed having the children there. I felt very self-conscious that I was the only woman present, but they were excellent hosts and it was a very pleasant evening. The children were brought back babbling incoherently about planes and things they had seen. We were driven back to the hotel in our Jeep, with outriders as before. The children were happy and had enjoyed themselves, although they were tired and ready for bed.

We got up early the next morning and ran down to the

beach to wave to the ship as it sailed away. It is sad that today neither Patricia nor Christopher remember anything about their dinner at the Captain's table on board what was then the largest aircraft carrier in the world. If they could remember they might be able to tell me how the US Navy managed to supply Christopher with a disposable nappy! They were a very rare commodity in those days and I would have given a great deal to have discovered where they had found it.

Two weeks had gone by and the fighting over the Suez Canal continued. I met several of the news correspondents at the bar in the Club and heard how things were going. There was one old reprobate who spent his time gossiping at the bar and sending the tales home to his paper before returning to his room, next to mine, at La Résidence, where I could hear him snoring loudly through the wall. I'm afraid he did not impress me much as a purveyor of first-hand news, though his capacity for gin and tonic was phenomenal. The old reprobate really ought to have retired, as he rarely left his bar stool, and that was to go to bed and not to gather news.

There was, however, a young *Times* reporter who worked really hard and seemed to wangle himself into and out of all manner of scrapes. He had pale blue eyes, I remember, and told us about his exploits with an intensity of excitement which really had a ring of truth.

One morning, as I was sitting in the shade at the Club watching the children dive off the raft, Christopher came to tell me he was going to the loo. After some time he had still not returned, so I went to see what he was up to. I could not find him anywhere and no one had seen him. I was getting frantic. Then I looked down at the sea – to see him lying motionless on the rocks some fifteen feet below the sundeck area, with the waves washing over him.

I screamed for help. A young man scrambled down to Christopher and passed him up to another man who was reaching down. There was blood pouring from his head and he was unconscious. I grabbed a towel, wrapped it round him and ran out to the street, where I hailed a taxi and was driven at speed to the hospital.

The Beirut Hospital was a teaching hospital and the doctors and nurses were mostly American trained so, at least, I had no language difficulty. Christopher was whisked away from me and taken to the X-ray and casualty departments. I remember that I was very cold in the air-conditioned hospital, I had not thought to dress before I ran out, so I was wearing only a rather damp bathing suit. Eventually I was given back the blood-soaked towel I had wrapped round Christopher. I put it round my shoulders in an attempt to warm up.

After what seemed a long wait, a doctor came and told me that Christopher had a cut on his head and they had stitched it up, but he had not cracked his skull. However he did have concussion, so they wanted to keep him in for a while. I was taken to see him and he looked very small lying in the white bed with his head swathed in a huge bandage. He was very dopey and did not seem to care if I was there or not. He was being well cared for, so I decided to take the opportunity to go back to the Club, to see what had happened to Patricia and get myself dressed. I felt a bit conspicuous standing on the pavement dressed in my bathing costume and no shoes, clutching a bloodstained towel. I also realised I had no money to pay for a taxi, and then I remembered that I had not paid for the taxi that had brought us to the hospital either!

I arrived back at the Club to find Patricia sitting with a friend having lunch. I told the Club manager that I would have to return to the hospital as I ought to be there when Christopher woke up.

Everybody was very kind to us. It was suggested that, as I spent so much time at the Club anyway, I might as well take over two of the rooms available for visitors passing through, as this would be easier for me to have help in keeping an eye on the children. I was allowed to bring Christopher home that evening, though I had to keep him in bed for the next few days. With the help of kind friends we managed to keep Patricia amused and Christopher quiet until he was back to normal. Certainly it was easier to manage with extra hands and eyes about, though I did miss my little kitchenette at the hotel.

Two weeks later John arrived in Beirut, and we were very glad to see him. The day after he arrived, we moved into a little villa in the Patrakia district. It was a pretty little house built into the hill, with three bedrooms and a living room with a dining area at the back with a vaulted ceiling. There was a tiled patio, large enough for the children to ride their tricycles, with tubs and troughs for flowers round the edge. We engaged a maid called Marie, who lived in a room off the kitchen. The Patrakia was a quiet residential area with a Catholic bishop living on one side of us and, we discovered at a later date, a rather high-class brothel on the other.

The Lebanon is a beautiful country with mountains stretching inland and the wonderful blue Mediterranean Sea lapping on the beaches. Beirut was a modern city with sophisticated shops displaying a variety of goods from all over the world. There were markets which sold fresh fruit and vegetables, grown in the gardens in the mountains and in the Bekaa valley to the east. There were supermarkets and department stores cheek by jowl with boutiques and small emporia beside tailors and hairdressers, a shoe shop next door to a jeweller, bookshops beside cafes, furniture stores alongside electricians. In fact it was a delicious contrast to all the places I had lived in to date in the Middle East.

The community was very cosmopolitan, speaking French, English and Arabic. As the Lebanon had been under French mandate, like Syria, the French influence was very evident in the buildings, with their pretty little wrought iron verandas, and in their inadequate plumbing arrangements. Most educated people spoke French and it was commonly spoken in the market, though Arabic was the native tongue. English was widely spoken too, as there were a great number of Americans working on various projects with the United Nations who had offices and ran refugee camps for Palestinians in the mountains. There was also a large rest and recreation centre where UN men and women came to recover and prepare for their next period of duty, mainly in Israel.

The political climate was very confusing all the time we were in the Lebanon. The various religious factions were feuding continuously. If a Lebanese was asked what he was, he would not reply that he was a butcher, baker, or candlestick maker. He would say that he was a Christian Maronite, Druse, Copt or Muslim Shiite, etc.

Not long after we arrived in the Lebanon, parliamentary elections were held. The various religious and political factions fiercely contested these. In the end Camille Shamoun, a Christian, was elected President, while the Muslim Sammi Solh was elected Prime Minister.

There were a great many Palestinian refugees in camps dotted about the country, where they lived without work or anything to do, and so had plenty of time to fume about their situation and foment trouble for all and sundry. They had been displaced when the state of Israel was formed and so had become homeless refugees, causing embarrassment to the hard-working trading Lebanese, who really did not want to have their cosy lives disturbed. There were more refugee camps in Syria and Egypt and they did not want to settle them either, as they were useful as a reason to stir up trouble for Israel. The situation was difficult enough because so many had to live as refugees in camps, though the United Nations was doing its utmost to cope with an insoluble problem. All this, added to the anti-British feelings provoked by the pro Egyptian Gamel

Abdul Nasser fanatics, and the Suez Canal crisis, made Beirut a difficult place in which to live at times.

Bombs began exploded in various embassies and offices all over the Middle East, and Beirut became inundated with European refugees fleeing from Syria, Iraq and Jordan. Most of the British people went on to the UK, but unmarried Bank personnel were billeted on those of us left in Beirut, as it was considered safe enough on the whole. The Rolls Royce agent in Damascus passed through on his way to the UK and left his dog Cindy, a corgi cross, with us.

We had two men from the Bank in Jordan staying with us. Things became a little difficult when we were unable to obtain replacement butane gas bottles for the cooking stove. I found a primus stove and, as I already had a pressure cooker, I managed to cope. It was summer, so hot food was not essential but thinking up a varied menu was a problem. One very hot sunny day I had an idea. I made a meringue mixture and placed small portions on a chopping board, a tumbler over each, with a stone under the rim of each glass to let the air out. The meringues dried beautifully in the sun and we had a very exotic variation to the menu. I called them "cloched meringues".

As there were so many people passing through Beirut, health control became a problem. An edict was issued that everyone must carry a certificate to say that they had been vaccinated against smallpox, cholera and typhoid. There were checkpoints all over town and if you were unable to present a certificate when stopped you were inoculated there and then.

Some people looked like boy scouts with rows of plasters up their arms where they had been re-vaccinated several times. I was always careful to see that we carried our papers at all times.

Guards were put on the entrances to all offices and public buildings and all bags were searched for anything suspicious. I remember being angry with the guard on the Bank door one morning. He allowed me to pass without turning out my shopping. I insisted that he inspect my onions and that he was to let no one into the Bank, whether he knew them or not, without searching them. After all, my husband was in that office and no risks were to be taken.

Unfortunately, for the first few months after we moved into our little house in the Patrakia one or other of us was always ill. Patricia had rheumatic fever, Christopher had bouts of bronchitis and we all had influenza, including the maid. Christopher had cyclical vomiting and had to be taken to hospital to be intravenously fed, as he had become dehydrated. At the same time the maid was ill and Patricia was recovering from another bout of illness. This was very difficult to understand as we had survived the problems of Saudi Arabia and had been reasonably healthy. Our diet was so much better in Beirut that it was difficult to understand why we should all be so unhealthy. The climate was not very hot in the Lebanon, so we did not require air conditioning, but it was very humid, and everything was damp. I became convinced that our house was damp as well as humid.

After a certain amount of argument we managed to

persuade the Manager that indeed we did have a problem and he allowed me to look for other accommodation. I looked at over 50 apartments and eventually found a ground floor flat in an old building, with a small garden, in the El Hamrah district, quite near the University. We moved, and became well again.

When the floor was pulled up in the little villa it was discovered that the floor tiles had been laid straight on to the ground and there was no damp course. One could squeeze water out of the sand in which the tiles were bedded. What had been taken for Beirut's humidity was in fact rising damp.

Our new flat was a great success. The children enjoyed the garden, as they had plenty of room to play. We made a sand pit and there was a small lawn where they could pitch their tent. Cindy enjoyed the freedom too. The main snag was the traffic, which ran on two sides of us, but we quickly got used to that.

The building was an old one and the rooms were large with high ceilings. The floors were cool tiles and there was a very efficient marble fireplace in which to burn logs in winter. The main bedrooms were double aspect and were fitted with fly netting to keep the mosquitoes out. There were security bars on the windows too, so we were not afraid to keep our windows open at night. We had the added security of having the Bank's Ras Beirut sub office immediately opposite us, so a night watchman could keep an eye on us at night while guarding the Bank.

There were many interesting places to visit in Lebanon, so we found ourselves a car, a very ancient BMW which had a long bonnet with a sort of "rabbit hutch" on the back. It was really a two-seater, but there was a bench seat in the back, which was fine for the children, and a fairly capacious boot, quite capable of holding tricycles and picnic baskets as well as flippers and masks etc. for outings.

Driving was quite terrifying and I never quite summoned up the courage to drive in Beirut. I found being a passenger quite frightening enough. I continued to travel about town by service taxi, as this was a very convenient way to get around. These were taxis which ran along set routes and set off to and from the centre of town whenever they had four passengers. One could stop them wherever one liked to get on or off, and the price was a set fee of LL1 per seat, however far one wanted to travel so long as it was on the set route.

Shopping was much easier from our new flat as a big supermarket, Spinneys, was a two-minute walk away. The Hamra, the Oxford Street of Beirut, was the next street along to ours and ran parallel to it. The English-speaking school Patricia was to attend when she was five was a short walk away.

Several children we knew went to the German kindergarten on the sea front and seemed to enjoy being there, so we enrolled Patricia for a term to see how she settled down. She already spoke some French and Arabic as well as English and quickly learned to make herself understood in German too. She was collected by bus each morning at 8.30 and returned at midday in time for lunch. This enabled the children to have a rest after their lunch and be ready to do whatever was planned for the afternoon after John and I had eaten. The next term we let Christopher join Patricia. We were very amused one day, after John and I had been conversing in rapid French so that the children should not understand, when Patricia said something in German to Christopher, which we did not understand, and Christopher replied, also in German, with a conspiratorial glance in our direction.

At weekends and on holidays we loved to drive out of town and up into the hills to explore. The roads were good and wide but often steep. Our elderly car would sometimes boil, so we had to park by the roadside and open the bonnet to let the engine cool down. On these occasions we scrambled over the rocks and found wild cyclamen growing in the most inaccessible places and anemones flourishing in the poorest of soil. Somehow things grew much larger and taller in the Lebanon than anywhere else. Cabbages were like footballs, carrots were like cucumbers and the insects were huge too. The umbrella pine trees were a feature of the Lebanon, with very tall trunks reaching starkly into the sky, and their greenery clustered right at the top. The famous cedars grew high in the mountains above the snow line, where one could ski in winter. It was said that it was possible to ski in the morning and swim in the sea in the afternoon. Well I suppose it was true, if one got up early, drove for four hours up to the cedars, skied, and drove down again for the four hour return trip to the sea. Personally, we did not try.

One of our favourite trips was a visit to the ruins of the Roman Temples at Baalbek over the mountains in the Bekaa valley. The six remaining pillars of the Roman Temple of

Jupiter, some 65 feet high, were especially impressive, as was the staircase, hewn from a huge single block of stone. We went there one night to see the Royal Shakespeare Company's production of The Merchant of Venice, with Robert Helpmann as Shylock. The ancient Roman stage or sacrificial altar was uneven, and the actors had to move with care. The eerie shadows thrown by the flickering torches fixed round the walls gave the action an aura of authenticity. Somehow the idea of Romans in their togas mingling with the audience seemed quite possible. It was wonderful to see this temple as it was meant to be seen, with the carved acanthus leaves decorating the capitals and the frieze lit from below, as originally intended. As there was no roof on the temple, except over the colonnade round the outside of the walls, in daylight the carvings were lit from above and therefore were not seen at their best.

The 65-foot-high pillars of the Temple of Jupiter looked as if they were made of gold lying on a bed of black velvet, floodlit against the night sky, presiding over the Temple of Bacchus in which the production was taking place.

On the way into the village, we passed a quarry where a huge 2,000-ton hand-hewn block of stone still lies, too heavy even for the resourceful Romans to move. It is said to be the largest hewn block in the world.

A short walk away stands the small, even dainty, temple of Venus, circular in shape with a double row of columns. French archaeologists had tastefully restored it. If only the stones could talk; they would be able to tell us about the various people who had built temples, mosques and churches on the site since about 138 AD, all to be destroyed by major earthquakes in 1664 and 1750.

Patricia and Christopher loved to play Lone Ranger and Tonto (characters in a cowboy film that was particularly in favour at that time), while scrambling over the stones. They were thrilled when a camel driver allowed them to ride on one of his camels.

Another favourite haunt was Nahr Kelb, where little boats took us about half a mile along an underground river into the magnificent caves of Jaheeta, to see the stalactites dripping from the roof of the caves deep under the mountain. They were much more impressive and the underground river was far longer than those to be seen at the Cheddar Gorge in England. It was wonderful to be in the caves on a hot day, as they were so cool that one really required a cardigan.

Round the shoulder of the mountain at the mouth of the Nahr Kelb was an ancient road with carvings on the rocks commemorating the passing of armies long ago. Among them was Nebuchadnezzar (605-562 BC,) the Chaldean King of Babylon mentioned in the Bible. There were several Assyrian memorials in poor condition, including those of Marcus Aurelias Caracalla (211-217 AD), and more modern commemorative plaques, including one about the British Liberation of the Lebanon and Syria in 1941, and the evacuation of all foreign troops in 1946. Opposite the road, high on the top of a peak, stood a huge, modern statue of Christ with His arms raised high, reaching to the heavens above.

Along the coast ran an autobahn from Nahr Kelb to Byblos, the next town on the coast. It was along this autobahn that we were once stopped for driving too slowly! You were limited to between 50 and 70 mph. Unfortunately our old car would not go fast enough, so we were requested to leave. It was a little ridiculous, as, apart from the police car there were no other cars to be seen in either direction. We felt humiliated, however.

Byblos is one of the oldest continuously-inhabited towns in the world, thought by many to be the oldest city. It was already a great commercial and religious centre in 400 BC and has played its part in Middle Eastern history ever since. The ruins of a small Roman theatre, some pillars of which still stand, are situated on the edge of the coast. A Crusader castle stood beside a Phoenician port, the remains of which stretch out into the sea. Neolithic pot burial grounds and several "god boxes," tall, thin obelisks, can be seen from the walls of the castle. It was at Byblos that we learned how the great stone sarcophagi were lowered into their graves. A deep hole, a bit larger than the sarcophagus, was excavated and then filled with sand. The sarcophagus was then dragged on top and all the sand was removed from around it, until the right depth was reached.

I was told that it was along this beach that Jonah escaped from the whale. We did not believe that whales were found in the Mediterranean, until a dead one was washed up on the beach one day near Beirut. We went down to see it so that I could legitimately use my very first Arabic word – "huout". It was a very smelly "huout" too.

After Byblos, the dual carriage way led on to Tripoli, the second largest town in the Lebanon.

Chapter Eleven

TRIPOLI AND LEBANON

The castle in Tripoli is balanced high on a rock overlooking the town. There is a splendid antique cannon patiently poised for the action which will come no more. From the ramparts we could see the circular area where the Whirling Dervishes practice their gyrating art.

We visited our Manager in Tripoli, Stewart Stott, for lunch one Friday, and managed to dodge the worst of a civil disturbance that had erupted that day. The Tripolitanians had a tendency to riot if given half a chance. I do not now remember the particular bone of contention on that occasion, but it was probably based on some religious injustice felt by one of the Muslim factions. The Manager was genuinely nervous for the welfare of his family and had a store of Molotov cocktails ready at the top of his stairs in case his home should be attacked. We were glad that we did not feel so threatened. At that time there had been very little rioting in Beirut and apart from the bag searching and the periodic car searches, especially of taxis at night, life carried on much as usual.

While at a coffee morning I heard about Christine Taylor, a British teacher at the university who had contracted Polio. I had not met her but I heard that she was very worried about her three-year-old son. He had to be left in the care of a very young Lebanese girl and without supervision. Her husband, Brian, was a full time professor at the University and was finding it difficult to do his work, as well as some of his wife's, and to care for little David at the same time. We contacted Brian and asked if he would like David to spend the days with us, then return to his own home at night. This worked well until David became ill and it was necessary to keep him in bed in our spare room. His father then came to stay with us to to be with him, and their maid came during the day to help, which made quite a houseful.

As we lived very close to the hospital we were able to take David to see his mother every day, as she slowly recovered. I would go to help her in the swimming pool where the physiotherapist tried to make her legs work again. Later she recovered enough to be allowed to come out to the beach on picnics. There was no room for a wheelchair in our car with all the children and their paraphernalia, so we had to park as near to the sea as we could and open the door to enable her to feel like one of the party.

After a couple of months, the wife of the manager of Middle East Airlines offered to take over the care of David. They were in a better position to accommodate his mother when she came out of hospital. It was a wonderful day when she was considered well enough to fly home to England, helped by Middle East Airlines.

Not long after David and his parents had returned home to England John's mother, Granny L, came out for a visit. It was wonderful to see her and the children were very excited and eager to show her all their favourite toys, friends and places to swim and picnic.

At first Granny L could not get used to every day being hot and sunny. She would greet people in the street with a cheery, "Lovely day isn't it," and to all plans she would add the proviso "if it's fine".

We took the opportunity to give a large party to introduce Mum to our many friends. This ensured that she was invited to any parties to which we were invited. The social life in Beirut even in those troubled times was hectic. We were invited out to some party or other most evenings, and when we were not, we were giving a party of our own. Our Manager, Angus MacQueen, was invited to even more of them than we were, and on more than one occasion he would ask us to go to a party to represent him as he had too many invitations that evening. It was not unknown for John and me to go to different parties and then to meet at a third and go on for dinner. Somehow we did not notice how hectic life was at the time, but our letters home, kept by our parents, have helped to jog my memory.

Mum arrived in time to see Patricia take the lead in a little play at the kindergarten, about a mother goat rescuing her babies from the stomach of the big bad wolf. I was very proud to see my child, aged about four and a half, acting and speaking her part in German so confidently.

John was working very hard at this time. Banking was not easy at the best of times and the political situation did not help. But there was very little noticeable trouble and we were free to move about and take Mum on trips out of town. One of the assistant accountants, Alan Ashmole, had just acquired a moped and asked to come with us, as he was unsure of himself and would appreciate some back up. I recall that it was difficult for John to keep down to Alan's speed, especially up the mountains. It was a question of going on ahead and waiting for him to catch up or sending him on ahead and catching him up. Coming downhill was a different matter. On one occasion we came upon Alan lying in the road after he had lost control on a hairpin bend. Luckily he was unhurt.

One afternoon trip we stopped at the salt pans on our way to Tripoli. We had not stopped there before, and were fascinated to see the sea water drawn up by windmills, poured out on the uppermost shallow tank, where it overflowed into the next tank, then the next, until the whole area was covered to a depth of about 6 inches. The water then evaporated in the hot sun, leaving the vast pans white with salt, which was collected before the process began all over again.

We had heard that there were fossils to be found in the mountains above Byblos, so we thought we would try to find them. We had good instructions and our old car managed to climb up the mountain until the road ran out. We had to walk the last 500 yards in the extreme heat. At last we saw the slate-like stone we were searching for. The little hammers we had brought to loosen the fossil bearing pieces worked easily and we quickly had a few samples. Poor Mum was not used to the heat and did not perspire easily, so she quickly felt faint. Luckily we had plenty of water with us and got her back to the car, but not before we had found several real fossils of small fish and shells.

We decided to go downhill and find some shade in which to have our picnic. The spot we found was a grassy slope beside the track under some oleander trees, overlooking the sea. There was a cool breeze blowing and the deep blue sea far below, with its scallops of creamy, lace-edged waves breaking on the long sandy beach, looked very tempting. We had a good view of the salt pans too.

After our picnic lunch we decided to go for a swim at the Deep Water Sea Club at Pigeon Rocks. The car was pleased to be running down hill as we drove round Beirut to the club, quickly slipping into our bathing suits and wallowing in the dark green cooling water. Mum was a little weary that evening, so we put her to bed and planned a peaceful day the next day.

We went to church most Sundays, where John sometimes read the lesson, and then had lunch at the St. George's Club next door. This enabled us to be free to go on outings in the afternoons. One day we drove over the mountains to Beit Eddine, the summer palace of the President. The drive took us past the small farms built on terraces up the mountainsides.

Dry stone walls held the earth in at each level, looking for all the world like contour lines on a relief map. The vegetables planted in neat rows were very reminiscent of the drawings of Mr McGregor's garden in Beatrix Potter's Peter Rabbit books.

The entrance to Beit Eddine Palace was through an arched gateway leading to a large dusty courtyard where we parked the car. We walked round the house, though there was little to see as it was being redecorated and was not furnished. The walls were covered with brightly-coloured glossy mosaic tiles, which must have helped to keep the rooms at a pleasant temperature. There was a primitive cooling system. Spring water trickled down over tiles to make a deep gurgle as it ploppled into a shell-shaped bowl before disappearing down a shallow runnel and out into the garden.

The views from the windows, added to the burble of the water, were very relaxing. The dome of the Turkish bath was studded with wine bottles that let in a speckled, mottled, eerie light when the sun shone through. I am sure the President found it a very therapeutic place, and felt better able to face the traumas that went with his high office after spending a few days there.

One day on a trip into the mountains, John did not see an unpainted traffic island hidden in the shadows, and... crunch! The sump hit the solid stone kerb. We were miles from anywhere, but there was a house a little way along the road. We could not see any telephone wires going to it, although that was not unusual in that part of the world, since not every house had phones in those days.

Suddenly we became aware that we had not seen another car, nor noticed any sign of anyone about for some time. It was a lonely spot. We all walked up to the house and much to our surprise and delight a woman came out to greet us. It appeared that this was a café, closed until the summer, but still able to provide us with a cup of tea. She told us that there was no garage in the area and it was some three miles to the nearest village. No, she did not have a car, but there was a bus twice a week and today was one of the days. It would be here in two hours' time. What luck!

The children were excited to think that they were to have an unaccustomed ride in a bus. Mum was pleased at the opportunity to experience a Lebanese bus too, though John and I were anxious at the prospect of the journey down the mountain with a Lebanese driver.

Eventually the bus arrived; it was nearly empty so we had a window seat each. The views were spectacular as the bus swung round the corners at Monte Carlo rally speeds. We picked up a few passengers on the way, but I did not think that the service could make much profit. We took a taxi home from the bus depot, then called a garage to ask them to collect the car and see what could be done with it. It was very annoying, as this would curtail some of the visits we had planned for Mum.

We hired a taxi and took her to see the stalactites in the caves of Jahita at Nahr Kelb, and visited the museums in Beirut, for which a car was not essential. The museums of Beirut were full of archaeological interest, as one might expect, and Mum was able to spend happy hours looking at things on her own. The children enjoyed the rather moth-eaten Natural History Gallery, but were too young to be interested in "stones", as they called most other exhibits.

As we had no transport, Mum decided that she would stay and look after the children and John and I could go away for a weekend on our own. We had not had a night away from the children since they were born. John hired a taxi and we went up to a hotel at Bhamdoon. It was strange to be on our own and we both kept thinking of the children. However we enjoyed having a proper breakfast without having to nag them. We also enjoyed our peaceful lie-in. It was lovely to walk in the mountains on our own, but we both were aware of the feeling that something was missing. It was great to get home again. I think we missed the children more than we had expected.

We got the car back before Mum left to return home, but the weather was beginning to warm up and she was feeling the heat, so reluctantly, we took her to the airport.

Not long after she had gone, things started to warm up in more ways than one. Bombs exploded in the business part of town, the British Ambassador's residence was attacked and then the American Embassy was bombed. I remember the new department store in El Hamra had its huge plate-glass windows shattered. The military were more in evidence and armed guards stood outside all foreign offices and embassies. There was one outside our Manager's house and we shared another with the Bank's sub-office across the road. People were wary of going too far from home unless it was really necessary, and everyone was nervous about the safety of their menfolk. The majority of the Lebanese people behaved quite normally, but the social life quietened down, mainly because the cocktail party set had begun to leave town to spend the summer at their holiday houses in the mountains at Allee and Dar Eshooair.

I found it interesting to learn about the different dishes produced in the various countries. Hommous was made from chickpeas, sesame seed paste, lemon juice, garlic and olive oil. Tabouli was made from cracked wheat, onions, chopped tomatoes and mint. Dolma was savoury rice rolled in vine leaves. Khubbe's main ingredient was chopped meat, the preparation of which made such a din in the flat above us. It was cooked on a charcoal fire which nearly always smoked us out. Delicious shish kebabs, made from pieces of lamb alternating with pieces of onion, tomato and green pepper, were one of our favourites, especially when served on a bed of rice with the yolk of a raw egg mixed in it, or sometimes with a green salad or a fresh piece of unleavened bread. The delicious fruits of the Lebanon, fresh figs, apricots, peaches, melons, oranges and grapes, made a wonderful dessert.

One evening, as we were holding a dinner party and had just reached the coffee stage, there was a loud bang. It was as if all our guests were puppets, controlled by one central string. They all rose at once and made for the door. I did not know where to go first. There was silence in the nursery and the maid was screaming in the kitchen. John went to the maid, and I went to the children, who were fast asleep but covered in broken glass. The maid was not hurt but all the windows on the road side of the house were shattered.

We gingerly opened the front door to see what had happened. People were rushing about shouting to each other. Cars were coming and going at speed. The bomb had gone off in the Bank across the road. John ran over to see if anyone was hurt, but it appeared no one had been. However there was a large hole in the wall of the office, above which a large poster invited people to visit Bonnie Scotland ... as if this was the route!

The money safe was intact, so the motive was not robbery, a comparatively rare occurrence in those days. It would seem that the attack was political.

Poor Jeanette, the maid, was in shock. The kitchen windows overlooked the place where the bomb had exploded. She had seen the flash and had been showered with glass, though thankfully she was not badly cut. As soon as it was considered safe to go out she said she wanted to go to see her mother, who lived a short distance away. She seemed all right, so we let her go on her own. She did not return the next morning, when I was expecting her to help me clear up the mess, as well as guard the house, while I arranged for the windows to be repaired. I went round to her mother's house to see if she was all right, only to be told that she was not there and had not been there. Nobody had seen her.

The following day one of the Bank's messengers brought her back to me, saying he had found her in the souk, recognised her as our maid and brought her home. Poor girl, she was lost and confused. I wanted to take her home to her mother but she preferred to stay and work with me. I sent her to bed, as she had not slept since the bomb, and said we would discuss what to do when she awoke.

Next morning she brought in our early-morning tea as usual and seemed fully recovered. I sent her to see her mother to let her know she was well. I half expected her to stay there, but she soon came back and we were back to normal.

Not long after this, Cindy, our adopted refugee corgi cross, gave birth to a black puppy on the chair in the hall. The children were very excited and chose the name Shadow. John built a kennel for the dogs and the children had a lovely time painting it. Unfortunately, when the rain came we found the kennel was not waterproof, so we draped the children's plastic paddling pool over it.

One morning John phoned me to say that he had had a cable from Peter and Molly Townsend, some Bank friends of ours who had just gone to Tangier. Their dog, Wendy, had escaped from its lead while being walked at Beirut Airport on its way to join them. We knew Wendy, and were very fond of her. We did drive out to the airport to see if we could find her, but we felt it was unlikely. Similarly we had little confidence that the advert we had placed in the papers would do much good. However, much to our surprise we did get a call from someone who had found a dog wandering lost. We drove out to see if it was Wendy and there she was, thin but safe. We were happy to send her on to Peter and Molly. It was certainly a piece of luck. The idea of a loved pet being lost in a strange country is very distressing.

The garden flourished and all the seeds the children and I had sown sprouted and grew to a great size. It seemed that most plants, flowers, fruit and vegetables grow to above average proportions in Lebanon. Certainly the loofah seeds I planted along the railings on the roadside of the garden grew and grew, rather like Jack's beanstalk. They grew up the telegraph pole and across the wires that stretched over the road, the loofahs dangling like cucumber-shaped decorations 30 feet up. The snapdragons grew four feet tall and the carnations spread over the path.

I remember the wind had blown a packet of sweet pea seeds off the window sill and they fell onto the flower bed below the dining room window. Before long they began to grow, up to the windowsill, and then past the window and onwards up to the second floor window. They had to be parted like a pair of external curtains, as they blocked out the light. Finally they reached the sill of the third floor window, where they could be seen from the inside as if they were growing in a window box. The scent wafting in through the windows from the flowers all the way up was really heady.

Christopher watered the garden one evening, having a wonderful time spraying the path, then he carefully put the hose down and came thoughtfully up to me and said,

"Mummy, is water broken or mended?" I was stumped for an answer, as I knew what he wanted to know, having watched him allowing the water to "splat" onto the path. Christopher was a thoughtful little chap. On another occasion he watched ants crawling in and out of an ant hill and wanted to know why ants were so little. He accepted my explanation that it was to enable them to get down the little hole!

Both children enjoyed the swing, trapeze and rings we had erected in the garden, and the rope ladder at the end of the frame. They and their friends enjoyed the garden, small though it was, because so many people lived in flats in Beirut, with no garden at all. We were especially fortunate to have the space to put a large paddling pool and a sandpit. Our house and garden were a popular place to park children when parents were out shopping.

The time was coming when we were again due for home leave. There were all the farewell parties to attend and to give, both for the children and for ourselves. There was a home to find for the dogs, always a sad business when we had to change postings. Then there was the packing up or sale of outgrown tricycles, pedal cars and other no-longer-required items, and the selecting of souvenirs to remind us of happy times. It was strange to find that when we came to unpack at our new home, it seemed we had packed the items from the wrong list. Everything looked old and tatty and badly in need of replacement.

This time, for once, we were all going to fly home together, so any problems would be shared with John. As luck would have it, all went very smoothly and we arrived at London Airport on time.

Birth of Christopher – Aleppo – the moment I discovered he
was a freak with eleven toes!

Granjo trying not to breathe in a wedding dress at the
Eggman's village, Aleppo, 1953

Eggman's 'Beehive' Syrian village, Aleppo, 1953

Inside the Eggman's house, Aleppo 1953

Saudi Arabia, our flat on the right - 1956

Christopher with falcon in the desert (Doha)

Doha 'Mutton grab' 1958

Our house in Doha, 1960

The Ruler's guest palace across from our house, Doha 1960

Trisha, Claire and Christopher in our house in Libya

Paintings found in the hole in the ground, Libya (Tripoli), 1962

Entrance to the hole

Libya – Mohammed's wife Fatima with Claire, 1962

Camel market in Goulamine, Morocco, 1969

The children in the tree house in the garden, Morocco

Tony on his motorbike in Kuwait, 1970

Phone box on the road to Basra from Kuwait, just above Mullah Ridge, 1977

Chapter Twelve

ON LEAVE IN ENGLAND, 1957

At the airport we were met by Mum, who had booked us all into the Regent Palace Hotel in Piccadilly. At once she telephoned John's sister Mary, and brother-in-law, Norman, who unknown to us were expecting a baby at any time. We were thrilled, if surprised, to hear that a new addition was expected to the family. We discovered that living overseas, as we did, people forgot to keep us up to date with important things like when babies were due! I think everybody assumed that someone else had told us. Momentous family events were discussed on the telephone and, in those days, phone calls to us were still impossible.

I remember that we did not require any supper that night as we had eaten so much, as usual, on the plane. The children were very excited and we took them out to see the lights of Piccadilly Circus, which fascinated them, and me. Eventually they calmed down and we took them back to the Hotel and popped them into bed. Both John and I felt "disembodied," as one often does after a long plane journey. Somehow the spirit takes some time to catch up with the body, and the disorientation persists for some time.

The next day John had to show his face at the Bank. In those days it was in Gracechurch Street, in the City. Mum and I took the children to Swan and Edgars (then on Piccadilly Circus) for some warm clothing and then on to Hamleys to goggle at the wonders in the toy world left over from Christmas. We all met up for lunch and then set off in Mum's car for Romsey. Before we left, we called Mary again, and heard that she had had a baby boy and all was well. Peter Allum was born on February 6th.

After spending a few days at Abbotswood, Mum took us all to visit Granny Dickson in Bournemouth. The children were a good deal older than the last time they had been there. Nevertheless I still spent a lot of time walking them on the golf course nearby, so that they could work off their energy at a safe distance from Granny's china cabinets.

We visited Granny Hill and Aunt Joy in Boscombe, and had good runs on the beach. Mrs Webb, Gran's housekeeper, provided wonderful meals for us all, set at the large dining table. Christopher sat on the beautiful Georgian polished high chair, which pushed right up to the table, so he really felt one of the grown-ups.

Patricia loved to wind the old napkin press up and down while standing on a chair. Over the fireplace in the dining room stood an Alabaster Pieta. Granny told us that it represented Bishop Poore, lying in the lap of an Abbess girlfriend!

Conventionally, a Pieta represents the Virgin Mary with the body of Christ. Where it came from originally is open to question. Some say it is Portuguese, and once stood in a niche in the wall of Hurstborne-Tarrent Church. Whatever its history, this Pieta was given to Romsey Abbey and now stands in a glass case with other interesting items. In the 1980s it was stolen from the Abbey, later being found by the police in a house in a London suburb, along with a selection of other stolen religious artefacts, and was returned to the Abbey none the worse for its adventure.

We stayed a few days with Granny Dickson. During that time she took the children to Poole Park, where they rode on the miniature railway and John took them out on the boating lake. Honey, Mum's beautiful blousey blonde Golden Retriever, enjoyed lolloping around with us all. However, Gran's Dachshund, Puck, did not like having the children in his home, and we had to watch to make sure he did not snap at them. Puck was a very spoiled animal who slept on GG's bed and was fed sugar lumps dipped in cream. The children were fascinated at the sight of GG in bed in the mornings, wearing a lace mob cap and a frilly bedjacket. There was a wonderful supply of biscuits and chocolates, though they were careful not to select Puck's favourite. Her bedroom was very warm and there was always a luxurious smell of talcum powder and perfume.

Soon after our return to Abbotswood we set off for Scotland to see Granjo and Gramps, my parents. They had organised for us to stay in their cottage down the road from their own. As we were to be home for at least three months, they had also arranged for Patricia and Christopher to go to the village school. This was a good idea, as they were able to make friends in the village.

Often, after the children had gone to bed, they could be heard talking to each other, but we could not hear what they were saying. We put the microphone of our tape recorder into their room one night. Before long Christopher started by saying,

"Teetah?" He always called Patricia Teetah.

"What?" Said Teetah, wearily.

"Djou know what I was thinkin?" After a pause.

"No, what?"

"There was a dragon with his tongue hanging out, and someone came and cut his tongue off. He just walked away and didn't say anything."

"Oh." Said Patricia. Silence. So now we knew!

It was a wonderful, relaxing time just lazing about doing nothing much, reading, walking and playing with the children. But before too long, John began to feel restless. A man can only do nothing for so long. Granjo and Gramps suggested that they would look after the children and we could have a few days' holiday, so we decided to go over to Ireland. John's elder brother Edward was building an earth dam near Armagh, so it was arranged that we would spend a few days with him and his wife Mary, and from them we could visit Loughry, the Lindesay ancestral home in Ireland.

John and I caught a train to Stranraer from Dumfries and

crossed the Irish Sea to Belfast, where we found the train to Armagh. Edward met us at the station and drove us to his bungalow just outside Armagh. Mary greeted us and showed us round her new home. It stood just above the site of the earth dam Edward was constructing. The house was built the wrong way round as it faced south, in line with convention, but the view was to the north. Sadly, the picture window looked on to a high bank some ten feet away, and the view could be seen best from the bathroom and the tiny dining room. The crop of thistles in the garden was very impressive.

We were taken on a tour of Edward's creation and admired the other dams and reservoirs. One bleak area, called Silent Valley, stuck in my mind. It was eerily quiet. Birds did not sing, nor was there any sign of life. The barren hillsides appeared quite lifeless, though they were majestically beautiful. The wind was so strong that Edward's hat blew off and into the water, much to the distress of little James, our nephew.

The Irish countryside was lovely, as spring was nearly upon us with the high hedges round the tiny fields bursting into leaf. The apple blossom along the roadside was particularly spectacular.

The next day we borrowed Edward's car and set off for Limavady to visit John's cousin-once-removed, Inez MacRory. She was John's father's first cousin. We found her in a flat in town overlooking the town square. She was an interesting lady deeply steeped in the complicated history of the family. There was much discussion with John about various members of the family tree. I wish now that I had taken more interest, as she was a fund of family gossip and information. She took us to visit a friend of hers, who lived in a large house nearby. The friend was, I suppose, typically Irish. The garden was a jungle and had not been tamed for years. The lady proclaimed it would cost her £5 per week to pay a gardener and she could buy all the flowers she wanted for ten shillings.

The inside of the house was amazing, the wallpaper peeling off the walls and the chairs draped as if she had been trying out swatches of material and had not got any further. I gathered that this was indeed the case. There was a thick layer of dust everywhere and there were heaps of books and magazines. We had a delicious tea in front of a lovely log fire. Inez's friend made delicious scones and cakes.

The next day we drove to visit the Giant's Causeway on the north coast. The wind was blowing a gale, but it was exciting to see the amazing rock formation of hexagonal pillars stretching out to sea.

On the way back to Edward and Mary we stopped off to visit the Lindesay ancestral home, Loughry, which means "King's Gift." The estate, near the village of Tullyhogue, was given to John's ancestor, Robert Lindesay. It was part of the plan of James I of England and VI of Scotland to establish a loyal Protestant presence in Ireland by granting estates, confiscated from local landlords, to the sons of his favourite courtiers. They would be duty bound to produce armed forces on demand to defend the area against rebel uprisings. The grant was made in 1611, and under its terms Robert had to build a stone manor, or castle, within a set time, and populate the estate with English or Scottish settlers who would bear arms to defend their homes. The first manor house was built in 1632 but was burned down by the Catholic rebels, supporters of James II, nine years later and not rebuilt till 1671. Robert became Chief Harbinger to James I in 1614 and, as Comptroller of Artillery was at the Battle of Worcester, between Charles I and Oliver Cromwell, in 1651.

Robert's son, also named Robert, succeeded to the property in 1674. In the rebellion of 1689 he retired to Londonderry for safety, with his family. The town was besieged by the deposed James II's Catholic troops. The breaking of the boom lifted the siege across the river by King William of Orange's ships, 105 days later. The Battle of the Boyne officially ended the rebellion in 1690 (but has been fermenting ever since).

There is a story that when the family departed from Loughry to take refuge in Derry, neither the three-year-old youngest child, John, nor his nurse, could be found. The nurse was a native Irish woman, the wife of a soldier in King James's army, so it was decided that the infant must have been kidnapped and killed. One day, sometime after the siege, when the country had settled down, a woman arrived at Loughry's door with a donkey with panniers on its back, apparently filled with oysters covered with seaweed (not an unusual sight in those days). One basket did indeed contain oysters, but from the other the woman produced the boy John, who was immediately recognised by his parents. The old woman was his wet nurse, who, in her devotion to the child and anxiety for his welfare, had hidden him in a cave, still known as Lindesay Cave. There she fed and watched over him, taught him a few words of Irish, and afterwards passed him off as her own son to the soldiers of King James' army. Finally, when all had quietened down, she restored him to his parents.

In the garden at Loughry stands a summerhouse where, it is said, Dean Swift, who was a close friend of the fourth Robert Lindesay to own Loughry, used to retire to write.

The last Lindesay owner died in 1893. After another fire, the estate was sold and became an agricultural college, now run by the Northern Ireland Ministry of Agriculture.

The manor we saw is not quite the same house as it was in the 1800s, but the pillars of the entrance gates still stand, surmounted by a swan and a griffin, the emblems of the last Lindesay owners. The locals call these "the Duck and the Devil." The manor had lost its top floor in the fire after its sale, which had had one principal bedroom, two nurseries and the servant quarters, but it still boasted four principal reception rooms, nine bedrooms and a banqueting hall with a musicians' gallery and turret.

In a field facing the village of Lindesayville stands the family vault. We had been told that John's father had been the last person to enter it, but he had thrown the key into the Irish Sea on his way home to Scotland, to prevent any further intrusion. The locals said that the coffins in the vault kept changing places, as if the occupants were taking part in some macabre cocktail party. We climbed the wall surrounding the vault and found the door firmly bricked up and surrounded by magnificent nettles.

We returned the car to Edward and left the next day for the ferry from Belfast back to Stranraer and then home to Glencaple and the children. It seemed that our young had been extremely good and their grandparents were still remarkably cheerful. The children did not seem to have noticed that we had been away. One comment Granjo made was that, when the children were asked what they liked best to eat for tea, they had said that they preferred pâté de foie. She really thought that I should not bring them up to have quite such expensive tastes! In Beirut pate was not very expensive, being the equivalent to meat paste in Britain.

Eventually the time came for John to return to the Middle East. Originally he had been posted as Manager of Muscat in the Sultanate of Oman, but news came through that the Manager of Doha in the Persian Gulf was ill and had to return home, so John had been diverted to Doha to take over. It seemed that I was not to go at once, as the new accommodation was not yet ready and there was nowhere for families to stay.

Chapter Thirteen

DOHA

After John had gone the house seemed pretty empty, but the children did their best to fill the gap. Christopher sat at table in John's place and exclaimed, "I'm Daddy, talk, talk, talk, two hundred pounds, three hundred pounds, talk, talk, talk." It seemed that he considered himself the man in the house and, as we had been discussing buying a cottage in the village, he had decided that this was the way the man of the house discussed matters. We saw ourselves as others see us!

The first morning after John left, both Patricia and Christopher woke me at 7 am. They had brought me a breakfast tray of tea, made with hot water from the tap (as they were not allowed to touch the kettle), and toast, which was burned to a cinder. (I like burned toast but this was a bit much even for me!) I had to eat and drink with a smile, because two little faces were eagerly awaiting my reaction.

After a further three weeks I took the children south to spend a few days with Granny L and to visit the Great Grannies to say our farewells. It was always traumatic saying farewell to the latter. Three years seemed a very long time and I always wondered if they would be there when we next returned.

When the day came for us to leave for Doha, Mum took us and our luggage to the airport. We sat talking trivia in the first-class lounge. We were very lucky because in our early days, all planes were one class only. When the airlines introduced economy class on their long distance flights, Bank staff continued to fly first class. A Consular Official complained that he did not think it appropriate that Bank juniors should travel first class, while the Foreign Office considered tourist class was good enough for Embassy staff, up to a certain rank. Changes had to be made. Fortunately John was sufficiently senior by that time to still qualify for first-class seats, which were more comfortable on long journeys.

I disliked being seen off at the airport because I have always hated flying, an irrational fear I know, but real enough to me. I suppose I subconsciously feel that planes, like bumblebees, should not be able to fly. While I am still on the ground I can control my destiny, in that I can always decide not to go. When I am up in the air, things are out of my hands and I am quite philosophical. I found that I seemed to lose confidence when I had the children. I suppose it was because I felt responsible for them.

We arrived in Bahrain to be met by the manager, Archie Butt, who welcomed us to the Persian Gulf. Almost at once we climbed aboard a little nine-seater Dove and took off for

Doha, a flight of about half an hour. We felt very hot and sticky in our English-weight clothing, and were pleased to land on the patch of desert, marked by a windsock and a wooden barasti hut, which constituted Doha airport. We were met by John who came out on to the tarmac to greet us, and by Ahmed, his driver. Ahmed was dressed, like almost everyone else, in a long white night-shirt and a crocheted skullcap, over which a soft white headscarf was held in place by a double loop of twisted black silk cord. In days gone by this "aqhal" (cord) would have doubled as a camel hobble.

We went through customs, which, in those days, consisted of a counter made of an upturned packing case beneath a barasti shade. The customs men wore khaki uniform, with guns in holsters on their hips and red-and-white checked headscarves draped round their heads. This seemed to be standard uniform for customs, army and police.

We climbed into the large American car and were driven the five miles or so to our new home. The house had only recently been built. It was a two-storey building with a veranda both upstairs and down, shading the windows. There were three bedrooms and two bathrooms, one en suite, and a long living room with two huge doors to shut off the dining end, which led into a servery and kitchen. There was a courtyard beyond the kitchen, with two servants' quarters and the garage.

The "garden" was an area of about two acres completely surrounded by a pink roughcast wall, about six feet high. The dry earth was covered in a thick layer of tiny shells, rather like pea gravel but very uncomfortable to walk on in sandals, and death to high-heeled shoes. Next door, in the same compound, was the accountant's house, similar to ours but with only two bedrooms.

We unpacked our cases and dressed in more suitable clothing. It was warm for us, although it was winter. John took us for a quick tour of the town and showed us the Bank, which was also newly built, on the edge of the sea. The souk reminded me of Jeddah. There were little hole-in-the wall shops and a cold store called Darwish Canteen where I could buy my frozen fillet of beef or lamb. As it was frozen into long strips, similar in shape to the French baguette, we bought it by the foot! The cold store also sold fresh vegetables, which came in once a week, and there were frozen loaves of bread available from time to time. It was the only place where one might find European articles of clothing, make up and huge bottles of perfume. It was a veritable emporium of assorted goods.

The local men wore the long white night shirts, or dishdashers as they were called, while the Indian or Goanese clerks, cooks and house boys wore white trousers and white shirts. The Egyptians, Palestinians and Lebanese tended to wear beige trousers and shirts. The labourers and fishermen wore cotton sarong-like garments and T-shirts, with coloured scarves wound round their heads like bundles of washing. The Arab women usually wore a long black abya or cloak, and a mask called a petula over their eyes and noses. It seems these masks were worn to protect their husband's honour, which is kept in the noses of their womenfolk and must be kept unseen. The wives of Indian clerks wore colourful saris and the few dozen British wives dressed in discreet European frocks. The upper arm had to be covered and skirts had to extend to the knee, at least while in the streets, so as not to offend the local inhabitants.

The Ruler, Sheikh Ali al Thani, governed the country. He had a British adviser, Geoffrey Hancock, and there was also the Crown Prince, Sheikh Ahmed, and his cousin Khalifa waiting to take over. The British adviser to the Ruler was head of the civil service and made suggestions as to how things might be done. The sheikhs, or heads of the leading families, each had their departments - customs, police, finance, public works and education for example, and each also had their British Technical Assistant. There were no Americans or other Europeans at that time. Most foreigners worked for the Qatar Petroleum Company or Shell Oil Company, or ran departments in the Government. The civil engineers built the roads and public buildings as well as the sheikhs' palaces. There were three banks, The Ottoman Bank, the Eastern Bank and ourselves, the British Bank of the Middle East.

The water department was in charge of the huge seawater distillation plant from which our drinking water came. The lavatories, however, were flushed with brackish water drawn from wells. The electricity department produced the enormous amount of power required to drive all the air-conditioning units in the summer and light all the coloured neon signs which brightened up the sand-coloured buildings at night. The money came from the oil revenues, and Indian, Egyptian and Palestinian staff did most of the clerical work. The labour was drawn from Iran and Bhutan with a few Pakistanis. The Qatari population was very small and the majority owned some business or other, which was run by a foreigner. All businesses and agencies had to have a Qatari sponsor or they were not permitted to operate. There was a vast civil list, all of whom could claim a salary from the government. Each male child born to the Royal Family became a wage earner at once.

The sheikhs all built splendid palaces for themselves, in some cases because it seemed to be expected of them and not because they really wanted to live in them. I knew of one who drove his Cadillac into the front hall, left it there, walked down the back steps into the garden at the back, and settled down for the evening in a Bedouin tent surrounded by his camels.

The Ruler built a guest palace across the road from our house. It was a huge edifice, with only four bedrooms, each with ensuite bathrooms and gold taps. There was an enormous majlis, or reception room, with electrically-drawn curtains and touching chandeliers along the length of the ceiling, surrounded by concealed neon lighting around the cornice. The floor was covered with wall-to-wall Persian rugs. Deep red moquette-covered chairs sat cheek by jowl round the walls. The grey Formica-covered coffee tables each had an advertisement pushdown ashtray on it. The Formica-topped dining table was capable of seating one hundred and one guests, with gold-plated cutlery and a Minton dinner service.

The kitchen had two enormous rice boilers, which could be raised out of the heater by a chain pulley and lowered to the floor, where a tall person could scoop the rice out. How the bottom was reached was beyond my imagination. I did hope that the people who did the washing up were careful, as I do not think that there was any spare china to replace broken pieces. I took an interest in the building of this guest palace and got to know the workmen.

Outside on the patio of the palace there were some concrete flower troughs. I knew Joe Stefan, the Egyptian, who was overseeing the building. He liked to visit me for an illegal cooling beer from time to time. I asked him if he thought he could supply some flower troughs for my patio and he said he would see what he could do. The next thing I knew, I had six enormous troughs plonked between the pillars on the veranda round the house. They were somewhat larger than I had planned, so we christened them the sarcophagi. They looked quite good once I had found some sweet earth, planted periwinkles in them and remembered to water them twice a day.

Alcohol was available to Europeans, on licence obtainable from the British Political Agency, bought in Bahrain at very reasonable prices. Whisky was about seventeen shillings a bottle and gin about twelve shillings. Beer was relatively expensive, and was, of course, the most popular. The rules were quite clear: it was for consumption in the home and for entertaining only. Heads of companies or government departments had an unlimited quota, while underlings had a certain ration for their own consumption, and it all had to be kept under lock and key. The sale of liquor to anyone was strictly forbidden, and if the regulations were broken the licence was withdrawn and the miscreant would probably be sent home.

All the time we were in Qatar there was an undercurrent of political intrigue. Sheikh Ahmad, the son of Sheikh Ali the Ruler, was destined to take over, but Sheikh Khalifa, Ahmad's cousin, also wanted power. In 1960 Sheikh Ali abdicated and Sheikh Ahmad became ruler, while Sheikh Khalifa became Minister of Education. During this bloodless coup the British navy dropped anchor off shore. They were very surprised to see us, in Ahmad al Othman's speed-boat, water-skiing round their ship while they were dressed for action. In actual fact the populace were mostly unaware of the events in the Palace.

In those days there was very little greenery to relieve the monotone of concrete. We had two scrawny thorn bushes near the house, which I watered religiously. The sun quickly bleached any effort to vary the grey of concrete buildings. I tried to plant a border of periwinkles but found the earth was too poor, or the water too brackish, for them to survive.

Before long the building errors in our house began to grate on our nerves. The stairs had an eleven-inch high bottom step and a three-inch high top step and the rest varied by an inch or so, which tripped us up if we were not very careful. The cupboard on the landing was three feet square with the door opening inwards, suitable only for storing fishing rods or similar tall slim objects that could be fed in either over or round the door. The built-in wardrobes were only eighteen inches deep and too narrow to hang coat-hangers. The 1 ft by 4 ft horizontal windows, high up near the ceiling in the living room, were meant to allow air to circulate, but could not be opened even if we had had a stepladder, and succeeded only in collecting dust. The huge doors that opened into the dining room left no room for a dining table when opened, as the room was too narrow.

We discovered that the drains were too long and lacking in "drop" and had a tendency to become blocked. We had to take a day each week to clear them. The accountant and I had to fill our baths, basins and sinks, while John stuffed sacking down the drain manholes. Then, at a given whistle, we would rush round pulling out all the plugs and flushing all the loos to cause a good head of water down the drains. John would whip the sacking out of the manholes and allow the rush of water to swoosh down to the next manhole, and on out into the main drain along the roadside, where it dropped six feet!

This last problem was not entirely the fault of the clerk of works, John Tester. He had been misinformed as to the position of the main drain and had dug trenches in three directions before he got the right place. We complained to London Office about these problems, but they thought the clerk of works was such good value for money that they could not believe things had gone wrong. However, eventually, he was sent back to sort us out.

In the meantime we arranged for Patricia and Christopher

to start at the English Speaking Shell School, handily situated across the lane from our back gate. Both children loved school and settled in very quickly. They had very good English teachers. The school was organised by the Shell Oil Company, based in Doha, which had the offshore drilling concession. The Qatar Petroleum Company had the inland drilling rights and was based at Umm Said, about thirty miles down the coast. Both companies had cinemas, and we were invited to shows. As this was the only "canned" entertainment in Qatar, we were quite happy to drive the sixty miles there and back to see a film in Um Said, or the 140 miles to Dukhan if there was a special film. These roads were tarmac and pretty straight. They could have been safe enough if they did not have lethal hidden dips. Frequently, cars and lorries would speed along and come over a small rise to be confronted by camels lying asleep on the road. This resulted in several nasty accidents. The mangled remains were left to serve as a warning to the unwary.

As the house was new with only basic furnishings, I had the job of buying curtains, chair covers and other soft furnishings. I tried hard to find some suitable curtain material in the souk, but found only small quantities of seconds. I was unable to find anyone prepared to make curtains for me. I decided that I would have to go over to Bahrain, where, I was told, there was greater choice.

We had two Goanese servants, Peter, the cook and Michael, the bearer. Both spoke English and had been trained in Army messes in India. Peter was a reasonable cook and the kitchen was quite well equipped. Both were Catholics, and therefore a little less unpredictable than the Muslim servants I was accustomed to, except that they were used to the Indian caste system and at first refused to sweep and clean floors, as this was deemed beneath their dignity. I managed to persuade them that if they did not clean the floors, I would have to do them myself. This was too much for them, and I was relieved when they agreed that perhaps less face would be lost if they did them themselves! People were unaware of the caste system in Qatar.

Michael was a strange lad, very interested in Shakespearean sonnets, and he asked me to complete quotations for him. I eventually supplied him with the complete works of Shakespeare, which delighted him, and relieved me from being forced to display my lack of adequate Shakespearean knowledge.

It was essential that John and I should find something to do to entertain ourselves, as there was nowhere to go, no restaurants, no local cinemas or theatres, in fact very little to do apart from eating, drinking, reading or painting and home hobbies.. We did play quite a lot of bridge but even that palled after a while.

We decided to join the Doha Players, who met in the civil engineers' furniture store, which was handy for props and ensured a ready supply of seats for the audience. The Indian upholsterers were co-opted to help dress the sets and they made the curtains so that the productions had an authentic appearance. The Players tried to put on at least three or four productions each winter. It was too hot in the summer, and many of the wives went home. The government's expatriate employees took their annual leave in the summer months, so the supply of people to act and work backstage was depleted, as was the audience.

John was working very hard at this time. The branch was growing fast and it was his first posting as Manager. As his predecessor, Ken Jeffries, had been ill, the handover had been brief and sketchy, not least because the Chairman had come out for the opening of the new office and Ken was preoccupied with him. There was no hotel in Doha, so everyone had to be accommodated in the incomplete Bank house. There was a traditional Arab reception laid on at the house. As there was no room indoors, carpets were laid on the ground at the back of the house (over the aforementioned drain hole covers!) where the traditional feast was set. It consisted, I am told, of huge trays of rice with whole roasted sheep and goat, surrounded by chickens and eggs, round which the guests sat and ate their fill.

When the Bank's new office was duly opened the outgoing manager, Ken Jeffries, set off for home, then John began to learn how to run his office. The Commercial Assistant, Ali Behzad, was Qatari, as it was necessary for John to have someone who knew the customers and their sponsors. He spoke good English, which was just as well as John preferred to use his knowledge of Arabic to check on the translation. It also enabled him to understand the asides the customers made, some of which were quite amusing, especially as John had not, at first, admitted that he understood Arabic, and no one suspected that some of the remarks had been understood.

As a bank manager is considered one of the leaders in a community, John was consulted on all parochial matters. As a newcomer to the community he was inevitably voted chairman of the latest communal project. In this case it was the Beach Club. The project had been started some years before and had reached an impasse in that the Ruler had donated a stretch of beach on the edge of town to the European community. A sailing club had been created, but its rules did not suit those in the community who had children and just wanted to swim and play on the beach. There was room for all, but insufficient money to provide the clubhouses to which each group aspired. In the beginning the club had a shed in which their boatbuilding equipment was kept. (The members built their own dinghies, from kits imported by enthusiasts.)

The Beacon, as the beach club was known, had two large packing cases as changing rooms and a barasti shade erected between them. Neither club had any water or electricity laid on.

One day the Ruler decided that he wanted to build a beach house for his wives on the beach next to the Beacon. This required a high wall to be constructed to ensure privacy. Sadly this meant that the Beacon would lose its site and packing cases. John, as chairman of the Beacon, was dispatched to claim compensation for our loss. The result was that we were allocated a space a bit further along the beach and were given a respectable sum in compensation for our packing cases.

Meetings were called and decisions made as to what we would

do with our windfall. The civil engineers managed to find some "condemned" cement and expertise was used to design and construct a clubhouse and squash court. The members helped by mixing cement and feeding the workers. In a remarkably short time the whole new clubhouse was ready for painting. When the plaster was considered dry some "condemned" distemper was found and a team of painters organised. We worked all one morning and painted part of one wall.

One day Joe Stefan, one of our Egyptian members, came to see how things were going, He said we should stop for lunch and he would get a team who would have it finished by evening. An hour later three Persian painters arrived and plunged towel-like rags into the buckets of paint and proceeded to slosh it onto the walls. We were horrified, as we were convinced that the smeared marks would look dreadful. In fact when it had all dried it was beautifully even, and looked better than the wall we had painstakingly painted with four-inch brushes.

The sand was very hot in summer and one had to sprint across the beach to the water to swim, or wear flip-flops. Usually we went down to the beach wearing bathing suits under suitable wraps, and carried sufficient food and drink in a cool box kept under a beach umbrella. The water was very shallow and warm and so quite safe for small children. The older swimmers had to wade about 25 yards before the water came above their knees. The Gulf is tidal, but the water rises little more than two feet. The sailing club welcomed the difference, as they had to drag their boats ashore, and it was easier when the tide was in. Anxious mothers with "swimming" children spent much of their time astride lilos, running herd on various heads popping in and out as their children cavorted 50 yards from the beach in the deeper water. Christopher spent a lot of time swimming under the water, appearing from time to time to gulp some air in preparation to dive again. I found it very stressful to balance on my raft trying to keep an eye on him.

Ahmad al Othman had a speedboat and was generous with invitations to some of us to try our hand at water skiing. We also were taken for turns round the Navy frigates when they came to call.

The next project was the Beacon's opening party. Eventually a fancy dress party was decided upon. The members prepared the food and transported it in cool boxes. Soft drinks (we were not permitted to drink alcohol outside our homes) were brought in large flasks containing ice.

John decided that he would dress as a devil, so I found cotton long johns and a long-sleeved vest in the souk and dyed them red. I made a helmet out of red material and created horns and a long tail. I painted his face green with some eye shadow and he looked very Mephistophelian.

I decided I would be a houri, and wore a floating chiffon gown with my face also painted green. When the green eyeshadow ran out, I added a bit of blue to my lips and eyes. I was amazed when Micky Mann, whom I knew well, could not recognise me and paid a sum to club funds to learn who I was!

We did not give many evening parties at the Beacon, mainly

because the catering was so difficult, and the paraffin lamps added so much to the heat. Barbecue lunches were more popular and easier to cater for.

We did however, have some fund-raising occasions as we were always in need of money. One evening we had a Beetle Drive and I was surprised how few people knew what this meant. Some thought it was literally racing cockroaches or the like. We managed to find enough card, garden tables, chairs, pencils and dice, while someone designed the sheets on which we played, showing the rules, and what the various numbers thrown on the dice represented. I remember the dour, serious Manager of the Ottoman Bank, a Palestinian called Zaroubi, declined at first to play, as he felt the game was too frivolous for dignitaries such as he. However he was persuaded, and once he got the hang of the game, played more feverishly and far more loudly than anyone else present, yelling "leg!" "head!" "feeler!" etc. In the end everyone enjoyed a really noisy evening.

The club was a very useful venue for children's parties and many were held there. The Shell Petroleum Company Club was also a popular place for entertainment for all ages, as it had two tennis courts. The school sports were organised there, and it was a great place for Patricia and Christopher to ride their bicycles in safety. The roads were totally unsafe, as not only did the Sheikhs like to drive their cars as if they were on a race track, but they bought sports cars for their children. The Ruler's son, at the age of 10, was given an Aston Martin, which he drove along the road leading to the Palace. Whenever the car was spotted everyone on the road drove off into the desert to keep well out of his way. It was also customary to stop and allow the Ruler to pass, which he did at great speed, with sirens screaming and guards clinging to the sides of his car.

While we were in Doha, traffic lights were installed at one of the more dangerous crossroads, the Kahrahba Street and Rummaila Road intersection. The changing lights generated great interest, and drivers would stop to watch them go from red to yellow to green and back again until they became bored. Then, regardless of whether they were red or green, they would drive on. As one can imagine, the chaos was considerable and there were several accidents. It was hoped that drivers might stop for a red light where they would ignore a policeman on point duty. At first they did stop if it was convenient, but they tended to ignore the lights if they were in a hurry.

From time to time the various heads of firms and departments were invited to dinner at the Palace with the Ruler, when he was entertaining visiting dignitaries. On these occasions, he seemed to regard them as his court, much as in medieval times. John would rush home from the beach, change into his dinner jacket and race up to the Palace, where he would meet the Ruler and the guest of honour. The "court" would sit for a minute or two, until it was time to go in for dinner. When the Ruler rose from the table they were free to leave. John would return home in time to dress more casually, go out to dinner, greet our guests, or perhaps go to a rehearsal. These royal "mutton grabs," as they were irreverently called, rarely took more than an hour and a half, door to door. They took place about three times a month. On one occasion, John managed to be back home in 45 minutes. I think the visiting dignitary was not considered worthy of a grander affair.

Chapter Fourteen

PICNIC IN THE DESERT

One Friday we were invited to go out for a picnic in the desert with one of the sheikhs, and asked to bring one or two friends with us. The children were invited, and viewed the prospect of a hot day in the desert with a certain amount of horror. However, they were especially invited, so go they must.

A guide was sent to lead us, as we had no idea where to go. The drive out into the desert was very strange. We were directed to turn right or left for no apparent reason, though perhaps it was to avoid a patch of soft sand or a rocky outcrop. Our friends, the Livingstone family and Alan and France Jack, in the following car, did exactly as we did. Eventually we crested a dune and there was a camp of several tents and a herd of camels. I had not realised that one could drive a car on these dunes, but the sand on the windward side is not as soft as one would think.

The Sheikh came to greet us, riding on his favourite white camel, and we were taken into a tent spread with a large Persian carpet and cushions. We were all given a cup of cardamom coffee, dispensed from a large brass Arab coffeepot. The spout was filled with what appeared to be unravelled rope to filter out the grains. The coffee was poured into tiny thimble-like cups. The tradition is to swallow the "potion" and accept a second cup, then rock the cup from side to side to indicate that one does not require a third helping. Though I do not like the taste, I must admit that it is a good tummy settler if one has the slightest upset.

The Sheikh then had some of his camels brought over to us and we were each invited to ride. First the men were put aboard. John mounted the saddle while the animal was kneeling on the ground making very disagreeable noises. It rose up, back legs first, so that the rear pommel on the seat hit him smartly in the back. This caused him to lean forward in time to be punched smartly in the stomach by the front pommel as the forelegs straightened up. This threw him back to receive a further bump in the back as the back legs straightened. I imagine one would learn the proper timing to avoid the bruising.

He looked very high off the ground, as the saddle is balanced precariously on the top of the single hump, and there is nothing in front or behind. John crossed his legs in front and, (as I also did when my turn came,) held onto the pommel like grim death. The walk is rather jerky and the trot or run is undulating, and I felt very insecure. The dismount is just as devastating as the rise, as once again one is struck firmly back and front.

We all had a ride and then were taken to see the baby camels, which managed to look quite attractive, while their parents were anything but. We were amused to see that some of the mothers wore a sort of bra. We were told that this was to prevent the babies from drinking all the milk, as the humans liked to drink it too!

After our exertions we were taken into the tent, where we sat on a carpet round a huge tray of stuffed whole lamb and goat, on a bed of rice with hard-boiled eggs and roast chicken. First we were offered a drink of camel's milk in a communal pint tankard. To me, it tasted like frothy sour cream and I thought it unkind to deprive the baby camel on my behalf. The way to tackle the food is to use the right hand only, make a ball of rice and flick it into the mouth with the thumb. Similarly, you have to tear a piece of meat off the carcass and hope that your teeth are strong and sharp enough to bite a piece off. Usually we found the meat to be quite tender and tasty. The meal was completed by a juicy orange, which we were supposed to peel with the right hand only. Our efforts caused much amusement and we were full of admiration for those who managed to do it.

When we had finished our meal the drivers and interpreters were invited to help themselves. I noted that our host, very democratically, sat down again with the second sitting. When they had finished, the servants had their chance. I thought that the food would be a bit congealed by then, but they seemed to tuck in quite happily. Finally when the servants were replete the tray was dragged outside and the three favourite camels were invited to clear up the remains, which they did with wonderful smiles on their silly faces.

Afterwards we watched the men try their hand at shooting

targets and cigarettes pinned to a pole. Our hosts were excellent shots. The children played with our host's son and his whipping boy. Apparently if the young sheikh misbehaves, punishment is meted out to his companion, who is supposed to see that he comes to no harm and is responsible for his behaviour. Some distance from the camp there was a large puddle created by the recent rainstorm. The boys had fashioned a sailing boat out of a petrol can and formed a sail from a handkerchief. The fact that the children could not converse was no deterrent to their game as they raced round the pond, each yelling in his own language. The young Arabs hitched up their long dish-dasher skirts, while our bare-legged ones ran through the water in their flipflops.

Qataris, on the whole, are very proud of their falcons, and on this occasion the birds were brought out for us to see. We were given pads to protect our arms and each presented with a bird to hold. I was pleased that they wore jesses over their eyes, as I was wary of their hooked beaks. Later we watched them fly. It is a magnificent sight to see them soar and then seemingly plummet to earth, though I must admit I could not see their prey.

All too soon it was time for another dose of the "potion". Then we climbed into our cars and set off home before the sun set. It would be quite difficult to find our way home after dark.

The next "mutton grab" we were invited to was out in a village called Um Salal. Again the children and I were invited to go along with John. Women were not usually included in these invitations, as the hosts' wives did not appear. We sat in the majlis with the men and drank the "potion" while John made polite conversation in Arabic.

After a while we were all taken in to sit on the floor and eat our lunch. Patricia and Christopher enjoyed the novelty of actually being allowed to eat with their fingers and being forgiven for being in a mess. After the meal a servant brought round a bowl with soap and a rose water sprinkler, to enable us to get the worst of the mess off our hands and faces. Then the children and I were taken to meet the wives in the harem. At that time I had no idea what to say to these women when I met them, as my Arabic was not nearly good enough for uneducated people to even try to understand, as these ladies were at that time.

The harem was a large building much like a granary, with piles of sacks at one end and a carpet and some cushions at the other. The children and I were invited to sit down and then we were subjected to close scrutiny, our faces stroked and the children's blonde hair fingered and discussed. Patricia's blue eyes were noted. My skirt was lifted and before I could move, my underwear was inspected. I made mental note to ensure I was wearing my most glamorous next time! Their children appeared, all aged under four and somewhat immodestly wearing their pants round their ankles (if they wore any at all) and their upper garments pulled up round their necks. I couldn't help feeling they were in for a shock when the girls grew up and were introduced to the petula mask and the long black jellabah.

Eventually the "potion" was brought and we were able to

return to the male majlis and John, and then to go home. I decided that I must take some advice on how to cope in the harems in future.

I did ask some of my friends for some ideas. I found that most wives were not invited on these occasions, but one who had gone found that it was useful to take glossy magazines with lots of pictures. The next time I went I took a *Harper's Bazaar* and spent a lot of time discussing the pictures with the wives. They were very happy when I let them keep the magazine.

At the Eids, the Muslim Festivals, it was usual to visit the Royal Sheikhs' wives in the harems to wish them "Eid Mubarak", similar to our Happy Christmas. On one occasion I went to visit the Ruler's wife and found her painting her legs with henna, making them appear as if she was wearing stockings with a shaped heel, a welt at the top and a seam up the back. She wanted to paint my legs too, but I managed to dissuade her, as I thought I would look a little odd on the beach in my bathing costume.

On a visit to one of the Sheikhas (as the Sheikh's wives were called,) it was decided that I should be taught how to belly dance. I was pulled up off my cushion and a scarf was tied around my hips. Then I was persuaded to wobble and sway and shake the tassels on the scarf to the best of my ability. I do not think my teachers were very proud of my prowess, judging by the hilarity my efforts caused. I think the Arab women must have been made differently from me, as I just could not bend and sway in the way they did. Anyway word spread round the harems that I was learning to dance and most places I went I was given another lesson. This was a good icebreaker and made my visits much easier. I did not mind making a fool of myself, all in a good cause.

While I was learning to be a banker's wife in an Arab country, our house was being put to rights. The door was taken off the landing cupboard and made to open outwards and some sliding rails were fitted to our wardrobes so we could hang our clothes AND close the doors. John had removed the huge doors dividing the living room so we could now seat people at table. There was nothing to be done about the drains, but the stairs were still dangerous traitors' steps and the clerk of works was being very slow in sorting the problem. After nearly six months, he had only got as far as removing the terrazzo treads and we were reduced to climbing the stairs on rough concrete. He was also building a tennis court between the houses. So far the base had been laid and strings stretched over the area to help make it level.

All this had been progressing between a series of people staying at the house when on business. John received cables from a salesman asking him to book them a room at the best hotel, as the travel agents could not do so. The reason was that there were no hotels in Doha at that time, except for the Darwish Emporium guesthouse, which was only available for Darwish customers. So I was often called upon to provide a bed.

Some men became regular visitors. On one occasion I was asked to accommodate an elderly Dutch Ghee salesman and his son. Apparently the old man wanted to visit his customers before he retired. This caused some embarrassment, as our house was a bit small to accommodate two total strangers for a whole week. Head Office had been quite clear that we should not make any charge for accommodating people and we were under no obligation to do so. That was all very well, but what were we to do when the Bank's customers arrived at the airport on business with nowhere to stay?

The Dutch couple gave me a gold watch as a thank you present. Others gave me silk scarves and one a mohair cardigan. A large box of prunes heralded the arrival of an arms dealer we knew from our Beirut days. We were asked to help with BOAC crew accommodation when planes stayed overnight. Not long after this started, a hotel was built. Thank goodness.

Christmas came round and there was the usual panic to try to supply the requests to Father Christmas. The completion of the tennis court prompted us to find larger bicycles, as there was now somewhere for the children to ride.

Both children had parts in the school nativity play. Patricia was the Angel Gabriel dressed in a long white "sheet" with polystyrene wings. I had spent half the night before cutting out and sticking "feathers" cut from airmail newspaper on to a polystyrene shape cut from some machinery packaging. Her head was wrapped in angel hair from the Christmas tree. She really looked the part! She sang solo *Who is He in yonder stall?* and sounded very well.

Christopher was to be a king. He wore "kingly" robes and

a crown made from the usual silver paper, but decorated with Rowntrees' Fruit Gums stuck on to represent jewels. He remembered his lines but had to maintain his strength by surreptitiously picking off the wine gums from his crown and eating them!

After the play everybody congratulated everyone else, and proud parents smirked with pride at the prowess of their offspring in the approved manner. I was no exception.

We were warned that the sheikhs and merchants would come to call on us on Christmas morning, so we should be prepared. I had no idea what was required, but the servants said they knew how to cope. We should buy about 12 tins of assorted fruit juice and a box of biscuits and a few sticky cakes. The drinks would be served with straws, which I should order from Bahrain.

On Christmas morning the children awoke at about 5 am, so fortunately we were awake early too. At about 6.30 there was a beating on the front door. John went down to open it and found a real Christmas tree on the doorstep and a grinning merchant wishing him a Happy Christmas. Michael, our bearer, appeared with our morning tea, so John sat in his dressing gown with our guest and supped tea. I quickly got dressed, as I could not appear in my night attire.

After a brief stay our guest departed. John rushed upstairs and got dressed while I went to the kitchen to hurry the servants to prepare breakfast and our visitor's drinks. John came down just in time as the next merchant arrived. Michael brought round a tray of tins of fruit juice and sticky cakes. More visitors arrived and soon our room was full. It seemed that when there were no more seats the first callers left, leaving space for the new arrivals.

As more and more visitors arrived I was panicking that our supplies would run out. The servants told me not to worry. Still the callers came and went. Still the drinks and eats kept coming. I made a mental note to thank the boys profusely when this was all over.

Eventually the 93rd visitor left and I went to the kitchen to praise the servants and to see how much I owed for all the extra tins. I was amazed and horrified to hear how the magic was worked. It seems that all they did was to pop a new straw into each tin when it was cleared away, cut any teeth marks from the slices of cake and served them again. It seems that the guests don't drink the drinks, they just bend down the straw to indicate they have had enough, take a biscuit and leave it on the plate. So the original 12 tins, still mainly full, remained beside the nearly empty box of straws. I was speechless and hoped, most sincerely, that no one would ever know. However I discovered that most people coped with the callers in the same way. I remembered all the tins of juice I had drunk on my calls and wondered if the Qataris coped with our visits at their Eids in the same way!

Christmas lunch was a family affair when the accountants and their families joined us for the traditional feast. We ate a turkey which had been given to us some three weeks earlier by a customer. It had been gobbling in the back yard while, Peter, the cook, fattened it up. He came to me on Christmas Eve and asked for a glass of brandy because he was going to kill the turkey. I was very surprised - did he really need a glass of brandy to fortify him before he killed the bird?

"No no, not for me!" he exclaimed, laughing, "For the turkey, to relax the tendons and make the meat more tender." I felt rather foolish, but thought this was an interesting idea.

When tea time came we had some more callers, so we gave them a cup of tea and the children were asked to pass round the sugar. I saw out of the corner of my eye Sheikh Nasser helping himself to spoonful after spoonful, and was very surprised. Then it was my turn and I discovered that the spoon in the sugar bowl was a joke one with a hole in the middle, sent by Gampy for Christopher's stocking. I often wonder what the Sheikhs thought, but my Arabic was not up to explaining.

For our first Christmas, we decided to invite the whole of the British Community to Boxing Day drinks and a finger food buffet. I remember there were 83 men, women and children on the list. We organised a Coca Cola bar on the tennis court. Children were invited to bring their pedal cars and bikes, as it was a safe place to ride. We also had games like pin the tail on the donkey and throwing rings on to hooks. It was a fun party, as we all enjoyed getting together and meeting up with the men who worked in the desert, whom we did not see very often. I remember that a pyramid was built out of empty beer cans and there was a dire penalty for the person who caused it to collapse.

After eighteen months the time came to take Patricia back to the UK to start boarding school. We had been warned that when children turned eight they were expected to leave the Shell School. We had been dreading this time, but it had to be done as she was outgrowing the school. She was looking forward to going, which was a help.

We decided that I would take Christopher with me, though he was not due to go to boarding school for another year or so. John came over to Bahrain to see us off and we stayed at the Speedbird Hotel and walked round the town. John had been posted to Bahrain in 1948 before we were married. It appears that it had changed since he was there. He lived in a town flat over the Post Office. There was no air-conditioning in those days and he often slept on the roof of the flat under a mosquito net, which may have protected him from mosquitoes, but did not prevent the heavy dew from soaking him. New bungalows had been built for the staff since then, with pretty gardens full of flowers. I was quite envious.

I had arranged for Granny L. to meet me in London as I wanted to order nametapes and buy Patricia's uniform at the school's outfitter. Granjo and Gampy had offered to have Christopher to stay in Scotland while the shopping was being done. I had said I would leave the decision until we actually got to London, as Christopher was only six and had never been away from me before. I had to buy him some clothes as he required some warmer items than he had worn in Doha. However when the time came he was very enthusiastic. He remembered travelling in a sleeper with me the last time he went to Scotland, and had a plan all worked out. He would drink his tea when the guard came to wake him up, then he would get dressed and go out to meet Gampy, and if he was not there he would ring him up. He was amazingly confident. I telephoned Gampy and he spoke to Christopher and they discussed how they would recognise each other. I took him to the train and tucked him in. The train did not leave until 11 pm, so he was pretty tired. The guard was an amiable chap and agreed to see he got up in time.

We returned to Romsey to enable Mum to prepare for her holiday in the Holy Land. We were to stay at Abbotswood while she was away and we had secretly decided to decorate her kitchen for her. After a week Granjo, Gampy and Christopher came south and joined us at Abbotswood and Granjo helped with the last of the nametapes.

The day I was dreading arrived, and Granjo came with me to take Patricia to Ridgeway. We were taken into the headmistress's room for a cup of tea and Patricia was sent off with a fellow pupil to explore. When the time came for me to leave she could not be found. Eventually she turned up and gave us a cheerful wave goodbye and was gone again. I was half relieved that she seemed quite happy and half miserable at leaving her. I remember I cried like a baby as soon as we had driven out of the school grounds, and Granjo made me stop at a pub to have a calming drink

The next day we set about painting Mum's kitchen. It had

been painted a dark bottle green by the previous owners and we planned to lighten the room up a bit. It was quite difficult trying to cook for the family on the Aga while tripping over paint pots, not to mention finding utensils, china and cutlery. We washed and sandpapered the walls and woodwork after carefully copying the height records of all the grandchildren, which were marked on the architrave of the kitchen door, so we could transfer them all to the newly painted door frame. We invited Aunt Joy to come and help us and Christopher joined in.

By the time Mum returned the kitchen had been painted a pale green and all the cupboards had been cleaned out and freshly lined and everything washed and put away. The spots had been cleaned off the floor and windows and we were pleased with our efforts. I think Mum was pleasantly surprised, even if she did find it difficult to find things for a while.

Meanwhile trouble brewed between the Dutch and the Government in Indonesia, which caused the Dutch Shell Oil Company to leave the island. They were sent to Doha and the British Shell Oil Company personnel were sent to Indonesia in their place. This meant that the Shell School would become Dutch, so there was a problem for English-speaking children. What were we to do with Christopher? Should I join the PNEU (the Parents' National Education Union,) and teach him myself with the aid of a correspondence course?

I decided to go to Walhampton School to ask their advice. Christopher was not due to go there for another 18 months or so, and I was worried that he might miss the company of other children if I taught him myself. Letters to and from John flew back and forth. In the end we decided to put him into his school even though he was only six and three quarters. They agreed to take him at half term provided I stayed in England for his first term to see how he settled down. More frantic uniform buying and sewing on name tapes and another heart-breaking parting, but I did see him each weekend.

However, both children settled down well at school. John and I decided that I should stay at home for the summer holidays, as it would be expensive to fly us all out to Doha. We felt that I should be there to see them in for their second term. I had been away from John for four months by then and he was missing us as much as we were missing him. We went to Scotland for some of the holiday and visited friends from time to time. Then the time came for the children to return to school. They were both quite happy to go, which made it easier for me to part with them, although I think I cried more than they did.

I felt very strange flying back to Doha on my own. It was the first time I had flown without the children for eight years, since they had been born in fact. The temperature was pleasant when I arrived.

The stairs had had half their treads replaced as, in the end, the concrete treads were replaced with wood. Not nice hardwood as I had hoped but deal, a softwood, which had to be painted and then carpeted. Shelves had been fitted into the store cupboards, and joy of joys, I now had a washing machine with an electric wringer. It was not a very efficient machine but our clothes were not really dirty, so it served its purpose.

John had organised a welcome-home party for me, so I was able to see who had returned from leave and meet a few newcomers.

The season was beginning to swing and the Doha Players were getting into production. I became "props" back stage and John was business manager for "Sailor Beware". It was a happy cast for once with fewer tantrums than usual, and the prima donnas were less vociferous, which was pleasant. One of my duties was to provide six china ornaments to be thrown about each night. At least two should be breakable, for preference. I went round the souk trying to scrounge broken figurines and animals which I could repair ready to be broken again. I had great difficulty in making my requirements understood. I would rummage about in the shops' storerooms and whoop with delight if I came upon broken items. I think the shopkeepers were convinced that I was quite mad. However they gave them to me with very peculiar looks on their faces. I think I got the reputation for being the meanest person in Doha, too mean to pay the price of unbroken goods.

After the play an invitation came from Cyprus Airways for a group of us to go on an inaugural flight to Cyprus. We left very early in the morning after the last night of the play and flew to Bahrain, where we picked up some Bahrainis. After a champagne breakfast on the plane, we landed at Nicosia

Airport and were driven to the Ledra Palace Hotel. That afternoon a fleet of taxis took us up a very steep and winding road into the Trudos Mountains. We felt the drivers must develop magnificent biceps hauling their cars round the hairpin bends. This was before the days of power-assisted steering.

At the top we reached the snow line. It was great fun throwing snowballs at each other and watching the Bahrainis experiencing snow for the first time. Back to the hotel for dinner, and on to a very seedy nightclub. I sat next to a Bahraini gentleman who had never seen the like of these scantily clad girls and applauded their every high kick. I was in hysterics watching him cheer and clap. He really enjoyed it all.

The next day we got up early and set off on an exploratory trip, again in our fleet of taxis. We stopped at Bella Paix Abbey and enjoyed the walk round the ruins and looking at the view. There was a wonderful tree in the courtyard which produced oranges, lemons, bitter oranges and grapefruit all at the same time.

On we went, up into the hills to St Helarian Castle perched round a pinnacle of rock. It was quite a climb to the top and the views from the windows in all directions were magnificent. It is said that St Helarian was the inspiration for Walt Disney's Castle in Snow White.

Back in Nicosia we were taken to hear President Makarios preach. The church was so full we had to stand right below his pulpit. It was an interesting service with many different actions that we did not understand. The floor was swept at regular intervals, and people seemed to burst into song for no apparent reason. Makarios changed clothes under a canopy and gave instructions by ringing handbells while the congregation ate sandwiches, chatted and even played cards. It seemed a very informal business.

The next morning we visited Salamis and watched some archaeologists digging up some little statuettes. It gave me a funny feeling to think that I was one of the first people to see those statuettes for hundreds of years. On the way back to Nicosia we passed through Kyrenia and had a cup of tea at the Dome Hotel and walked round the castle. We were invited to a Cypriot wedding in a village we passed through and joined in the celebrations for a while. How friendly the people of Cyprus were, they made us all so welcome. It was a lovely interlude and I was only sorry that John had not been able to come too. The notice of the trip was too short for him to ask permission to leave his post. He could have done with the trip, as he had spent only one night out of Doha in two years, and was getting somewhat tired. One more year to go.

Chapter Fifteen

A VISIT TO DUBAI

Sheikh Ahmad al Thani, Ruler of Qatar, announced that he was to marry the daughter of the Sheikh of Dubai, Sheikha Miriam. Of course we were not invited to the wedding, but we were invited to visit her in her new palace in Dubai. About twenty of us were asked to appear at the airport early one morning, where we boarded a plane and were flown to Dubai. John borrowed a cine camera from a customer, Saab Salaam, so we could record it all. Unfortunately he found that the eyepiece had fallen out and he was unable to see what he was taking. We searched the floor of the plane without success.

We were driven to the palace in a fleet of smart American cars, to be greeted by the Sheikh and given the usual "potion" coffee. Then we were ushered into the huge dining room, where we sat at a table groaning with roast baby camels, sheep and goats, one of which was right opposite me. I found the baleful gaze of its eye and the grizzled whiskers of its beard rather disconcerting. I do wish that the servant, stomping on the table tearing off lumps of meat for everyone, had washed his feet more recently. However the food was very good and the gold-plated cutlery and gold-rimmed plates looked very elegant. There were tins, with straws, of Fanta and Pepsi Cola to drink, which slightly spoiled the effect. It was a good meal, and the rumour that honoured guests are forced to eat the sheep's eye appeared to be unfounded, thank goodness. At least the Political Agent, John Moberley, who was sitting next to me, was not offered one. If this was the custom, I am sure he would have been asked to share it on such an auspicious occasion.

When we had finished we were taken on a tour of Dubai, which was a thriving Arab town and has a creek dividing the commercial area from the residential. We watched the ferrymen sculling their abras, or narrow rowing boats, across the water, carrying pedestrian shoppers to and from the souk. Nowadays there are some bridges and the roads are wide and modern with grassy roundabouts and tree-lined streets - a scene hardly imaginable on our first visit in 1958. John bought me some 22-carat gold earrings, shaped like Arab coffee pots, as a memento of the occasion.

We were taken back to the Palace, where the ladies were taken to Sheikha Miriam's Palace across the courtyard. Her majlis was nearly as palatial as that of the Sheikh. The large, heavy, deep, red plush-covered furniture was arranged around the walls in true Arab fashion, which is not really very sociable. If one wants to talk to anyone other than one's immediate neighbour, one has to shout. The beautiful Persian carpets stretched almost wall to wall and the deep red curtains with their gold tasselled edges reached from floor to ceiling.

After the obligatory thimble of coffee a loud voice made us all jump.

"Would the ladies please return to the main Majlis as it is time to go." Shades of "the train standing at platform 3...!" We all looked at each other, imagining ourselves being summoned by a Tannoy system in our own drawing rooms! We did as we were bidden and joined the men. Then we were immediately swept off to the airport, where we boarded our DC9 and flew back home. On the way home, John found the eyepiece of the camera, which had fallen inside. The pictures he took blind are not brilliant, but they serve as a reminder of the day we flew for two and a half hours to have lunch with a sheikh.

The day dawned when the children would fly out for the holidays. This was going to be the first time they had flown on their own. Granny L. had collected them both from their schools and taken them to London Airport. There she completed the VYP forms required by unaccompanied minors and handed them over to a ground hostess, who saw to it that they, and several other children on the same flight, all got on the right plane. How pleased we were that British Airways flew direct to Doha. There were stops on the way but no changes of plane as we had had in Bahrain when we first arrived.

I spent days cleaning their rooms, setting out their toys and games and buying their favourite foods. I wondered if their tastes had changed and if they would hate to be back here after all the wonderful things the UK had to offer them. Somehow I could not believe that just being with us was going to be enough. Doha seemed such a dull place: hot, sticky and dusty. What was I going to do to compensate for all they had left behind? We had no cinemas, ice rinks, amusement parks, nor even fun places to walk. I worried about making their holiday enjoyable and secretly dreaded the day they might say they did not want to come out for the holidays. In retrospect, I am very glad to say that that day never came. The thought kept me on my toes though.

The plane landed smoothly and on time. Other parents were there, craning for the sight of their offspring walking gingerly down the plane's steps. They were all dressed in hot UK clothing, clutching blue BOAC bags bulging with books, pencils and sweets bought by fond grandparents who could not imagine what the children were going to do for the seventeen hours' duration of the flight.

We picked out Patricia in her grey blazer and cotton frock, clumpy shoes and socks and wearing her round steel-rimmed National Health glasses. She had recently acquired these and I had forgotten about them, so they were a bit of a shock. Christopher followed in his royal blue blazer and long grey corduroy shorts, just showing his knees above his long woolly hand-knitted socks. They looked so small as they half ran towards us. Patricia told me much later that she was in a panic in case she did not recognise us nor we recognise her, as people kept telling her how much she had grown. We couldn't wait to get them home and have a good look at them.

It was so wonderful to have them back again and they were

glad to be there. All previous misgivings were quickly dispelled as they gobbled up their favourite pâté sandwiches and glasses of Coca Cola. Cook Peter had made them a special cake and Michael was hovering in the background with his hands behind his back, one leg stuck out to the side as was his wont, wearing a broad grin. He was pleased the children were back, to provide a bit of life about the place.

In the evening there was lots of chatter and "Do you know, Mum...." and excited exclamations of "Dad!" as if they were practising the words. We all had an early night as the children were tired after their flight and we were ready to sleep after our restless previous night.

The next day the holidays began with the usual potter in the souk to try to supply outgrown wants like flipflops for the beach and T-shirts to swim in, until they were used to the hot sun. It was strange how quickly they developed tans and the fine hairs on arms and legs bleached white. It was fortunate that both had dark skin which seemed to be able to withstand the heat. We saw some poor mites who were lobster red and sore in spite of suntan oils, T-shirts and sunhats.

I need not have worried about entertaining the children as they quickly found their friends and spent the time visiting and being visited. Parents organised picnics at the beach and sports meetings, where we discovered that Christopher was a speedy sprinter, winning all the races he entered. Patricia was very game but found her disproportionately long legs hard to control when running. However, she came into her own when swimming. Car rallies were organised and the oil companies laid on the odd cinema show and swimming sports at Um Said.

One of the entertainments the children much enjoyed was to slide down the "soft" side of the sand dunes. Once we took tea trays and tried to toboggan down. It was good fun but hard work climbing up again.

The Dutch Shell people organised a "tulip car rally". Competitors were given a "strip map." This was a line with the turnings you needed to pass marked on the left or right. For example a right turn at a cross roads, meaning two turns would need to be passed on the left, would be shown as two marks on the left of the line. A lot of people got very lost! There were various questions to be answered en route. It was a lot of organization and hard work, but everyone joined in. It was a happy community and most people got on well. Possibly it was one of the happiest places we lived in.

All too soon the dreaded time came to put them back on the plane to return to school. Clothes were washed, ironed and packed, and presents to be taken home were found and labelled. Cables were sent to confirm flights, and after a restless night children were taken to the airport and handed over to a stewardess. Dressed in their hot UK clothing they looked so small and vulnerable as they walked out to the plane holding hands. Oh, how I hated sending them away. Life seemed so empty when they were away and John was at the office. But I would not have been permitted to work even if I could have found something to do.

I spent some time arranging plastic flowers in vases in Ali

bin Ali's new supermarket, so they would sell well. I was amazed to find them all sold the next time I went in. I decided to try a little window dressing in one of the small shops. While my effort was better than the shopkeepers, I decided that there was a bit more to window dressing than appeared!

When the tennis court was finally completed John invited the staff to use it on Thursday afternoons. This was almost a half-day holiday. I think about six of the Indian clerks made use of it, which was nice for them. There were tennis courts at Shell but ours became quite an asset for the community and made a change of entertainment from picnicking and swimming.

I found a hairdresser in Um Said, the oil company town, and spent a morning travelling the 30 or so miles to have my hair cut, which had previously been done by John and his Rolls razor. Afterwards I would visit a friend for coffee or lunch, which made an outing.

On one occasion the driver heard that there had been a bomb on the pipeline and Palestinians were suspected of sabotage. Indeed, we could see a column of smoke in the distance across the sand dunes. I had to hurry home, because we were organising a get together to raise funds at the Beacon in the evening. I called in at the Bank and spread the news about the bomb, as I had been one of the first to hear of it.

That evening we had a good barbecue supper and returned home fairly late. We had just got into bed when the telephone rang. It was a policeman saying that John should go down to the Bank as there had been an accident, though he would not say what had happened. Reluctantly John got dressed, muttering that probably Ali, the night watchman, had fallen off his chair or something.

After about 20 minutes the phone rang again. This time it was John asking me to go next door and wake up Jack Thompson, the accountant, as there had been a bomb in the Bank strongroom.

Jack was alone at this time, as his wife had flown home. I knew that he kept a gun under his bed for protection, after someone had broken into Ken Jarvis's house, and there had been a fight during which knives were used. I was reluctant to disturb Jack knowing how nervous he was, but I took the key we held to his house and tiptoed, dressed in my night clothes, up the stairs to the bedroom. I called his name loudly and banged on the door, while keeping well out of his sight. Poking my head round the door I saw the gun come up against the moon lit window.

"Don't shoot, it's me!" I yelled, and explained that John wanted him in the Bank at once. Startled, Jack drove off and I returned home to await developments. Before long both men returned with the codebook to try to code a cable to Head Office explaining what had happened. They found that they could send a message saying, "So and So had left by camel train today," but bombs in strongrooms were not catered for. There was, however, a way of saying "Read the next word backwards." So they decided to compose a message that way, although the word "bmob" did not look very encoded. There was little we could do that night, but we did not get much sleep. The next day we went to the Bank early to see what had happened. There was very little to see from the outside, beyond a bit of plaster which had fallen off the wall. There were police guards on everything and no one was allowed to go in until the Chief of Police had arrived. In those days, an event like this was quite a phenomenon. No one was quite sure how to begin.

The chief of police, Ron Cochrane, was very anxious to see if there was a body in the strongroom. John was anxious to get into the Bank to see what state the office was in. When he opened the door the most amazing sight met him. The bank was strewn with a fine dust and the strongroom door was firmly shut. There was what appeared to be confetti strewn all over the banking hall. This turned out to be 100 and 1000 rupee notes, which had been crimped up like crepe paper. The notes had been squeezed through the very fine gap round the heavy strongroom door by the explosion inside. One could take a scrap the size of a postage stamp and gently stretch it out into a complete note.

John organised a sweep up of every scrap, and they were placed in some of our tin trunks usually used to contain our heavy luggage as we moved around the world. The Manager of the Eastern Bank was very helpful and offered the loan of some cash and some space in their strongroom for the time being. John consulted one of our senior managers in Bahrain, though no one had any experience of such an incident before. In the end the National Bank of India sent two men who sat in the bank painstakingly smoothing out all the scraps of notes that had been salvaged, noting the numbers of each note. The National Bank of India promised they would refund the bank with the full value of every note, provided two numbers had been found. If only one number was found then half the value would be refunded. I think in the end, over 75% of the money lost was salvaged and replaced.

The force of the explosion was such that clear imprints of coins could be seen on the plaster on the walls of the strongroom. It seemed that the bomb had been placed inside the safe that stood in the strongroom. This also contained jewellery which had been placed in the bank for safe keeping. I remember I sat and sieved the pyrites to try to find some of the gold. This was a hard task as it was difficult to distinguish real gold from the fool's gold which had lined the safe.

John was quite pleased that with the co-operation of the Eastern Bank, he was able to open for business that afternoon. The post mortems and inquiries went on and on. The conclusion was that the bomb could have been put in with some late, uncounted cash, and therefore either the Cashier or the late customer knew more than they were saying. However, the police were unable to come to any satisfactory conclusion. If it was intended to rob the Bank it was a complete failure. If it was a Palestinian attempt to demonstrate against the British, then I suppose it did cause some irritation. I did hear later that it was an attempt by a customer to cover up and confuse some enormous debt he had incurred.

About this time Hazel Lough, one of our Bank wives living in Dubai, asked if she could come and stay with us, as she was expecting her first baby. Doha had a magnificent hospital by Middle Eastern standards and was about an hour's flight away. Richard would be able to come to greet his offspring fairly quickly. Baby Jennifer was, of course, late. But John was able to stand in for Richard, and duly paced the hospital appropriately when the time came in the middle of the night.

Christmas came and we were eagerly awaiting the arrival of our own children again. And so began the mad round of Christmas parties, too much food, and the indulgence of parents striving to make the children enjoy themselves. We had 'our' new baby for Christmas and Richard came to join us.

Hazel decided to return to Dubai by sea with her new baby. We all had the exciting duty of putting them aboard the Dumra, which was an old coastal steamer that plied up and down the Persian Gulf. There were no docksides for her to tie up to in those days, so we had to scramble, baby and all, on to a small barge to be ferried out some distance offshore. There was a cold wind, I recall, but the babe lying asleep in her carrycot, perched on a heap of luggage, looked very unconcerned by all the noise and bustle going on around her.

When we got on board, one of John's customers asked us all to join him in his cabin for lunch. This proved to be real "mutton grab," seated on the floor. As usual the food was good, and very welcome, as we had not thought of bringing any. There was a restaurant of sorts, but it in no way came up to this standard. We waved goodbye to Hazel and Jennifer and returned to the shore. The next trip the Dumra sailed was to be her last, as she caught fire and sank off Muscat.

Then came the tearful farewells and the drowning of sorrows, as all too soon peace fell on our homes as the children flew back to school.

About this time BOAC began to land larger planes at Doha Airport. "Cats Eyes" Cunningham brought the Britannia to show off its paces and we were invited to go up for a trial flight. John was too busy to go, so I arranged for our bearer, Michael, to take his seat. As he had arrived in Qatar from Goa by boat, he had no experience of flying. We took off and flew over Doha and looked down on the desert below. It looked like a relief map, showing the lace-like edge of the sea and the sparseness of the sand cut by the road to Dukhan and Ahmadi, and was reminiscent of pictures of the moon. Michael enjoyed it immensely, although I noticed he gripped the seat until his knuckles showed.

The new airport building was, to my mind, reminiscent of a huge, old-fashioned train, complete with cowcatcher at the front. The circular control tower on the roof had blue glass windows all round, and stood at one end of the new building - a vast improvement on the barasti hut that served as a departure and arrival lounge when we first arrived. The architect had arranged tiles bearing his wife's footprints to be laid in the arrival and departure halls, to indicate the direction people should follow. At this time I believe the idea was as original as it was novel.

The Government civil engineer, Alan Jack, became quite

paranoid, as each time the jet planes took off from the new runway the afterburn destroyed the tarmac, and it had to be repaired before the next plane landed. The sun tended to melt the tar anyway, as I found to my dismay one day when we were standing awaiting the arrival of King Ibn Saud when he came to visit the Ruler of Qatar. My high heels sank into the soft surface and I could not take my feet out of my shoes in time, and so found myself flat on my back, unable to move. Very embarrassing.

It was interesting to watch the Ruler and his "Court" milling round the King. I have a cine film of the crowd surrounding the King and Sheikh Ali, trying to shake their hand. Paul Ensor, head of QPC, is evident, wearing his very British bowler hat. Alistair Livingstone is also easily picked out by his very white hair. John is also there, but as his hair was still dark, he is less easily spotted. They were very hot in their lounge suits.

The Police Pipe Band played jolly tunes on the bagpipes and the troops stood to attention. After this greeting the invited guests gravitated to the guest palace near our house. The state Cadillacs drove at speed (they never seemed to drive anywhere without screaming tyres,) to collect their passengers, then screamed off again to the palace, with guards hanging dangerously on the sides and all the aides following in hot pursuit. Trucks loaded with more soldiers followed behind. John avoided the traffic jam by returning home via our back gate, and then walked across the road for the party at the palace. This was not really considered a sufficiently dignified method for important people to arrive. They should join the queue of cars waiting to drive up to the front door. However, John, ever practical, decided he would join the hoi polloi and walk. On this occasion the mutton grab was served at the long table rather than sitting on the floor. That night there was loud Arabic music far into the night. Knowing, as I did, that the huge palace had only four bedrooms, I wondered where everyone fitted in for the night. Perhaps tents were set up in the garden behind.

The next day John was summoned, with most of the male foreign community, to the Ruler's Palace for dinner. John said it was an enormous crowd. When the time came to leave, he had to climb out of the window with several others (including the owner of the bowler hat), or they might have been there all night. Fortunately, on this occasion he had taken the driver, as there was a colossal parking problem. Somehow Ahmed, the driver, had got wind that John was leaving and was there ready waiting to drive him home.

Not long after this occasion we noticed that the mode of palace entertaining was changing. A most uncomfortable "modernisation" was introduced, a low table some fourteen inches off the floor beset by cushions. It was nigh impossible for the diners to sit comfortably and reach the food, which was still a "mutton grab". There was nowhere to put one's legs, as to stick them straight out under the table was very hard on the back. Kneeling quickly gave one pins and needles. To lounge on one haunch, like a Roman, was not much better, as it left little room for one's neighbour and it was impossible to reach the food. The best way of coping was to sit cross-legged, which made one too far from the table to "grab" easily. So you had to hope that the servant, who walked up and down the table in his bare feet, would tear off a succulent morsel and drop it on one's plate. This new table was not considered an improvement and fortunately was soon abandoned.

I am sad to say that by the time we left Doha, palace food had deteriorated to burned chops, soggy chips and overcooked peas, at least for the European guests. I am sure the sheikhs continued to "mutton grab", which was much better.

We decided that we could not afford to fly the children out for the three weeks of the Easter holiday, so they went to grandparents and had a wonderful time. We were due to have home leave that summer, so we felt we would see them before long.

Then John fell ill.

The doctors were unable to decide what was wrong with him. Some said he had tuberculosis and others lung cancer. All said he was too ill to fly home. It was a dreadful period, as he found it too painful to sleep lying down, so I propped him up with pillows leaning on a card table and he slept fitfully. I sat beside him, trying to ensure he did not fall off the pillows. He was given a massive dose of some antibiotic. He became allergic to this and came out in a series of wheals all over his body. He was given Piriton to counteract this and promptly became addicted to it.

After a short while Bunny Robbins was sent to take over the

branch. I was greatly relieved as I was expected to act as go-between for the day to day running of the Bank. John was far too ill to cope and decisions had to be made, although Archie Butt, the Bahrain Manager, came for a brief visit to help. I was very relieved to see Bunny, our relief. He stayed with us and was such a help as he sat with John and tried to take over the Bank, poor chap, while I packed up our belongings.

Eventually it was deemed safe for us to fly home. John was very weak and pale, but with much help we arrived at the airport. There was quite a "send off" party but I'm afraid John was not really aware of what was going on. He was presented with a huge crystal chandelier, as a parting gift, by one of his very well-meaning customers, but it was not quite what was required at that time.

When we boarded the plane the BOAC staff really came up trumps and did their utmost to see that John was as comfortable as possible. An ambulance met us at London Airport and John was taken to the Brompton Chest Hospital while I was installed in a small hotel nearby. After many tests and x-rays the doctors at the Brompton decided that John had pleurisy, with an effusion which accounted for the blood in the sputum.

During one of the examinations John said he had a bronchoscope during which he swears he heard one of the doctors say, "Oh look, he has only one where he ought to have two!" When he came round from the anaesthetic John forgot to ask what was missing. His imagination boggled, and he has always wondered what it was.

Before we left Doha we had arranged to take delivery of a

Dormobile, which we had bought at a discount through one of John's customers, who was a motor agent. I took delivery of it just before John was allowed to come home from hospital. I felt very brave as I drove this large vehicle through the streets of London to collect him, although it was not the daunting task it would be today.

Not long after John came home he went back into hospital to have a cartilage removed from his knee. Poor John, it was not his year. However we made good use of our Dormobile, both for visiting people and for lovely picnics with the children.

Chapter Sixteen

LIBYA

When John had recovered sufficiently we set off to our new posting in Libya. We were quite pleased to be getting back to work. John was feeling much better and found time hanging heavily with nothing specific to do. We set off together by air, an unusual thing to do as we preferred to fly separately on the whole. The journey was comparatively short and uneventful, compared to our dramatic flight home from the Gulf.

The Mediterranean looked very blue as we flew over it. This was quite a contrast to the snow on the peaks of the mountains when we passed over the Pyrenees. As the coast of North Africa appeared, the sandy beaches seemed to be edged with white lace as the waves broke on the shore. There appeared to be a wide strip of vegetation along the coast that faded into desert brown as it got further inland.

Our plane came in to land on the tarmac and trundled up to the airport buildings of Idris Airport, once known as Castel Benito. As we stepped on to the platform at the top of the steps we were hit by a blast of hot air, as if we had opened an oven door. We had forgotten the contrast after stepping out of the air-conditioning in the plane and into the full North African sun. Whew! We were back.

Tony Panter was there to greet us and it was good to see him again. We had shared a house in Amman while on the Arabic course, but he and his wife had separated since then.

After immigration and customs we were driven along the country road, lined by wattle bushes and eucalyptus trees struggling to survive in the dry sand. On the edge of Tripoli we passed through the suburb of Collina Verde, where bungalows with green gardens lined the sandy side roads. Soon we drove passed a very high wall, which, we were told, hid the palace of King Idris, who ruled Libya at that time. We could see the gold dome peering over the turquoise tiles along the top of the wall, and a few treetops struggled to be seen. There were traffic lights outside the palace gates ready to stop the traffic whenever the King went in or out. Sentries stood at the gate much as at Buckingham Palace, but we could only catch a glimpse of the building inside through the gates.

We drove round the wall and passed the Russian Embassy, which was one of our near neighbours. They had armed guards on the gates, which were probably a good thing for us, as they would deter any would-be burglars in the vicinity. We drew up outside a wooden gate set in a high, brick wall. Tony opened the gate with a key. A brass plate proclaimed that this was Villa Bactria. The path up to the house was some 10ft wide and made of paving slabs. The gardener had valiantly tried to level the builder's rubble, but it was evident that our new home was very new.

Mahommed, our houseboy, greeted us and carried in our cases. Tony told me he was untrained but seemed fairly willing. He said he did not have a permanent cook, as he preferred to eat out most of the time. However he did have an itinerant cook who came in whenever he had to entertain at home. He had asked him to be there today to greet us.

The first impression of our new home was that it was impressively spacious. The entrance hall was vast, with a grand marble floor covered, in part, by a splendid Persian carpet. There was a long wooden Swedish screen dividing the hall from the dining room. It had a "trough" along the hall side of it, filled with assorted indoor plants, while the dining room side had a seat with a lift-up lid to store tablemats and linen. On the left was a wide marble staircase. Beyond this were two concertina doors that led into the drawing room. This was another large room, rather sparsely furnished, but had an enormous fireplace which, we were told, gave out a tremendous heat in the winter when fed with logs. The large patio doors opened on to an open terrace leading to the garden at the back. A flight of five steps led us up to an area about the size of two tennis courts, which was badly in need of organisation.

Mahommed brought us a tray of tea and biscuits, which was very welcome. I was somewhat daunted by the task of making these marble halls homely. Perhaps it would look better when we had some curtains and a few pictures.

We climbed the marble staircase to explore the upstairs. There were four bedrooms and two bathrooms. The en suite to the master bedroom had very jolly spotted tiles, which would take some getting used to, but the family one was a plainer creamy colour. All the rooms were large and airy with rugs over terrazza tiles. Probably cool in summer, but I hoped that the winters were not too cold. All the rooms had vast built-in cupboards, but the furnishings were sparse. Tony had ordered curtains for all the bedrooms, thank goodness.

The Bank was closed when we arrived, otherwise John would have wanted to visit his office. Instead we were taken on a tour of the town. Tony drove us first past the office, which was in no way impressive. Apparently a splendid new building was conceived. It was intended to build this in the main street, but it was in the planning stage as yet. This was yet another new office for John to build. Did Head Office think he needed more practice? I hoped it would be easier than in Jeddah.

The main street of Tripoli was called the Istiklal and here most of the upmarket shops were to be found. The road was wide and there were covered pavements with pollarded oleander trees adding a bit of colour to the pristine whitewashed buildings. The road parallel to the Istiklal was called 24th of December Street to commemorate Libya's Independence Day. After World War Two, the British controlled Libya and the army was much in evidence, but they had diminished by the time we got there.

Turning right at the entrance to the souk we came into the

town square. The castle was to our left and housed the museum. High in the wall were two huge windows from which, we were told, Mussolini harangued the populace after he had landed at the steps up from the sea. As at the entrance to Piazza Marco Polo in Venice, there are two tall columns said to mark the road to Rome, which often are found in Italian ports. In Tripoli, at that time, Romulus stood on the top of one and Remus on the other. At a later date these were swapped for a star and moon, the Libyan insignia.

Turning right again, we drove along the Corniche, a spectacular wide road lined with palm trees on the right and a low stone balustrade overlooking the blue Mediterranean on the left. The British Embassy and the Ambassador's Residence overlooked the Corniche and the Mediterranean. We next turned right again at the end of the road and passed the American Embassy, arriving eventually at our own back door. John opened the garage and we drove in.

Entering the kitchen we met our cook, whose name was also Mahommed. How confusing, I thought. He was a friendly chap and wore the dark red brimless hat sported by the majority of Libyans. His English was quite good and he was busy preparing our evening meal. Tony told us that he had invited the accountant and the assistant accountant to come to dinner. We had one hour to prepare ourselves before they arrived.

I hastily unpacked our cases while John became acquainted with our spotty tiles in the bathroom. Thank goodness for my crease-resistant frock. Clean and refreshed, we came downstairs just as the two young men arrived. We sat and talked and drank Libyan wine and then sat down at the table, where we had an enormous meal – I remember that the starter was followed by a pigeon each. Both accountants liked Tripoli and found the staff reasonably efficient. The accountant, Jim Mc Murray, lived in the old Manager's house, Villa Viviana, a pleasant villa in a mature garden in Collina Verde, a suburb of Tripoli. The assistant accountant, Bob Clunie, had a flat above the bank downtown. We chatted until quite late and retired about one in the morning.

Neither John nor I slept very well that night. We put it down to the very hard Swedish beds. The mattresses were unsprung and the bases of the beds were reminiscent of duckboards, each one of which we could feel through to our bones.

Next morning John set off to the office with Tony and I set out to explore our new home. Boy Mahommed was capable of cooking a simple breakfast and had a routine for doing the household chores. I told him to carry on as usual. Cook Mahommed was not in evidence. So far I had hardly spoken a word to him. Boy Mahommed told me that Cook Mahommed would be in later to cook lunch for me. The Masters would not be in for lunch, he said, so I would be on my own. It seems that we were all invited out for dinner that evening, so would it be possible for him to go home that afternoon? If indeed we were going out for dinner, I could see no reason for him to stay in, so I said that he could go.

I was at a bit of a loss to know what to do with myself. I

finished my unpacking and wandered about the house absorbing the situation. I tried to converse with the gardener, but Salem's English was non-existent and I had forgotten the little Arabic I knew. So we held discussions as best we could, with much laughing, gesticulating and head nodding.

I decided that I would walk downtown to the Bank and find out what the programme was to be. The second language in Tripoli was, of course, Italian, of which I had very little experience, apart from my short sojourn in Ethiopia. I decided that if I got lost I could at least ask for the bank in Arabic. I passed the Russian Embassy and was greeted with a stony stare in response to my greeting to the Russian guards. Oh dear, this did not augur well if indeed we were beset by burglars.

I walked past the palace wall and peered through the gates into the palace grounds. It was a pretty garden and the grass was lush and green. I walked down the Istiklal and looked in the shop windows. There were dress shops displaying Italian clothes and beautiful shoes, Gucci handbags, wallets, belts and luggage. The display of materials for curtains was evident but I did not feel prepared to start on that task yet. I felt I ought to wait at least until Tony had left. I know how one feels when handing over to someone else. Almost anything the incomer does to change things can be taken as a criticism, so it is probably more diplomatic to bide one's time. I stopped at a café and was just about to ask for a "caffe latte per favore" when I remembered, just in time, that I had no money. It would have taxed my linguistic capabilities to explain that away!

I walked down the street looking in the windows, impressed by the variety of goods available. It was all so different from the shops in Iran and down the Gulf. Suddenly I came upon the crossed palm trees and three coconuts symbol which heralded the presence of the Bank. I went into the office and found it quite busy. Jim, the accountant, spotted me at once and took me to see John in his office. I asked Tony what our programme was and was told that they were going out to lunch with a customer and would be home in the early afternoon. I was offered Abdulla, the Bank driver, who could show me where I might do my shopping, and as his English was quite good, he could translate if required. Please could I have the car back for them at 12.30 pm?

Abdulla, like all bank drivers, was a fund of information. I found that in those days there were few supermarkets in Tripoli. I did my shopping at various small shops, grocers for groceries, butchers for meat and so on. It was important to know the religion of your shopkeeper, as they tended to close on the day of rest as dictated by their religion. Arabs closed on Fridays, Jews on Saturdays and Christians on Sundays. It was helpful to have Abdulla who had driven for several Bank wives before me, and was well aware of these useful tips.

I was relieved to see that Cook Mahommed was there when we arrived home, as I did not have a door key to get in. Having given Boy Mahommed the afternoon off, I had forgotten this little problem. I suggested that for the time being it would be as well if the Mahommeds took their orders from Tony, until we took over properly.

We dined out nearly every evening, as people were saying goodbye to Tony and were welcoming us. As usual we found this a great trial, as so many people knew who we were, but we had difficulty in remembering who was who. John and I usually sat up in bed and tried to remember names as soon as we got home. We found it helped if we could tie them to their spouse in some way. It was also helpful if we could have a little thumb sketch of people – for example "tall hair and curly teeth."

Finally we were able to wave farewell to Tony and start to make our own life in Libya and settle into our new home. As soon as Tony left our social life quietened down, and we stopped drinking so much wine every night. We also started to sleep better, but whether it was because we had become accustomed to the beds, or the fact that we no longer drank large quantities of the local wine (which may have been rather too indigestible), we shall never know.

At long last our overland luggage arrived, and we were able to hang a few pictures and make the bookcases look more useful. I enjoyed displaying some of the treasures we had accumulated in our sundry postings. Some things looked so sad and crumpled after being packed in our trunks for so long. However they conjured up memories and made the house more homely. I was glad that the children's things were there to welcome them. Inevitably there was a great need for me to find where I could replace their outgrown clothing. Fortunately, shorts and T-shirts were the order of every day with flipflops and bathing suits. These were the days before designer wear became a necessity, thank goodness.

The children were about to arrive for their first Libyan holiday. I enlisted the help of new-found friends to find furnishings and fittings to complete the house and to prepare for their arrival. As usual I was nervous that our new home would not quite come up to the children's expectations, or that we would not find the sort of things that would interest them. We discovered that most people went home for the summer holidays, so there would not be very many children for our young to meet. However there were so many things to do we were a bit spoiled for choice. There were beach clubs where we could go to swim in the sea and have lunch. The children could meet such others as there were and their social life would begin. There was the Old Town to explore. Tripoli means three towns - Leptis Magna, Sabratha, and Oea (which was the old Roman name for Tripoli). Tripolitania was once the name of western Libya. The eastern part was called Cyrenaica. The ancient ruins of Cyrene were there, hence the name.

Both John and I were impatient for the children to arrive. We had not had much time to explore ourselves, beyond visiting the old city, which held the traditional souk. Unlike the Gulf States in the 1950s, Libya had a fair number of tourists. The shops in the souk made typical brass ornaments and trays for them to buy. There were also rugs and woven blankets in tribal designs. The courtyards off the main souk were tiled and encircled by tiny stalls glittering with gold jewellery. As in all Arab countries gold was much sought after. Many of the courtyards had small ponds with fountains playing.

The museum displayed a variety of Roman artefacts, for example there were complete mosaic floors, some of them brightly coloured and others faded and incomplete. There were coins, statues and pottery lamps, some of which looked as if they might contain a genie ready to grant three wishes if the right formula could be found to release them. They had been removed from Roman excavation sites in order to preserve them from the sun and rain, not to mention souvenir hunters. Apparently there had been many earthquakes over the years and much had been destroyed.

Near the port of Tripoli there was a magnificent Marcus Aurelius arch, not quite wide enough to have a modern road through it, so it stood on an island and the roads ran round it. The National Bank of Libya was down by the port too. I was told that as the building was of such historical interest, it had been filled with sand during the Second World War, in order to preserve it from damage. This seemed to have worked as the building is of considerable beauty and the mosaic ceiling inside was well worth a visit.

We first visited Sabratha, some forty miles east of Tripoli, one afternoon after John had finished work, as it was within such easy reach. Sabratha had never been a grand Roman metropolis, but was more of a market town. As one walks into the site along a dusty road, the plan of the buildings can easily be seen outlined by the foundations of the thick walls. The rooms appear to have been small by present-day standards.

A little further along we came to the remains of a Christian basilica, complete with an altar, which must have been a later addition as it seemed to be made of several overturned bases of pillars. There were some sarcophagi and a baptistery with steps down into it for total immersion and more steps up the other side. Moving on were the remains of the Antonine Temple, surrounded by pillars, which had steps up to a flat marble area which lay spread out on the dusty ground. We were told that the beautiful mosaic floors had been removed to the local museum.

The forum is a large area, and at the time of our visit it was much littered by fallen columns and large blocks of stone, evidence of the earthquakes which over the years had destroyed so much of the Punic and Roman remains. There was a magnificent Portico leading to a 14-seater lavatory. The seat was made of marble. Once upon a time the floor might have been marble or mosaic, but now it was modern concrete. I was told that this latrine probably would have been a town council meeting place, where many serious discussions had taken place.

The theatre had been considerably restored and the monumental stage had been painstakingly rebuilt. A wooden platform for the stage had been constructed in front of the row of pillars on the wall at the back. A French company was intending to present Shakespeare in French, which we very much wanted to see. Beyond that stood another Christian Basilica, said to be of the 4th century, probably built on the ruins of a Roman Temple and of more modest proportions than the first we had seen. Beside the sea we came to the magnificent amphitheatre, reputed to be the largest in Africa. Certainly we were impressed by the acoustics. After a run along the beach we went to the museum, to look at the mosaics and statues. They were moved there both for protection from the weather and safekeeping from the souvenir hunters, from whom nothing seems safe.

At last the day arrived and we went up to the airport to meet Patricia and Christopher. We scanned the people clumping down the steps from the plane. Why weren't our children the first, or were they? It is so hard to recognise people when they are laden with coats and bags. There they were and we waved madly. At last they reached immigration and the stewardess helped them through into customs, but they were not stopped. They were smiling shyly, clutching bags, coats and sundry books and papers, excited and eager to see their new home. Abdulla took hold of as many bags as he could and we made our way out to the car. We were eager for news of home and all the family.

When we arrived at the house, the two Mahommeds were there to greet us. They shook hands with the children and took the luggage upstairs. The children were impressed with the house and garden and remarked on the possibility of being able to swing several cats. We showed them their rooms and they immediately changed out of their hot school uniform and into shorts and shirts.

We thought that a swim would be the first thing to do.

John said he was not going back to the Bank that day, so he would come with us. The Piccolo Capri Officer's Club was some distance away beyond the suburb of Giorgimpopoli, which we named "Georgium pot-holey" as the roads through it were full of enormous potholes, which made progress very slow and difficult.

Eventually we arrived at the club. After buying the inevitable Coca Cola at the bar we showed the children where to change in the row of huts along the beach. The tide was in, not that it made much difference, as there is very little rise or fall in the Mediterranean. It did however make a bit of difference to the size of the breakers on the sandy beach. Much to the children's annoyance, I made them wear T-shirts for the first few days, as I was always anxious that they did not get burnt before they got acclimatised. We all had a wonderful time and were quite ready for our evening meal by the time we returned home.

The next few days I showed them as much as I could. The afternoons were spent swimming or exploring the town with its fascinating souk, or paying visits to Sabratha. The children had their photographs taken with their heads showing over a statue of a headless Roman soldier, which stood at one side of the Forum.

We were able to go further afield at weekends. We were all longing to go to Leptis Magna, a large Roman metropolis lying some 70 miles along the coast. Taking a picnic lunch, we set off. We said we would stop in Homs to try to find some freshly cooked Arab bread. The village was a bustling little place and the children found the souk interesting. I bought them some wide-brimmed straw hats on our way to find the bakery. It was interesting watching the flat pancakes of dough blowing out on the roof of the domed oven and falling off as soon as it was cooked. We would open the "bags" of bread and fill it with whatever fillings we chose. These were nicknamed "handbags".

As we drove up to the gates of Leptis Magna a camel train loped round the corner. The animals were laden with huge sacking-wrapped bundles, probably rugs and carpets that had been woven by the Bedouin women who lived in tents in the desert. This appeared in complete contrast to the large car in which we had just swept into the car park. After a short walk over the dusty car park, we came to the imposing remains of an archway. The guidebook informed us that it was named after the Roman Emperor Septimus Severus.

The early history of Leptis is somewhat vague as it appears it was a town in the Carthaginian Empire and in spite of its size does not appear to have been very important at that time. However we found the ruts in the streets made by the chariot wheels of long ago very exciting, reminiscent of tramlines in our own towns. Walls of huge hand-hewn stones, about four feet high, lined the road, with tufts of long dried grass growing in the cracks. It was very hot, so we were glad of our sunhats.

As we walked along the road we came to a large open space littered with huge carved stones lying where they had fallen after one of the earthquakes. The children enjoyed playing leapfrog over Ionic capitals and chunks of marble pillar. I suspect they were a little young to really appreciate the wonders of the vast ruins. Indeed there are many adults who remain unimpressed, and who should blame them? John and I have always taken a great interest in archaeology and all things antique.

However the children were very interested in an inscription on a fallen pulpit. "Septimus Severus died at York." We have no idea why it was written in English. Beyond the fallen stones we came to an enormous, 38-seater lavatory. The seat was made of a long shelf of marble with holes at suitable intervals. It seems that the Romans were in no way prudish. In fact we were led to believe that, as in Sabratha, important council meetings were held here. I can't help feeling that it must have been a chilly place in winter, though summer may have been more bearable!

Passing through the lavatory, we came to the baths. We could see where the hot steam flowed beneath the baths through the hypocaust to heat the water. There were several statues of Roman ladies and gentlemen standing decoratively round the baths, draped in folds. It was as if they were waiting for the baths to fill up to enable them to dip a toe in the water. There was evidence of pipes where steam would have warmed the water. Some of this was in reasonable repair and it was possible to see how the system worked. There was much more excavating to be done, but the port was evident along the seashore, though the sea had silted up the harbour itself. Waves crashed against the base of the lighthouse. It was a wonderful thought that perhaps Romans had watched waves rolling up the beach much as we were doing now.

Along the sand we came to the Basilica of Septimus Severus and the Byzantine Church, with its wonderful carved marble pillars. Fingers could be hooked behind the carved vines that wound around the pillars with various animals, hunters and huntresses intertwined in the fine tendrils amongst the leaves. It was impossible to explore the whole of so vast an area in one day, so we set off home just as the sun was setting. We would have plenty of time to explore further at a later date.

The time passed all too quickly and it was time to take the children to the airport and send them back to school.

Princess Alexandra paid a visit to King Idriss and stayed at the Embassy with her husband Angus Ogilvie. Prince Michael was also in Libya on a military exercise in the desert. I happened to be visiting the Military attaché's wife one morning, when Prince Michael rushed in looking very scruffy. He was desperate to find a razor and to iron his own shirt before he met his sister. Somehow it was amusing to see the young Prince having domestic difficulties and being afraid of his sister's displeasure.

Princess Alexandra showed great consideration to a friend of mine, Mary. There had been a visit to Leptis Magna and Mary had been in the party. While they were there the heavens opened and everyone got soaked. Mary was upset as her hairstyle had been ruined and she was due to go to the reception at the Embassy that evening. There was a knock at the door and a lady announced that she was the Princess's hairdresser. It seemed that the Princess was going to wear her toupe that evening and had asked that her hairdresser should find Mary and set her hair for her. What a kind thought.

John and I went to the reception. I was now expecting my third child, and when I met the Princess she gave me a hand up from my curtsy. I was to meet her again at an Embassy Reception two years later in Teheran and was amazed when she asked me whether I had a baby boy or girl. I was so surprised I was almost speechless. However I think that she must have been primed, as I cannot imagine she would remember me.

I would soon follow the children home, as, in line with medical advice, I was to return to England in time to give birth. As luck would have it John's younger brother Bob, who worked for International Air Radio, had been posted to Tripoli Airport. As was common practice when taking an overseas posting, married accommodation was not provided during the first tour. We decided it would be good if Bob and Jenny moved into our house and looked after him while I was away, thus allowing Bob and Jenny to be together and John to have company.

I flew home to stay for a few days with Granny Lindesay, taking time to visit Trish and Chris at school as well as seeing the Grannies. I then went up to Scotland to await my baby's arrival. On one of my weekly check-ups at Cresswell Hospital, Dumfries, I was advised to go into hospital, as my blood pressure was a little high. I was very pleased that the end was in sight, as I had huge abscesses on my front teeth, and the dentist would not take them out because I was too near my time.

The doctor asked me which day I would like my baby to be born. For no particular reason I thought it would be appropriate to give John a wedding anniversary present of his new baby. I was put on a drip to try to hasten things along but, annoyingly, Claire was in no hurry to put in an appearance. Finally, 36 hours later on May 27th, much to everyone's relief, I was delivered of an 8lb bouncing girl. Very soon my dentist removed my offending teeth and fitted me with a bridge, which still works very satisfactorily today. Incidentally I was very nonplussed, on a recent visit to Dumfries Museum, to see the very dentist's chair in which I sat being displayed as veritable museum piece.

I had a problem when I tried to register Claire. The Registrar could not accept John's address as being a postbox number. In the end she settled for Villa Bactria, Tripoli, Libya. It was just as well that she had no need to write to him, as I think the Post Office would have had difficulty in delivering it.

My next problem was to arrange for Claire's name to be added to my passport. Apparently I had to obtain written permission from John before I could take her out of Britain. I became quite cross at all these difficulties, after all there was no doubt at all that the child was indeed mine. However letters were duly written and papers put in order. I took leave of my parents, who had been immeasurably helpful and supportive throughout the whole business, and set off back to Libya to introduce our little daughter to her dad.

I went to London by train. Granny Lindesay came to meet us and took us to see the Great Grannies and to pay a quick visit to Patricia and Christopher before we took off from London Heathrow. I could hardly wait to show Claire to John. Landing at the airport was all very exciting and it was wonderful to be met by John, as well as Bob and Jenny, all eager to see the latest addition to the family. Claire was a lovely baby with a rosy complexion and large brown eyes. She was very placid from birth and a good sleeper at night, which was a great joy.

One evening she screamed loudly from her cot upstairs. I raced up to see what was wrong with her. She was lying on her back grasping her tuft of hair in her little fist and was pulling it as hard as she could. Her face was puce and her mouth was as wide as it would go. She was very angry!

At first we were able to take her with us in her carrycot when we went out in the evening. Our hosts were always happy to see her as she was so little trouble. It was easy for me to feed her as she was on the "demand feeding" system, the latest fashion, which worked very well.

Bob and Jenny were given a villa in Collina Verde and set up their own home. They found a boxer dog, which they named Stubby. It was fun having them there as we were unaccustomed to having real family near at hand.

The summer holidays were soon upon us and the children

were due to join us. This time they were escorting Granjo. They arrived at the airport, grandmother and children eager to meet their little sister, to see how much she had developed. She was quite a novelty for the first few days and turns were taken to bath, powder and dress her. They also enjoyed showing their grandmother around. We had bought a pushchair and a parasol that clipped onto the frame and could be suitably adjusted to protect Claire from the sun.

We had discovered the Botanical Gardens, an interesting place to wander. Apart from the wonderful variety of shrubs and bushes there were some magnificent Uaddan gazelles. These large, goat-like animals had long hair hanging from their throats, reminiscent of the tassels on a Scots sporran. There were also monkeys, which were a source of great amusement. They had acquired some little mirrors from somewhere and enjoyed using them to peep round corners at visitors. They had also learned that they could catch the sun and make "Tinkerbell" appear in each other's eyes. The bougainvillaea that climbed some of the trees was very spectacular, especially the mauve variety.

It was the tomato season and the roads were blocked with lorries laden with tomatoes, queuing at the factory gates. These dripping loads were to be made into tomato paste, or tinned. It was a truly messy and smelly sight.

Granjo really enjoyed swimming in the warm Mediterranean seawater, but, because she had lovely red hair and the very fair skin that went with it, we had to be very careful of her in the sun, as she burned so easily. She also enjoyed our visits to the Roman sites and exploring the town and souks.

We arranged for Granny Lindesay to fly out to visit us while Granjo was still with us. Bob and Jenny had her to stay with them. This gave us an opportunity to have Claire christened with family there to witness it. The Garrison church was there at that time (though it closed shortly afterwards) and the Reverend Wilkinson (who, incidentally was a friend of our vicar at home, the Reverend Canon Sam Boothman), was prepared to christen Claire. We had a lovely day and it was so special that we had so many of our family present. Our cine film shows both Patricia and Christopher taking turns to carry Claire from the church (which as a result had to happen twice!) Granny Lindesay had brought the family christening robe with her for the occasion. The Villa Bactria lent itself to holding large parties and the lunch to celebrate Claire's christening was no exception.

Shortly after the christening it was time for Granjo to return home. Gampy had been very noble allowing her to be away again for so long. It was sad that he was too ill to be able to join us. It was while we were seeing Granjo off that suddenly, John lifted Patricia into the air and stamped his foot hard. We all looked at him in amazement and then saw the reason for this sudden action. A scorpion, albeit squashed and very dead, was lying just where Trish had been standing in her open sandals. This was the first scorpion we had seen.

We were sad to see Granjo go, but we all had enjoyed her visit, and we had Granny Lindesay to introduce to Libya.

One morning Boy Mahommed was late and seemed in a bit of a state at breakfast time. His wife Fatima, who was expecting a baby, had started haemorrhaging. It seemed he had not called a doctor but had sent for her mother to help. I was worried about this, so I sent for Abdulla the driver, and leaving Granny L. to look after the children, Mahommed and I set out with Abdulla to see what we could do. Mahommed lived in a one-storey house in the middle of a plot of land on the edge of a village beyond Collina Verdi. It was a pretty spot with flowers in the garden and vegetables at the side. The house had stone floors with a colourful wool carpet in the centre. A tall cupboard stood against one wall and a chest of drawers against another. There were neither chairs nor a table, but several brightly-coloured cushions were scattered about. One could picture people lounging Roman style, especially as the Libyan national dress is very reminiscent of the Roman toga.

Poor Fatima was still haemorrhaging and was rather distressed, lying on a mattress in the other room. Her mother was there and was relieved that we had come to collect her. We got Fatima into the car and drove her to the hospital in the centre of town. She was admitted and we were not allowed to stay with her. Even Mahommed was asked to leave, so we all returned to Villa Bactria. Later in the day we sent Mahommed to make enquiries. He came back grinning from ear to ear; he was the father of a very small son.

That evening Mahommed invited us to visit his son and heir in the hospital. It was an enormous building and very full of patients, so full that we found Fatima lying head to tail in a bed with another mother. However she seemed content and was very pleased with her tiny son. Although he was small he seemed fairly lusty, if his cries were anything to go by. However the doctors were quite happy for her to remain in hospital for a day or so as the infant was so small and Fatima had had a bit of difficulty. Normally Libyan women do not go to hospital to have their babies and probably Fatima would not have done so if we had not taken her. I told Mahommed that I would get Abdulla to take his family home in our car when the time came.

A day or so later Abdulla arrived one morning in great excitement. One of his farmer friends had been trying to move some very large stones from the field he was ploughing. In doing so he had uncovered an underground cave with a hole just large enough to allow one to wriggle inside. The farmer had fetched a torch and crawled in. He found that the walls were decorated with paintings of animals and dancing figures. They appeared to be hunting scenes and one wall was taken up with an angel rising up to heaven. We couldn't wait to go and see this exciting find, and Abdulla couldn't wait to show us.

We all climbed into the car and drove into the desert. Mahommed took us to a small farmhouse which stood miles from anywhere. His farmer friend squeezed into the car with us. We bumped over the ground and stopped in the middle of a dry, dusty area. We had to walk the rest of the way. Claire was in her carrycot fast asleep and Granny L. was eagerly making her way towards a heap of stones some distance away. There was the hole in the ground with a built-up low wall on either side of the entrance. The farmer urged us to crawl into the hole. He was wearing his best suit, I suspect in our honour, and did not really wish to demonstrate the way in.

John lay on his stomach and wriggled forward, easing his shoulders into the hole. We had remembered to bring a torch, which was just as well, as the inside was pitch black. This was probably the reason the paintings had remained in such good condition and the reddish brown colours were still clear.

We all took turns crawling into the cave, which was quite cool in contrast to the hot dusty sunshine outside. We had no idea how long the tomb, if indeed that is what it was, had been there before it had been opened the previous week. The farmer did not wish to inform anyone about it at that time, as he felt he might lose his land, so we were asked not to tell anyone where it was. Actually we would have been taxed to find the spot in the desert without any landmarks, so I think his secret is safe with us. I do, however, have some photographs of what we saw.

After more visits to Leptis and Sabratha and their museums, and many bathes in the sea, the time came for Granny L. to return home. We were sad to see her go as her enthusiasm to see everything available inspired us to get out in spite of the heat.

On one of our trips out and about we discovered a place

where we could park and watch the American military planes landing at Wheelus Airbase. Patricia and Christopher were fascinated when the parachutes billowed out of the backs of the planes as they roared in to land. They also loved to watch them doing aerobatics over the sea.

Not long after the children returned to school we had the sad news that our Manager in Benghazi had suddenly died. As this was in John's "parish" he wanted to get down there to see how things were. We made arrangements with the accountant in Benghazi for us to stay in the Manager's house. We had been told that the best hotel in Benghazi, the Berenice, was not to be recommended. We flew down for a weekend taking Claire with us. I don't recall much of that visit, except the awful night we spent being eaten by bed bugs. I had not encountered them before; it turned out that both John and I were allergic to them and we were both covered with bites and had swollen limbs. From where the bed bugs appeared has remained a mystery, but I do recall that orders were given for the beds to be burned and new ones bought.

The next holiday was Christmas. There were heaps of parties for us as well as the children. Claire was now too large for her carrycot, so we were in need of a baby sitter. Mahommed was reliable enough, provided she was asleep, but was at a loss if she did wake up. We made inquiries and a girl called Minette was found. She spoke a bit of English, so we felt that she could cope. Claire was very good and usually slept well enough. Minette had experience with children, having two of her own. She lived in Collina Verdi and was prepared to work during the day for Jenny. This arrangement should work well. She worked well enough and Claire quite liked her. Then I was told that Minette had small children of her own and she left them at home, alone and tied to the table leg, while she worked for us. The idea of a child being left in such conditions upset me greatly. Apparently Minette's husband was away a great deal (if, indeed, she did have a husband). I told her that I could not continue to employ her unless she made arrangements for her children. Sadly we next found that she was stealing from us and we lost confidence in her. Babysitting became a problem, but Bob and Jenny stepped into the breech, so long as we were not invited to the same parties. Sometimes the Bank bachelors would help out in return for a square meal and a bottle of wine!

All the time we were in Libya John was struggling to build his new Bank on the Istiklal. There were unexpected difficulties right from the start. While digging for the foundations they struck water. This meant that steel pylons had to be driven down all round the plot. This was pretty unpopular as the thumping of the giant hammers could be heard all over town for days on end. Poor John had a very frustrating time with the architects and contractors, while at the same time trying to run the Bank.

About a month before Claire's first birthday I had been using some drawing pins and had dropped the box on the floor. I had gathered them up carefully, or so I thought. That night Claire awoke and screamed and screamed. I tried gripe water and a hot water bottle on her tummy, patting her as we walked up and down. Nothing would pacify her. I then began to think of what I had given her to eat that day. Then I remembered the drawing pins. I called John and we drove to the military hospital. We were not really supposed to use it, but I did not fancy the local one from the little I had seen of it. We arrived at the military hospital at about 5.30 am. The doctor on duty was very kind and gave her an X-ray to try to spot the drawing pin if it was to be seen. Nothing. So far so good.

By now she had been screaming so much she had a roaring temperature. She was put in an oxygen tent and kept in hospital for several days before I was allowed to bring her home. I had to keep an eye on her temperature and return her to hospital if it rose to 40 degrees. This I did twice and she was given oxygen. Eventually I took her to the Evalina Hospital in London, but to this day we have no satisfactory diagnosis as to why she should spark this high temperature from time to time. She seemed perfectly happy, so we all learned to keep a wary eye on her and to live with it. Eventually, whatever was causing it went away.

Mahommed gave the children a ginger cat as a Christmas present. I am not very fond of cats on the whole but this animal was quite convinced that he was a human, and did his best to behave like one, much to our amusement. He would sit on a chair like a human with his legs hanging down and leaning against John's thigh. Mahommed had gone to all the trouble of house training him first. The result was that Kitty Wee or Winkle Cat, as he was named, would miaow loudly when "caught short" in the garden and when let in would speed, cross-legged, to his sandbox. Somehow the idea that the world was all a huge sandbox did not enter his head. He was a very playful cat and enjoyed swinging on the curtain pulls and playing goalie with a marble, the goal posts being a gap between two rugs on the drawing room floor. Kitty became a great pet with all the family.

John decided that we would have the children fly to Malta for their next holiday and we would fly to meet them there and spend ten days exploring the island. There was plenty to see as we explored the villages, each with its huge cathedral. They seemed quite disproportionate to the size of the congregation they served. We enjoyed a visit to the Blue Grotto, where the water was really blue and clear. We sat in our little boat and gently drifted in and out of the caves watching the fish about their business far below. Then we beached the boat on a little sandy beach and dipped into the water for a wonderful swim. Claire was not in the least afraid of the water and floated about in her rubber ring full of confidence.

One day we crossed on the ferry to the island of Gozo, where the streets were lined with women making lace. They were twiddling their bobbins, which were pinned to cushions, at a tremendous speed. The most intricate patterns appeared and they all made it look so easy. I was tempted by some creamy table linen that I found to be ridiculously cheap. We all enjoyed the view of the harbour with the Royal Navy ships tied up alongside, some of them dressed overall. The local Dicer boats were being sculled backwards and forwards across the harbour, their distinctive high bows ploughing proudly through the water.

We were all very pleased to flop into the hotel pool after the trips out and about. Claire loved having her big brother and sister there to be impressed by anything she did. In fact it was in Malta that she took her first steps, staggering between big brother and sister. Everyone was very pleased they had been there to witness her first lurching paces. There was no holding her back from then on.

When we returned to Tripoli I took Patricia and Christopher out to the military stables I had found. A retired British Army Colonel ran it and had invited me to take the children out for a ride during the holidays. As both children rode at school I wanted to see how they were progressing.

The children were excited at the prospect. I had been before and ridden out with one of the grooms. It had been some time since I had ridden, and I was a little stiff afterwards, but I enjoyed it. Two quietish horses were selected for the children. Patricia had a smart little pony called Apollo and Christopher was given a large stallion called Willing, which he had some difficulty in mounting. However, with the aid of the mounting block he was soon in the saddle with a broad grin on his face. I rode the same little mare I had ridden last time. The groom came with us, mainly because I did not know the routes to take. It was a wonderful experience and we enjoyed several rides throughout the holidays, sometimes taking other children with us.

On one occasion, after Patricia and Christopher had returned to school, I took three other children out on a ride. Two of them were mounted on stallions, both of which I thought I knew. Suddenly the horses decided to fight. I had never seen this before and was quite horrified and unsure as to the best course of action. First I decided I had to get the children off, so I slipped off my mare and beat her with my whip hoping she would race home. I then grasped the bridles of the fighting stallions and managed to pull the ring on the snaffle bit into their mouths and then hung on for dear life. The terrified children slipped off. I asked the third child to ride home as quickly as she could to summon help. As she was a beginner and not very confident, she did well to go as quickly as she did.

Before very long, though it seemed a lifetime, a groom came galloping into sight. He had been alerted by my riderless horse and came to try to find us. I am happy to say that none of us were hurt and the children came out with me again, but I think it was that experience that caused me to lose some enthusiasm for riding lively horses - although I did ride with the children again when they came out for the holidays.

On our next trip to Leptis Magna we drove a bit further on and came to a huge Roman sports arena which was in the process of being excavated. The floor had a deep oblong pit in the middle. We were led to believe that this was where the lions were kept before being let loose on the unfortunate Christians, in the name of sport. All round the basin of the arena, the remains of tiered seats could be clearly seen. We climbed right up to the top and found what must have been the best seats. There was a wonderful view of the arena, and if one turned round there was a spectacular view across the beach where the chariot races were held. If one became bored of Christians being eaten by lions, then there were always the chariots, drawn by wild galloping horses, to cheer on. Perhaps the marvellous view over the Mediterranean Sea, with its cooling breeze bringing sailing ships into port, might calm the over excited audiences. There were partially-excavated tunnels beneath the stone seats, but we were reluctant to explore them too closely for fear of meeting smaller antagonists such as snakes or scorpions.

On another occasion while walking in the desert looking for wild plants, we were very startled to hear the sound of rushing water. There had been a sudden rainstorm a while earlier and we were walking round the base of some small hillocks. Suddenly a wave of water was coming towards us, bowling quite large boulders before it. Evidently the rain on the plateau above us was sufficient to reawaken an old riverbed and the water was trying to flow again. We quickly climbed up the slope to the car and were in no danger, but it was strange to see the flash flood go pouring past us, along the seemingly long-forgotten course.

Salem, the gardener, had been feeling unwell for some time and went into hospital to have his gall bladder removed. Abdulla had been to see him and brought me the message that Salem would very much like me to visit him in hospital. Although I could converse with him in the garden, our language was very much of the "tic tac" school. I was in no way confident that I could cope at his bedside. However I went and found him in a bed of his own (!) in a ward with many others. He showed me with pride his gall bladder, which he had on his bedside table in a jar. We managed to converse with the usual arm waving and head nodding, punctuated with much laughter. He and his friends about him seemed to enjoy my visit. I am told that I earned him much kudos and that his social standing was raised because he had a European visitor. Remember this was in the time of King Idris. I doubt if it would have been the same under Gaddafi.

Our time in Libya was drawing to an end and the new Bank was nearly complete. A date was set for the opening and Bank directors were organised to come and wave the flag. A huge reception was organised at the best hotel and hundreds of invitations were sent out. Then the man who cut the marble got a splinter in his eye, and was unable to finish the entrance hall. Of all places to have incomplete, this was the most noticeable. Marble cutting is a very skilled business and there was no one available to take over. It was such a pity, as the office would really look good if the entrance were finished. However the show had to go on and the Bank was duly opened. The customary reception was held for some 300 people and life returned more or less to normal.

Shortly after this we were to move on again, this time to the Bank of Iran and the Middle East in Teheran. John handed over his new office to Kenneth Bradford. For the second time John had suffered all the problems of building a bank for someone else to enjoy.

Chapter Seventeen

TEHERAN, 1964

John's home leave came to an end about seven weeks before our fourth child was due to be born, and he was posted to Teheran. Because I had had problems when Claire was born two years earlier, I was advised to remain in the UK for the birth to ensure that all went well. This was a popular move with my parents and they invited me to stay with them, as this would enable them to get to know their second granddaughter better. Poor John had to fly to Teheran and live on his own again. In a way this was a little easier for him, as it meant that he could concentrate on taking over his new job without worrying about us settling in. This also meant that Patricia and Christopher would come up to Scotland for the Easter holidays. This pleased everyone, as staying at Glencaple was a happy time for all the children.

I developed toxaemia again, as I had with Claire, and so had to go into hospital to have the baby induced. This happened to be exactly the same date as when Claire was due. Unlike Claire, Tony was in a hurry to come into the world, so he arrived the day before our wedding anniversary. The poor child's face was so squashed he looked as if he'd been in a fight with Cassius Clay, as the world boxing champion Mohammed Ali was known at that time.

Again I had trouble registering the birth at the Registrar's Office. The lady in charge simply could not understand that the Bank's post box number was the only address I had and it would have to do. She muttered that my husband did not live in a post box and it really wasn't good enough.

During this period Claire and her grandparents were developing a wonderful relationship. My father would load Claire (wearing her reins) into the car and take her to places of interest. One of her favourite places was the Duke of Norfolk's duck pond, where some pinioned wild barnacle geese were kept. Claire loved to feed the birds, which she called "bardies." Some years later when my father was talking to Claire he used the word. When Claire picked him up on this, and asked why he said "bardies," instead of birds, he gave a lovely smile and said that he once knew a little girl who used the word. "Oh" said Claire, none the wiser.

When Anthony William was six weeks old, we prepared to fly off to introduce him to his father. First we paid a quick visit to Granny L. and the great grannies, and called at the schools to see Patricia and Christopher so that they could meet their new brother. As the Bank always sent us first class, the twelve-hour journey out to Teheran was relatively painless and the children slept most of the way.

John was there to meet us and we were whisked away to our new home at Tajrish, a village some 1000 feet above the town of Teheran, up in the lower Alborz Mountains. The villa was up a side kutche and, we were told, next door to the Shah's mother's home. The high wooden gates opened into a paved courtyard, surrounded by tall lime and eucalyptus trees. There were also a number of flowering shrubs and plenty of zinnias and marigolds in a flowerbed that bordered the lawn. There was a small swimming pool at the end of the patio, with a low fence round it to ensure the safety of the children. Several wide steps led up to the front door. Inside the hall on the right of the door, was the study with an interesting corner window overlooking the garden and gate. Straight ahead, a flight of stairs with a solid concrete banister led to the upstairs. To the left, through double doors, was the drawing room. A large marble fireplace was the focal point, with comfortable looking chairs spread around the room on a large, beautiful cream based Persian carpet. A pair of folding doors opened into the dining room. The kitchen was at the back of the house where a courtyard led to two servant's rooms, their washroom and the laundry. Upstairs there were four bedrooms and two bathrooms.

The two servants were there to greet me as I arrived. Jamilah, which means beautiful in Farsi, was the housemaid and Zohrah was the cook. Jamilah came daily while Zohrah slept on the premises, which meant that we had a resident babysitter once the babies had accepted her.

The gardener was named Gulam Reza. He maintained the

265

garden and generally kept the outside looking clean and tidy. John's driver was called Sadek and he kept our large red American car in immaculate condition. Sadek was the only one of our "staff" who spoke any English, and that was pretty basic. However I was pleased to discover that the vocabulary I had learned when we had lived in Isfahan, some 10 years earlier, was still buried in my mind, and I was soon able to cope. This was just as well, as there was only three weeks before Patricia and Christopher arrived for the summer holidays. Educated Iranians spoke French if they did not speak English, so conversing was not really much of a problem socially.

John had already met several European families and we were invited to join the "Travellers". This was a group of parents with children coming out for the holidays, who all had the same problems of how to entertain the teenagers and to give them the opportunity to meet others. Patricia and Christopher were among the youngest, but we felt they could fit in with help. Various entertainments were organised, including a fancy dress party to enable the youngsters to meet each other to start things off. A programme of events was drawn up from mini golf at the Hilton Hotel, tennis at the tennis club, bowling at the Bowlarena and swimming at the Bank's huge pool downtown. There was country dancing and even archery classes were organised at various embassies. We were very fortunate, as once Sadek had taken John to the Bank in the morning, he was at my disposal until it was time for John to come home again.

The introductory party was a fancy dress affair to be held at the Hilton. Needless to say all the children dreaded it and were very shy for the most part. Patricia and Christopher went as cave man and woman. I had made a sort of bearskin shift for Chris out of some fur fabric I had found in the bazaar. Patricia was similarly clad, but I fashioned a long plait of hair from some unravelled string. She lay along a toy trailer with her "hair" wound round the handle, so that when Christopher pulled her, along it looked as if she was being dragged by the hair. I thought this was a wonderful scheme, but both children were a bit sceptical! However they made their mark and were duly accepted into the Travellers.

I organised a games party one evening - parents were welcome so long as they joined in the games. There was to be no sitting on the sidelines watching. We made the invitation from 7 pm to 11 pm. John and I spent a lot of time inventing games, writing lists, wrapping presents as prizes and planning our programme. Everybody arrived on time. I think there were about 30 people in all. The first game was "names on backs", where everyone had to try to read the names on each other's backs, while at the same time guarding their own. We went on to team races with oranges under the chin and matchboxes passed from nose to nose. After supper we played "Stations." When players had found their partners, they rushed round the lists of places I had stuck to the wall, until they found their way back to the station from which they had started. Then more team games until well after "home time". John and I were most amused as, while the young were wilting and we were exhausted, the parents were clamouring for more games. I think the last guest left at 1 am. We fell into bed tired, but happy that the children's first party had been a success.

Tony was a very good baby and was adored by all the servants. I was able to leave him with them between feeds and take the others with me when I went downtown shopping, or to take them to the "activity" laid on for that day. The traffic in Teheran was extremely chaotic and everyone drove at speed. The roads were wide and dangerous to cross. If the shop I required was on the other side of the road, Sadek would make a terrifying U-turn to ensure that I did not have to cross the road on foot. He also insisted on pushing my supermarket trolley with Claire standing up at the front, like Boadicea directing the way. It was considered rather smart to have a chauffeur-driven trolley and I was the envy of many of my friends. Later on, when I first came home to the UK, I would still automatically turn around in the shops when I heard someone speaking English, as I always did in Teheran, where the supermarket was a usual meeting place. The cooks and houseboys did the bazaar shopping while the "Khanoums" (the English wives) did the tins and packets, much of which were unfamiliar to Iranians.

When we first arrived in Teheran we all found that even the smallest effort made us feel breathless and going up stairs made us all puff a bit. This was because Teheran is some 5,000 feet above sea level. However the body quickly became acclimatised and we were all able to rush about quite normally. We were even able to cope with country dancing and Scottish reels at the Teheran Club.

On one occasion a group of us decided to spend a weekend at Ziba Kannah on the Caspian Sea. We packed the car with all the paraphernalia required for a weekend for a family of six. Arrangements were made with the other families to meet at a Chai Khane (café), over the first pass through the mountains. There we could buy refreshments and stretch our legs. It took about an hour to reach the meeting place. The climb through the pass had been fairly slow, as the road was quite steep in places and very twisty. We pulled off the road when we met oncoming lorries, as they tended to demand more than their share of the road, which was quite narrow. Fortunately there was very little traffic in either direction.

The views were quite spectacular between the craggy hills and down the deep ravines to the Chai Khane where we were to meet. This was a very rough and ready place, but they provided a loo of sorts and sold cold drinks. We were rather distressed to see a brown bear standing in a cage swaying back and forth as it stared at us gloomily. I'm afraid that animals seem to have a hard life in Iran. But then, since many humans do too, I suppose animal welfare is a bit low on the list of Iranian priorities. It was cooler in the mountains and the cold drinks and leg stretch did us all good.

We climbed into our cars again and set off down the winding road. It was less steep this side, and the views over the plain stretching into the distance seemed endless. Before too long though, we were driving between green fields. Not perhaps as green as those in the UK, but after the dusty plateau round Teheran it was good to see some vegetation.

The sandy beach of the Caspian Sea came into view. There were a few fishing boats dotted on the water, and a group of donkeys stood, heads lowered, dozing while they waited for customers to come to bargain for a ride along the sand. There were very few buildings of any substance to be seen, so we headed for the largest, imagining it to be the hotel. It wasn't. It was the summer residence of one of the wealthy Iranian families. Our hotel turned out to be a group of chalets stretching out along the beach. They were more or less self-contained, and one could cook for oneself, or hire a cook. We had a conference and decided to have a barbecue on the beach, so some of us went off to see what we could find in the shops, if anything. We found a wonderful fish market with really fresh fish, still flapping, and some lovely hot Iranian bread, naan, and crisp lettuce and tomatoes. The fruit was limited to oranges and some strange flat peaches. We must have looked doubtful, but we were urged to taste one, and found it to be delicious. It had a skin like a peach and the texture was rather like an apple, with a delicious flavour of its own. None of us had ever seen this fruit before, though I did find them again in Tajrish market. We christened them feaches. To drink there was the local Abjo beer and the inevitable Coca-Cola.

On returning to the beach we found that John and the

others had organised the children to have rides on the donkeys. Claire was very importantly sitting up very straight with her little brother Tony perched in front of her. The grin on both faces made it quite clear that this *was* the life. Trish and Chris were flapping their legs unsuccessfully trying to urge their mounts into something more than an amble, as were all the others in our party. A cook and a waiter were busily preparing the site for our meal. Tables and chairs had appeared and glasses of foaming Abjo were already being consumed.

When the children had been put to bed, the teenagers and adults wandered along the shore to a restaurant which turned out to be much more upmarket than it appeared from the outside. There was a stage, where there was to be a cabaret later in the evening. There were a few other European guests sitting around and the room was filling up with Iranians. Before long the jangling music became louder and faster until suddenly three energetic dancers sprang on to the stage, jangling little bells fixed to their ankles and wrists. They swayed and wriggled and contorted their bodies in time to the music and in time with each other, their colourful swirling skirts billowing this way and that. When the applause had died down they began again wagging their hips in a provocative fashion. Next the music softened and the lights went down, a voluptuous girl dressed in a long black and gold ribbon skirt leaped onto the stage. She was barefooted and wore a black and gold yashmak over her face. Just her dark eyes, outlined with kohl, glittered beneath a fringed headband. Her skin was very pale and she wore a bra top with tassels over her nipples. When the music stopped so did she, dead still with her hands on her hips, one of which was thrust forward. Slowly she started to twitch a muscle in her thigh, then the twitching moved to her belly, where the tassel in her belly button started to twirl. Soon the tassels on various parts of her body were twirling independently. It was truly an amazing sight. Finally she stood, knees bent, hands on hips, belly thrust forward, while the tassels on her bosoms twirled round and round, one clockwise, the other anticlockwise. The applause was deafening and well earned.

I discovered later that when we had all gone back to the privacy of our rooms, we had all tried it for ourselves in front of the mirror, but we still could not work out how she did it!

The next morning we all went into the sea for a swim. The shallow water was warm and very salty - not as salty as the Dead Sea in Jordan, but pretty buoyant all the same. The fishermen were standing in their punt-like boats, twirling the weighted net above their heads and letting it fly some ten yards away, where it splayed out in a circle over the water where it sank. The boat was then poled towards the spot, the net raised and the small catch loaded into the boat, when the process began all over again. I did not discover whether the sturgeon fish was caught in this way. The method looked very biblical, so it might be that the method had not changed since time began. We made a note to acquire some caviar before we left. It was supposed to be sold under strict licence, but we expected there would be ways round the regulations. There was little that could not be acquired at a price in Iran. The most annoying thing was that one had to bribe people to obtain what one should have, never mind things one shouldn't. For example John had to pay to have his driving licence put into the authority's in-tray, and then pay again to have it stamped. There was a time when the police had not been paid and they asked for payment to allow cars to move along the road. If one remonstrated, the tyres might well be punctured with a shot from a traffic policeman's pistol.

There were many methods of bribery and corruption at that time in Teheran. One paid protection for one's car to ensure that hubcaps, wipers and even wheels remained in place. I think the drivers arranged to pay a small sum to someone, then if something was stolen, this "someone" would ensure that it was returned. Similarly night watchmen patrolled the kutches at night, blasting a whistle from time to time to keep in touch with each other and say all was well. So long as one paid, little was stolen, though we did lose the cart Chris had used to drag Trish to the party.

Our swimming pool was about 25 feet long and four feet deep all over. Patricia and Christopher had fun teaching Claire to swim. She had little fear and would leap into the water wearing her rubber ring. Tony however was content to wallow in a small paddling pool, so long as it had warm water in it. He, like most babes, was not enthusiastic about cold pool water even in the height of summer.

As always, the holidays were too short and the children's departure for school came upon us too quickly. We always hated these partings, but thought it was lucky we lived in the current "air" age, rather than during the days when children were sent away to boarding school by ship for years at a time. I knew of one couple who sent their child home to boarding school at five years old. I couldn't have done that. As it was, we came to the decision that flying them back for the Easter holidays was going to be too expensive, for the less than three weeks we would see them, so we asked if Gampy and Granjo would have them. Needless to say, this idea was welcomed by all.

Easter came and I decided that I would have an Easter egg hunt for Claire and Tony. I invited about 20 children. I arranged for a mini merry-go-round, which I had seen in the bazaar offering rides for one rial, to come to the garden for Tony's baby friends. I asked Gulam Reza to select a couple of better-looking donkeys to come and provide donkey rides for the two and three year olds. I made buns and jellies and all was ready. I decided to leave the hiding of the eggs until the last minute, as the sun would surely melt them.

In the Middle East one is not accustomed to considering the weather, as it is nearly always sunny. At Easter the temperature is usually very pleasant and rain at that time would be considered a luxury. I could not believe it when after lunch, just before the guests arrived, the sky became dark and the heavens opened, and it poured with rain.

What was I going to do? The house was not really big

enough to hide all the eggs for so many children. They would all be found in five minutes. The rain showed no sign of abating, and even if it did stop the garden was too soggy.

There was nothing for it. I had to hide the eggs all over the house as best I could. First they would look downstairs and then when all were found we would send them upstairs. While they were upstairs the parents would be enlisted to hide more downstairs. Then we had tea.

While they were eating I did a surreptitious crawl under the table and stole some eggs from the fuller bags and hid them again! By this time the rain had stopped. The merry-go-round had arrived and the donkeys were brought out from the garage where they had been sheltering. The sun was shining and the ground was steaming as it quickly dried. Grinning chocolate faces whirled round, seated in a variety of cars, trains and elephants. Others bumped, two at a time, on the carpet covered donkey's backs, while anxious mums ran awkwardly alongside, holding them on. The sun was shining and the sky was blue just as it had been for the last six weeks, and was to remain for the foreseeable future.

Teheran was a very large and cosmopolitan community. The embassies had large compounds along the roads up to the hills, where the staff lived in the summer months, in family-type groups. There was usually a communal swimming pool and a tennis court where families could meet. Tajrish, where we lived, was some 1000 feet above the downtown shopping area, where we stayed when we first went to Teheran some ten years earlier. In those days most of the Bank lived in Haftdaska, an urban compound of seven houses surrounded by a high wall. This arrangement had its disadvantages, as like all families there were the inevitable sibling rivalries, and some wives felt slighted at times for no apparent reason. The result of, perhaps, not having enough to do and trying to "better" their position. I suppose John and I were lucky in some respects, as we never lived in a compound on any of our postings, so I just accepted whatever was given to me. Usually our accommodation was good and pleasant. Perhaps I was naive in many ways, but I enjoyed a quiet life with my husband and family and managed to get on with most people.

Outside the compounds few expatriates lived within walking distance of each other, so a car was essential for shopping and socialising. My usual daily routine was to organise the "staff" to clean the house and polish some of the considerable collection of brass and copperware we had collected. This was done with half a lemon dipped in salt. It made things shine well enough, but the humidity was such that they soon became tarnished again.

There was the laundry to be done, including nappies to be boiled. This was before the days when disposable nappies were widely available. I remember feeling reluctant to allow my babies to wear plastic pants. The idea of wet bottoms encased in plastic simply did not appeal to me, except of course for party occasions, when my baby girls wore voluminous frilly plastic bloomers decorated with little lace frills over their towelling nappies with "marathon" liners. Very short pretty embroidered frocks completed the ensemble. While my baby boys wore romper suits, which were really smocked, puff-sleeved frocks with a buttoned gusset and elasticated legs over plain plastic pants. I remember I loved the all-in-one stretch towelling Babygros when they came in for my grandchildren, and wished they had been invented when my babies were born. They kept "body and soul" together so neatly.

We did not have a washing machine, so all the laundry had to be done by hand. John usually wore at least two shirts per day, one for the office, one for sport or playing with the children and a third if we went out in the evening, or entertained at home. He wore lightweight trousers that required to be washed rather than dry-cleaned. Similarly I changed clothes to suit the occasion. All this necessitated a considerable wardrobe for each of us. I spent much time making the children's clothes myself, mainly because European clothes were very expensive. With two children at boarding school, we preferred to spend any spare money on them rather than waste it on overpriced frippery, as I half-longingly called it! Fortunately I have never been particularly fashion conscious so this has never worried me unduly.

Other domestic chores included the planning of meals. The shopping had to be done daily. We had a very rudimentary icebox still. Tony's solid food had to be made daily and "moulied" by hand, as we did not have an electric mixer or blender. I did everything for the children myself with the exception of the laundry.

People often say "Oh it must have been wonderful to have

servants to do everything." Well I agree up to a point, but often it was very frustrating to see things done badly or improperly. Often these servants were really a pair of hands with little brain on top. Frequently they were unreliable, forgetful, careless and at times incompetent, causing more trouble than assistance. I suspect that this was probably a combination of cultural differences and language problem. However I think that on the whole, they did make life easier, so long as they were overseen.

The one time we did rely on them was for babysitting. We were obliged to sack Zohra when we returned one evening to find Claire screaming in her bed. Zohra had crossed the road to visit a friend, leaving the child alone in an unlocked house. Zohra was very sorry when she realised that not only had she lost her job, board and lodging, she would not have a reference to enable her to find another job. John and I were real softies and let her sweat for a couple of weeks and then took her back again. Learning to trust a new maid was considered more nerve-racking than giving Zohra another chance. Anyway the children knew her and were happy with her. She never let us down again.

My friend Ruth and I got together and decided to organise a Music and Movement class for our two to four-year-olds. Permission was obtained to use one of the rooms in the English School. There was a piano and the facilities were put at our disposal. Ruth was a brilliant piano player and we began with nursery rhymes and progressed to musical games. The children loved to fly like birds, gallop like horses and jump like frogs, as the music dictated. We all enjoyed the weekly one-hour sessions. It abruptly came to an end when Ruth moved the piano and it toppled over on her leg, causing a dreadful gash down her shin.

John enjoyed a lot of sport in those days. We played tennis and swam at the Teheran Club and John played golf. I was unable to join him on the golf course as I had the small children to look after. We did go to watch him bat in the inter-company cricket matches. There were squash courts available and we enjoyed playing matches with the various embassy and commercial teams. One of the hotels had a ten-pin bowling alley, which was very much a novelty at that time. The Bank had a huge swimming pool behind the main Bank building, and there were many swimming galas and barbecues there in the summer.

In the winter we belonged to the Teheran Little Theatre Group. John played the lead in plays like *The man who came to dinner* and *For love or money*. He once played the part of a short fat Lancashire comedian in the Christmas Pantomime, *Ali Baba and the forty thieves*.

We planned to give a Christmas party for the little ones as soon as Christopher and Patricia arrived for the holidays. They had a lot of fun planning the games and helping to choose the prizes and presents. We had heard of a Father Christmas outfit and had arranged to borrow it.

In 1964 Teheran was well supplied with Christmas decorations, as there was a large Christian and Armenian

Community. So we had fun decorating the tree and getting into the Christmas spirit. The afternoon of the party, John went to try on the Father Christmas suit. Horrors, the trousers were much too short. What were we to do?

Christopher came into the room and we had an idea. With cushions stuffed down his front and a big belt round his middle, Christopher would be splendid. All he had to do was say "Ho Ho Ho" in a deep voice and we would do any talking that had to be done. I think Christopher enjoyed his roll. The children loved a small, fat Father Christmas and we had no tears. One little girl was terrified of Father Christmas so we invited her to secretly come and watch Christopher get dressed up. She was quite happy from then onwards. Claire did not guess who he was and the other children did not know him anyway. The small fat man was talked about for some time after, and many children enjoyed their first introduction to the great man.

One morning, Gulam Reza took Claire for a walk down the Kutche when one of next door's guard dogs broke free from its chain and rushed out at them. Gulam Reza grabbed Claire by her snowsuit and swung her up above his head. He ran back home with the dog snarling at his heels. Poor Claire was terrified and Gulam Reza had a torn jacket, but mercifully neither had been bitten. Claire however became terrified of all dogs and would run screaming if a dog appeared on the pavement. This would not do, as it could be dangerous if she ran into the street. The dog of a friend of ours had a litter of puppies, so we introduced Claire to them. Slowly she began to touch them, one finger at first, then she began to cuddle them. Eventually she fell in love with one and we adopted him. Claire christened him Solomon for some reason. This seemed quite appropriate as he showed much wisdom in his behaviour with Claire. John and I were unenthusiastic about owning dogs, as parting with them when we moved on was so painful, added to the fact that rabies is rife in the Middle East. However we felt that this was one time when perhaps we might stretch a point. Dear Solly went to a lovely home when we left Teheran, as his behaviour with children made him very popular.

Tajrish, being so much higher than Teheran, had significant falls of snow in the winter. I recall one morning waking up to a white world with about three feet of snow in our garden. Gulam Reza was already half way down the kutche, digging a path for John to get out to go to work. Snowploughs were out clearing the main roads. Sadek had fitted the chains on the car, as the hill was quite slippery all the way downtown. Patricia and Christopher got dressed and ready to make the inevitable snowman. Claire was very excited as she had not seen snow before and her siblings were in a hurry to introduce her. Tony, at six months, just looked wide-eyed at everything his siblings did. The maids were busy lighting the log fires in the downstairs rooms, as we had no other means of heating the house. These fires were very efficient and the house was soon warm and comfortable.

Our predecessors had left a toboggan in the garage, so

Patricia and Christopher were soon towing each other and Claire up and down the garden path. I did not notice when they progressed to whizzing down the kutche at speed. The first I knew about it was when Christopher, gasping breathlessly, rushed in to inform me that Patricia had been arrested and that I should come quickly. In a panic I called Gulam Reza (not that he could speak English, but more for moral support.) We ran down to the main road, where I found Patricia in tears and a couple of policemen looking slightly embarrassed, as a crowd had gathered at the spectacle of a European child in the hands of the police.

I rushed to comfort Patricia and to try to discover what had happened. Inevitably, everyone tried to talk at once, and my Farsee was very basic. So far as I could understand it with the help of a bystander, who spoke a little English, the children had shot out of the kutche into the road on their toboggan, and had frightened some pedestrians and narrowly escaped being run over. The snow caused enough problems without children on toboggans adding to the confusion. I felt sick at the thought of what might have happened, but managed to pacify everyone and took my chastened children home. They had had a fright too, as I don't think they had realised just how far and fast they were going. Anyway they were happy to settle down by the fire to play snakes and ladders with Claire.

At the weekend we all set off to Ahb Ali, a spot high in the Alborz Mountains where a rudimentary ski pull had been erected. We hired very basic skis for Jay and the children and set off to try our hand. I had learned to ski at school in

Switzerland and had brought my skis to Teheran in anticipation of this moment. The road up the mountain was very slippery. We had put the chains on the front wheels of the car as it was front wheel drive, and they were there to enable the wheels to grip. However on rounding a bend we were flagged down by police, who ordered us to change our chains to the back wheels like everybody else. No amount of arguing would change their minds, so we gingerly drove round the first corner out of their sight and quickly changed them back again.

Finally we arrived at Ahb Ali. These were the beginners' slopes, supplied with a button pull for the brave, which pulled people to the top. There was plenty of space for everyone as the area was not too crowded. There were a few small boys whizzing down the slopes with plain planks of wood tied to their feet and with tree branches used as ski sticks. They were amazingly skilful. I had tried to teach Patricia and Christopher what basics I could remember, like how to snowplough down a slope, and to do a kick turn, and to keep knees bent and transfer the weight to steer. This was all very easy to do while stationary in the garden, but hilariously amusing to try on a slope. We had brought the toboggan for Claire, so she was happy being towed about by any willing "horse". Probably it would have been better if we had had all the proper equipment, but it was hardly worth the expense at this time, as they were due to return to school so soon. There was a more upmarket ski club further up the mountain, but we felt that it was a bit advanced for us at this stage.

Then Christopher caught measles. We had to send cables

to the school and to Granny L. to let her know that he would not be returning. We sent a cable to Patricia's school to let them know the situation and we received a cable informing us that "as Patricia had had measles of course she should return to school". Patricia was upset, as this meant that Christopher would have a longer holiday than she would have. Our Iranian doctor was upset, as he was worried about Tony. It appeared that there was a brand of measles going around Teheran known as black measles and this was a killer of babies. Tony should be given gamma globulin. This was duly done. Then Patricia came out in a rash the day before she was to fly. She was having measles for the second time. She was pleased. We sent more cables, and as none of the children were really ill, we settled down to enjoy the extension of our time together.

Some time after the children had gone back to school both Claire and I caught flu. We both had high temperatures, so I decided that I could nurse both of us better if we were in the same room. Claire moved into our double bed and Tony played about on the floor. I had just given us both our medications when I noticed Tony scuttling away rather suspiciously. I noticed that Claire's dolls-pram had moved. When I picked up our medicine bottles ready to put them away in the cupboard, I noticed that mine seemed a bit light. Tony at this time was out of sight in his room. I discovered that the little monkey had drunk nearly all my medicine while I was giving Claire hers. He had climbed on the doll's pram to enable him to reach the bottle.

I telephoned the doctor to check what action I should take. He was very concerned and told me to keep him awake and to bring him to the hospital downtown at once. I telephoned John to send the driver. I got dressed and very shortly Sadek was at the door - he had driven like crazy to rescue his beloved Tony.

The drive down to the hospital was quite terrifying. We rushed a now drooping Tony into casualty, where they were expecting him, and they proceeded to stomach pump the poor child. Eventually all was well and we drove a very startled and subdued child home again, where he slept peacefully for the rest of the day. Apparently my medicine had a very high opium content which could have been lethal for a baby. It was fortunate that I had noticed him scuttling away.

A letter arrived from an elderly friend of my parents, one Winnie Russell. She had been staying in youth hostels around Australia and Japan and had just had her 60th birthday on a cattle boat in the middle of the Indian Ocean. She was about to catch the Indiaman Bus in Madras and expected to arrive in Teheran in a week or so. Time was up and she must be due, so we drove down to the Indiaman Bus Station to make enquiries. They did not know when the bus would arrive as it had broken down in the desert some miles south of Isfahan. It was hot and we did not envy the poor people stuck out in the middle of nowhere. We were assured that everything possible was being done for them. We hoped that what was possible was of some help.

Some days later we were informed that the bus was due that afternoon. We went to meet it and saw Winnie's nut-brown face grinning at us from the front seat of the bus.

"Keep upwind of me," she yelled. "Open all the windows

of your car!" She held her nose expressively. She was right. We drove her home and asked which she would like first - a whisky and soda or a bath?

"Whisky and soda IN the bath, please. Can you lend me some clothes? All mine are beyond the pale."

She was a remarkable old lady. She kept us amused with all the tales of things that had happened to her and regaled us with descriptions of the appalling discomfort of the trip she had just undertaken. She had lost her toes many years ago and wore surgical boots, which were in serious disrepair. Did we know anyone who could make her a new pair, before she set forth again on the bus to visit Crak du Chevalier in Syria and Petra in Jordan? John located a cobbler of sorts through the Bank. There is a saying "Miracles we achieve at once, but the impossible will take a little longer." The boots were ready for fitting the next day. She thought if she wore enough socks they would do!

We took Winnie sightseeing to the Gulestan Palace, where the most amazing clock, donated by Queen Victoria to the then Shah, was on show. Cocks crowed, wings flapped, bells rang, little figures scuttled round from left to right and animals popped in and out every time the hour struck! The grand Peacock throne was also on display amid a large variety of royal bric a brac donated to the Shahs over the years.

The Crown Jewels were well worth a visit. Cartier had especially arranged them in magnificent display cabinets. There was a particularly splendid emerald casket, about three inches long and two inches wide with a hinged lid. It was quite stunning. There were also many quite vulgar brooches, necklets and coronets, encrusted with jewels of every description. This display was said to be the backing for the Iranian currency.

John was quite concerned that Winnie would not survive the rest of her journey, and offered to buy her an air ticket home. She would not hear of it, maintaining that now she had had a few good nights' sleep and her clothes had been washed, armed with her new, if uncomfortable, boots, she was ready for the fray. So we put her back on the bus. She was an amazing lady. We were to meet her again.

John came home one day with the news that my mother, Granjo, was very ill as she had had a brain haemorrhage. John decided that I should fly home as soon as he could get a passage. Bless him, he had already contacted friends, who had agreed to look after the children at their home, if Jamilah went with them as an extra pair of eyes. Communications were so slow in those days and as my father was pretty unwell with a heart condition we agreed that it could be helpful if I flew home for a short time. Poor John, it was his birthday, March 4th, when I rushed to my mother's bedside.

My plane took 12 hours to reach London and I managed to get a standby passage up to Glasgow. There was a snowstorm in London and my flight was delayed. Finally I arrived at Mother's bedside in Killearn Hospital, only to be told that I could not see her as my being there could well be too much of a shock to her! Eventually I was allowed to see her and she berated me for taking so long to come and look after my father. Well! I knew she would expect me to come if she needed me. We were "that sort of family." I stayed for a week or so and saw her on the mend, and my father back home and prepared for her homecoming. Then I flew back to Teheran with, I think, a job well done. My little family was pleased to see me back and I was very happy to see them.

We decided that the next time the children came out we would take them to Isfahan to enable Patricia to see where she was born. As luck would have it Claire came down with chicken pox, so I had to stay behind to look after her and Tony. John decided to take Sadek to share the driving, as it was a long journey. The journey there was not without incident, as they had a flat tyre in the middle of nowhere. The road was tarmac, which was a vast improvement on when we first drove to Isfahan more than 12 years earlier.

Dr Peter Wild and his wife Mary, who were still there, invited them to stay, so Patricia was able to see exactly where she was born, and to meet the doctor who had brought her into the world in the Mission Hospital. The beautiful Masjhed Shah Mosque and the pretty little Lutfullah had not changed. They visited the "Shakey Minarets" and Christopher says he remembers seeing the music room in the Ali Kapoo, where the acoustics were remarkable. The walls were decorated with cut outs of musical instruments, which do not seem to have altered since the days when they were built in the 16th century. They saw as much as they could in the three days they were there. John said much had changed, and our house was no longer there.

Peter and Mary's daughter was given a lift back to Teheran as she was flying back to the UK. I was very sad not to have seen Isfahan again, but at least Patricia had seen where she was born.

Not very long after the children had returned to school, word came that we were to go home on leave and have a new posting in Tunisia. We were quite sad that our tour was coming to an end. We had enjoyed our time in Iran, but were ready to see the families at home and to prepare for pastures new.

Chapter Eighteen

TUNISIA, 1965

While we were on leave John took delivery of a new Vauxhall VX 490 which he had bought at a discount via an agent in Doha. We used it for our leave in the UK, though the left hand drive was a bit of a nuisance, then drove it to Tunisia, which was to be our next posting.

While on leave we met Rosaleen, a distant cousin of John's from New Zealand. She had been ill, and wanted to have a chance to recover her strength, so we decided to take her with us as a nanny-cum-companion.

Rosaleen, Claire aged 3½, Tony, aged 18 months, John and I, all packed ourselves into the car and set off to Dover to catch the boat for Calais. There was no "Chunnel" in those days. We had booked a passage for the car from Marseilles to Tunis, but had not left much time to get there. We had to stop from time to time, of course, to stretch legs and eat, but it was a tedious drive to Bayeux where we spent the first night. We took the children to see the Bayeux Tapestries. It was the first time we had met the "wand guides" which "talked" us round the length of the tapestries. I had not realised at that time that the whole battle was shown in a long strip, and not a huge wall hanging.

The next day we drove to Blois and parked by the river. It looked very pretty, but was really rather smelly. This was a bit of a shock as the town and the river looked so inviting, and we wanted to walk along the banks and let the children run off some steam. However the air was quite nauseating that particular day, possibly because of the low water and the heat.

The hotel was adequate and Tony had a wonderful time turning on the bidet in the room he shared with Claire and Rosaleen. He really enjoyed the great waterspout that hit the ceiling. This discovery was unfortunate, as from then onwards he made a beeline for every bidet he came across. I am afraid we left a trail of wet floors behind us, as most rural French hotels had bidets in the bedrooms. This was before the days of en suite bathrooms. French plumbing has improved since those days, when most rural lavatories were the "hole in the floor" variety. Notices were hung over the washbasins informing people that the water was "non-potable." All drinking water was provided in bottles.

After a long and tiring drive, the following day we reached Nîmes. The remains of a Roman amphitheatre stood right in the middle of the town, with the traffic weaving round it. Sadly we had little time to see it properly as we were all tired and probably a little cross and hungry.

The next morning we drove on to Marseilles, where we had to leave the car in the port over night. We were not very happy about this. There was a great deal of luggage that had to be left in the unlocked car, with the keys left in it. It was not a drive-on ferry so the car had to be craned on board in a huge net. We did not see this take place, which was probably just as well. We were very proud of our, to date, scratch-free car.

Having booked into a hotel we then had the rest of the day free, so we decided to take a boat out to Chateau D'If, an island where, it is said, the "Man in the Iron Mask" was once imprisoned. It was a beautiful day and the sea was very blue. The launch or open ferry had about twenty passengers sitting around the sides. Claire, as usual, made her presence felt and was soon perched in front of the captain steering the boat. Tony, wearing his reins, was leaning perilously over the side, fascinated by the water rushing by. We explored the island and climbed the castle. The view from the top was spectacular and the skyline of Marseilles across the water was very picturesque. We were able to walk along a stone gallery and peer into the dark dungeons where the unfortunate prisoners often died centuries ago.

After leaving Marseilles Airport we crossed the Mediterranean to land in North Africa once again. It was hot and we felt we were home once more. Mary and Emile Marshi were there to meet us and take us to our new home in Gammarth near Carthage, on the outskirts of Tunis.

Dar el Diaf was a villa set on the hillside overlooking the sea. It was an unusual house. The front steps led up into a small hall with a tiny kitchen on the left. A large L shaped living room lay straight ahead, with huge patio doors that led onto the wide patio, overlooking the garden. A plot of open land at the end of the garden in front of the house, led down to the sea at the bottom of the slope.

Two sliding doors opened from the dining area into the master bedroom, with an en suite bathroom. This bedroom was nicknamed "the orgy room", as when the doors were opened wide the huge double bed was in full view of the reception area. A study at the back of the house looked out on the drive that led down the slope from the road above. There was a strange, windowless bath room at the foot of the stairs and three more bedrooms opening on to the garden. The large double garage and servants' quarters faced the sea under the patio to the left of the front door. All the windows were barred with very decorative ironwork. The bars on the windows ballooned out at windowsill level that allowed space for window boxes. They certainly were more attractive than straight burglar bars and made it safe to leave the windows open for fresh air. There was no air-conditioning in Tunisia. The plan of the house was indeed very strange, but we had to try to learn to live with it.

There was a cook/houseboy named Mahommed. Actually "boy" was a misnomer as he was probably in his 50s. His ability to produce good meals in the tiny cupboard of a kitchen was remarkable. The driver named Sharif and gardener Hammed completed our "staff."

The children and Rosaleen explored the house and garden

while Emile and Mary gave us some tips and hints about life in Tunisia. Mary had her own car and was very helpful by showing me round the local shops. I was delighted with the local markets in Gammarth and La Marsa. The souk in Tunis was very interesting and the cleanliness of the streets, the cheerfulness and friendliness of the Tunisians impressed me. This was in contrast to the general air of indifference often shown by the Libyans in our last posting.

Our car was soon collected from the port and I became independent. John was driven to the office each morning in the Bank car by Sharif, so I was free to entertain the children, Rosaleen and myself.

At first I found having Rosaleen around useful, in that I could leave the children at home while I explored the souk and various shopping centres on my own. Having children in tow was not ideal, as they soon got bored as I explored the variety of things available in the market. In the afternoons, when John came home, we loved to explore our new countryside.

Over the road and up at the top of the hill was a military cemetery. The regimented white crosses marched across the hillside in silent remonstration against the awful loss of life in that area during World War II. We visited the amphitheatre in Carthage where General Montgomery had harangued his troops. The whole area was steeped in history, from Punic civilisations to the modern day. There is little of Carthage standing now, as much was destroyed by the Arabs in Punic times and more has been damaged by earthquakes and marauding armies as various tribes struggled for position over the years. The ruins to be seen in Carthage are the remains of the cellars below ground. It is said that the Arabs "razed Carthage to the ground and ploughed salt into the land". There is one enormous carved capital lying, half buried, in the sand. The pillars of the original building must have been very impressive to support such a huge carving.

Below Carthage, down by the sea, lie the remains of the Punic Port of Salambo. It was a fascinating pastime to sit on the shingle beach sorting through the stones, looking for small Roman intaglio stones that occasionally became washed up on the beach. We had been shown some that had been found there, though we were not so lucky whenever we tried.

Many Roman artefacts were on sale in Tunisia, but it was very difficult to distinguish between the genuine article and those that had been "made yesterday." Pottery "Ali Baba" oil lamps were plentiful, as were the potteries where very realistic copies were made.

There were so many places of interest to visit that we were spoiled for choice. Sidi Bu Said, in contrast to the Roman remains, is a comparatively modern Tunisian village built on a hillside overlooking the sea. All doors and windows must be painted light blue by law and all the walls were whitewashed. The windows were protected by decorative ironwork, also painted light blue, with shutters opening inwards. It was a tourist village and a favourite place to buy "bombalinas". These were real doughnuts made while you watched, deep-fried in hot oil and then dipped in sugar. Delicious, once they were cool enough to eat. Often on the return from a trip we had to divert via Sidi Bu Said to have a bombalina before we drove home.

At weekends we liked to explore the countryside. The Punic remains at Utica were interesting in that they had unusual female capitals to the pillars, said to depict Diana the Huntress. Utica had been the capital of the area in circa 300 BC, before Carthage was destroyed by the Romans.

There is a magnificent Roman aqueduct which brought water from the hills to Carthage in Roman times. We traced it into the hills where it went underground. I am afraid we were not brave enough to crawl through the tunnel, as we were not sure what we would meet in the darkness. The wild flowers that grew in the stony earth were very delicate. There was a steep escarpment called Jebel Resass near the tunnel, which provided a good place to fly gliders, often to be seen swooping and diving in the area.

Another of our favourite outings was to the little Roman town of Dougga. This is an interesting place as it gives a good insight into what ordinary Roman urban life may well have been like. There were simple shops and houses and a small temple. Stalls depicting their wares could be distinguished in the marketplace. The fish stall had a dolphin carved into the supports at each end of the counter. The grain salesman had a sheaf of corn and a marked bowl cut into the counter. This had a hole in the bottom, which could be plugged. Grain was poured in to the requisite level and then the plug removed to allow the grain to flow into a container below. The poulterer had a cockerel carved on the legs of his stall table. If one closed one's eyes one might imagine ordinary Romans living in the town, rather than the grander residents so often depicted in the temples and houses found in most Roman archaeological sites.

We also liked to visit the little unpretentious Roman market town of Thuburba Majus. There was very little of note here, but it showed that not all Roman remains were temples and theatres, and that simple lives were lived in simple towns.

The Bank where John worked was in Habib Bourguiba Boulevard in Tunis. This was a wide street with a space down the middle where market stalls, shaded by oleander trees, offered a wide variety of goods. There is a wide variety of beautiful flowers in Tunisia, so the flower stalls were easily the most spectacular. Flowers grow easily in Tunisia and were on sale in abundance and in a great variety of colours.

This street led straight into the souk, where we could buy an impressive array of clothing. The loose-fitting kaftans appealed to the girls, as they were so cool to wear. Tricia also found a camel hair burnous decorated at the sleeves and pockets with ric-rac braiding which was warm and useful in the winter. Both Christopher and Patricia bought long black flowing hooded cloaks and wore them in London at their colleges. It seemed that the "anything goes" of the late 1960s had begun.

The summer weekends were usually spent at one beach or

another, as the sea was so tempting. However in the cooler weather we drove out to places like El Djem, a huge Roman amphitheatre in the middle of the desert, miles from anywhere. It was said to be in as good order as the Coliseum in Rome. However, as I have only seen pictures of the Coliseum, so I cannot compare. It was three storeys high and one could walk round the first floor much as in Roman times. With eyes closed one could imagine gladiators battling away with clashing swords, or poor old Christians being pursued by ravenous lions. There were the remains of cages in the basement where the lions could have been kept. Much of the beautiful mosaic flooring had been preserved in the museum nearby and in the Bardo Museum in Tunis.

Tunisia produces a great deal of pottery. Nabuel was one of the villages given over mainly to producing highly-decorated mugs, plates, jugs and bowls. We went to look round it one day and the children climbed up an enormous vase that had been constructed round a tree in the village square. They wanted to know if the pot was full of earth. It was, and there was a hornet's nest! They jumped down with great alacrity on discovering this.

As Tunisia is so close to the UK we were able to have the children for all their school holidays. Sometimes they brought friends with them. One weekend, when Patricia had her friend Ginny to stay, we all went to the Sinbad Hotel in Hammermet. There the children rode camels along the beach and forced their legs to propel pedalos on the sea. Judging by their red faces this required a great deal of effort with very little result. The beautiful water was so clean and blue, though a lot of jellyfish floating about caused a certain amount of consternation. The sand was white and soft and kept beautifully clean. We slept in chalets, surrounded by oleander bushes and with the sound of the sea lulling us to sleep.

The next day we were invited by one of John's customers to visit a tourist village which the Bank had helped to finance. There were several "cottage" industries being demonstrated. Weaving of traditional Tunisian rugs and examples of the potter's art were on display. A man and his horse performed circus tricks. A woman was grinding corn on a large flat square, by turning another stone, which closely resembled a Scottish curling stone, in short circular movements. She invited people to try their hand. It was hard work and we all found it very difficult to get up any speed. It seemed that it helped to shout "Hya Hya" while turning the stone. It required more muscles than we possessed, I fear.

We were provided with lunch at a long table and served by ladies dressed in Tunisian costume. The food was the traditional couscous, with lamb or goat meat and stewed root vegetables. It was a potted example of village life.

At home in the garden we had a small kidney-shaped pool. It was too small to swim in, but it was ideal for Claire and Tony to doggy-paddle. It was tiled with pale blue mosaic and looked pretty in the middle of the lawn. It was pleasant to have a real grass lawn to sit on, surrounded by wonderful flowers. As in the Lebanon, all plants seemed to be outsized. Our zinnias grew to stand six feet high, while the hibiscus, oleanders and wattle made a screen round the garden. I was very upset to discover that the gardener had set traps to catch birds in the garden. It seems they were considered a delicacy. I soon put a stop to that. In the migratory season many small birds arrived across the sea from Europe. The largest flocks arrived at Cap Blanc, the most northerly point of Africa, and could be seen flopping about trying to ease tired wings. Sometimes they arrived in our garden. It was interesting to watch them limbering up. They would swoop and dive and perch on a branch to flap their wings, then, after a day or so, they would all agree to depart on their journey south together.

Our house was close to the beach and Patricia and Christopher liked to invite various young people to come to breakfast after an early morning swim. Mohammed made "briques", which they all enjoyed. "Briques" were made with filou pastry folded over a raw egg to form a triangle and then deep-fried in hot oil. They were very difficult to eat without dripping egg yolk down one's front. The children made several friends and we all enjoyed their company.

Claire was nearly four and was ready for some sort of schooling. I started a little nursery group with some friends nearby, and five children came to me each morning for two hours. We sang songs and painted pictures or did some handwork. Four children were English-speaking and one little boy, Ahmed, was a Tunisian whose parents wanted him to learn to speak English.

I was most amused by the way Claire took it upon herself

to make sure that Ahmed understood what had been said. Sometimes she could be heard trying to help him to do something in a mixture of French and English. She learned this from the servants and from me, as all shopping was done in French. It was at this time that I learned how to make "play-dough" from flour, salt, water and cake-colouring. I remember creating owls out of fir-cones with sequins for eyes. These were stuck on to a piece of wood and a calendar was added. A dab of white paint sprinkled with glitter created a home-made Christmas present. The children enjoyed it all and Ahmed learned to speak English.

Owing to a shortage of foreign exchange, the Tunisian shops were not very well stocked with foreign goods on the whole. There were what I called feasts and famines of various items. I recall a shortage of loo paper and tissues. The Airmail Times newspaper was not a good substitute, as it tended to block the drains. The end result was that we asked visitors to bring loo rolls with them or we were reduced to stealing lengths from visits to hotels. There was a potato famine too, so we just had to live on rice. Decent meat was hard to come by, but I found a butcher in a village 40 miles along the coast and drove there with friends once a week to buy from him.

People liked to come with me as the journey was interesting. Just beyond Gammarth there was a small Bac (ferry) that carried about 6 cars across the river. The road then wound through farmland until we arrived at a small village where the butcher had his shop. He would cut the meat to order. I think the reason his meat was so much better than any other was that he understood the need for meat to hang for a while. He also sold plucked chickens and fresh eggs, which were hard to find in the market.

We were fortunate, as we had a small fishing port about a mile along the coast, near where we lived. I could buy live crayfish and prawns there, as well as flapping fresh Mediterranean fish. I disliked cooking the crayfish as it always sounded as if they were screaming as I popped them into the boiling water.

One morning we lost Tony. We could not find him anywhere, so we all spread out to search for him. Hammed took his bike and sped off down the road. After about half a mile he came upon Tony coming back from the little shop that sold sweets and coca-cola. He was quite happy half running along the road dressed just in his nappy and no shoes. When asked what he was doing he said "No sweeties, no money, no pocks", patting the sides of his nappy. He was quite unaware of the panic he had caused and was in no way distressed at being out on his own and, although under two years old, he was perfectly confident. Actually I felt that all the children were quite safe in Tunisia. Tunisians love children, like most Arabs, and at no time did I feel that they were in any danger.

One day the government announced that if a plot of land was not enclosed by a fence, it could be taken over and built upon. As one of our predecessors had acquired the land below our house to ensure that our sea view remained unobstructed, we thought we should put a fence round it. We also asked Hammed to dig the plot and plant sweetcorn and so put it to good use.

About this time the Israeli Six Day War broke out. This did not affect us very much as Tunisians did not seem to be unduly disturbed at that time; there was little anti-British feeling. There was, however, one day when a serious riot erupted downtown and the UK Embassy was burned. John was in the Bank and rang me to say that he was going to stay there until things had quietened down. I was worried about this. I rang him during the day to see if all was well and I could hear, down the phone, the roar of the crowd outside the Bank. John was very calm and said he felt the demonstration was calming down. I was to keep the children at home and not go out. It was quite late when John got home that night.

It was rumoured that the Tunisian Army was recruiting men to go to fight against Israel with the Egyptians, but I suspect that was mostly patriotic rhetoric. There were Jews living in Tunisia quite amicably. Most Tunisians appeared to be happy and peace loving. There was no oil, and therefore no great wealth, and little or none of the corruption it could bring.

One morning Hammed came to me to complain that the plot of land below the garden was very stony. I did not feel that he was the hardest of workers, so I just told him to dig it as best he could. Then one morning he staggered up to the house lugging a rather beautiful Ionic capital. I was surprised and went to see where he had found it. True the ground was very stony, but then it had not been dug for a long time. As the place was so near the walls of Carthage I imagined that it was part of the destroyed town. There was, after all, plenty of evidence of the existence of grand buildings at one time all over Gammarth. I told him to continue to dig.

Soon after we arrived we felt that something had to be done about our house. The bedrooms downstairs and the internal bathroom beside the boiler room were not very convenient. I spent a lot of time redesigning the place. I thought that three single bedrooms could be built at the front, opening on to the garden, with a bathroom at the end. A large double bedroom could be made out of the large existing room which overlooked the rose garden at the side of the house. An en suite bathroom with a fifth bedroom/dressing room would complete the sleeping area. The "orgy room" would become the dining room and the old bathroom would become the servery. The study would become the kitchen and the tiny existing kitchen would make an excellent storeroom. Building the bedrooms along the front would extend the already large patio from which the magnificent view could be appreciated. It would be ideal for entertaining. A flight of steps would lead down to the garden.

Was it too much to hope that the Bank would sanction such a huge operation? Much to our joy, after a few suggestions and advice from the architect, we were allowed to go ahead.

About this time the Tunisian Government decided that they required me to pay duty on my car. The amount required was nearly double what we had paid for it in the first place.

This was a blow. My lovely car, the first new car I had ever owned, was set up on bricks in our capacious garage and the clutch pedal secured with a customs seal. I eventually sold it to a Romanian diplomat who was not required to pay duty. The next time I saw my car it was in the garage having been quite badly smashed. I was very sad.

I required transport, however, and John set out to find me a cheap substitute. Obviously we could not afford anything exotic and I could always have the use of the Bank car for "state occasions." In due course an inexpensive Renault 4L was found. It was not the prettiest vehicle on the road and it had an almost obscene gear stick that stuck out of the dashboard. However it "went," and what is even more important in my eyes, it "stopped." I was mobile again.

The time came for Rosaleen to return to the UK and I set out to find a local maid to help in the house and look after the children when I was out. We found Zohrah, a pleasant girl, but she did not speak English. The children could understand French well enough and Claire was actually quite fluent. I required help to keep an eye on the children as the trenches dug in the garden for our building foundations were quite deep and dangerous.

When the builders got to the drains and electrical stage, John suggested that I take the children and Zohrah home for a break while he lodged with some Canadian friends who lived next door. Arrangements were made and Granny Lindesay met us at Heathrow. I remember Zohrah asking,

"When are we going to get out of this big park?" as we drove home. It made me realise how we all take our green and pleasant land for granted. Tunisia is mainly barren desert and the little greenery is confined to parks and gardens. To Zohrah, England was one big park.

Claire took it upon herself to be Zohrah's interpreter, translating very well when required. On one occasion I drove them all into Southampton to do some shopping. I suggested to Zohrah that she could do some window shopping and walk round the block and come back to where I had parked the car, while I went into Sainsburys'.

When I returned to the car there was no sign of the children. I decided that they must have been doing another circuit. Then I saw them coming. Zohrah was carrying a large dress box and all three were wearing broad grins. It appeared that Zohrah had seen a suit in the window of a boutique and had gone in to purchase it. The salesperson did not speak French, so Claire had successfully translated. I was truly amazed.

My parents invited us to go up to Scotland. As my father was not very PC about coloured people I was a little apprehensive about what he would say when he saw Zohrah's black face - she was unusually dark skinned for a Tunisian. I need not have worried as he became firm friends with Zohrah and greeted her each morning with "Bonjour, où est la plume de ma tante?" Zohra replied "Bonjour. C'est dans le jardin." Both laughed uproariously.

Every day Dad took Zohrah and his grandchildren out on

a jaunt to some interesting place or other, Claire acting as interpreter. One day Tony managed to cut his forehead on a swing in the park. He was taken to the Infirmary and stitched up by an Arab doctor. Zohrah was in her element and took charge of the situation, happily chattering away in Arabic. Tony was very proud of the "sewing" on his forehead. Poor Grandad was more shaken than Tony and was very impressed by Zohrah's capabilities. He was so impressed that when the time came for me to return south to attend a function at Patricia and Christopher's schools, he suggested that Zohrah remain up there with the children, and he would put them on the train the following week. Zohrah was quite happy with this arrangement, so I set off myself to spend a little time with the older two children.

My father put the children on the train at Carlisle and spoke to the dining attendant to arrange for them to be escorted to the dining car for lunch. I had given Zohrah a letter to give to a policeman, if by any chance I was not there in time to meet them at Euston Station. I was there, however, and escorted them to Waterloo Station and on to the train to Winchester. I was amazed at the number of people on the train who greeted the children by name. It seems that Claire had gone up to people on the train from Scotland and explained that Zohrah couldn't read, so would they please read to them. It appears that she gave everyone a turn! How kind people were.

We said our goodbyes to Patricia and Christopher and Granny Lindesay and returned to Tunis. John met us and we were in a hurry to see how the house had turned out. I was thrilled. Everyone had worked hard to prepare for our return and the whole project was a success. The children were pleased with their rooms and I loved our new reception area and the lovely kitchen. I couldn't wait to have a party and show it all off.

Not long after my return Hammed came up with another Ionic capital and said that he had come across some sort of wall very near the surface. We thought in terms of an Italian pillbox left from the war. Then Hammed reported a mosaic floor! This was too smart to be a pillbox, we decided, so we asked the Bardo Museum in Tunis to come and have a look at what we had found.

They were very excited, because usually things were only discovered when builders were digging foundations of houses and they were reluctant to report findings lest they be delayed in their work. The Bardo Museum said that they would send a team to dig the site for us. This was very exciting and Hammed was very pleased too. He was relieved that he had to struggle with the digging no longer!

The children and all our visitors were interested to help the archaeologists who arrived every weekday to gently brush and scrape the hard clay soil from the remains, which turned out to be of Punic origin. They uncovered a bath and a well from which the water had been drawn, as well as a mosaic floor. It was not a picture, as in the Roman remains. It was made up of small one inch tiles of a rust colour, randomly interspersed with cream ones. There was a doorway leading on to a step into the street that was paved with stone slabs. In the doorway there were pyramid-shaped holes where probably a door hinge had been. There was also an amphora-shaped pot lying, set in the wall, to act as a drain from the room into the street.

Lower down the hill they uncovered a large stone cube with a groove along the top. The experts said that this was the base of a Punic olive oil press. There were the remains of vats where the oil had been collected and then there was a store room with holes in the floor where large amphora had stood. There was evidence of decorated plaster that had been stuck to reeds on the walls and ceiling, and low bench-like seats set around the walls of the room. Very little pottery was found, but we were given a pot lid about four inches across with a knop intact.

It was very exciting to have our own dig in our garden and the family got up early in the morning, as soon as it was light, to try their hands at excavating in the cool. One day Christopher hid a Roman coin in the ground for the archaeologists to find. The discovery caused great consternation as it upset the dating of the construction. Chris' confession that he had planted the coin was greeted with relief. Sadly no coins or anything really valuable came to light, but it was exciting to visualise the people working there so long ago.

Then, about three months after the house was completed, John was posted to Morocco.

Chapter Nineteen

MOROCCO, 1969

Our house in Morocco was called Kasr el-Kheir and was large and spacious and stood in a pleasant garden. It was furnished with heavy Spanish furniture. There were four bedrooms and one bathroom but there were basins in the bedrooms. A marble staircase led from the large hall to the upstairs. There was a large modern kitchen and the servants' quarters were out the back.

The people before us had run a gambling casino in the house and a lot of people had the key to my front door, as I was to find out. I remember opening a cupboard door and being knocked down by a whole lot of packs of cards, stripped as if used for poker.

Our cook was called Fedela and she was a suitable build for her profession. She wore a voluminous kaftan and a copious apron. The maid was called Ouza. She was of a slighter build and wore a slightly more European-type frock, but was still old fashioned. The gardener was called Laarbi. It turned out that Laarbi was also assistant gardener to the King, and he "imported" several Zinnias to my garden from the Royal Palace. We were not to find this out until we noticed that our flowers were diseased and we discovered that the King's flowers had the same problem! The garden was fairly large with a banana tree and two orange trees at the back. Another orange tree at the front had a lemon tree grafted on to it, which was handy for gin and tonics. There was a large tree in the centre of the lawn in which we eventually built a tree house for the children, who delighted in telling of an occasion when I climbed into the tree house, up the rope ladder. I have no head for heights but I wanted to make sure it was safe and secure for the children to play in. When I got up there I panicked. I simply froze in terror because I couldn't get down. I told the children to phone their father and to ask him to come at once to get me down. The children nearly died with laughter, which did not help me one bit. Eventually John arrived and was not pleased with me for making such a fuss. I made a mental note not to do anything like it again. I felt very stupid but I was very glad to be down on terra firma.

At one point we invited the Chandlers, our next door neighbours in Tunis, to come and stay with us. My instructions to them to get to our house were to drive round the coast of Africa until they found a round house on stilts, and then to turn first left and then left again– we were the first house on the right. Amazingly enough they found us!

The other notable landmark near our house was the Anfa Hotel, where Churchill, Eisenhower and Stalin met during the Second World War.

Fairly early on in our time in Morocco, we bought a second-hand Vauxhall Cresta car for me, which we nicknamed the Old Lady. It was useful for taking Claire and Tony to school. Claire went to a Catholic school, run by very strict nuns, who taught in French. Later on she was to make herself very unpopular at school in England, I was told, by correcting her French mistress when she made an error when speaking in French. Claire spoke French better than English at that time.

Tony went to a boy's Catholic kindergarten. Much of the morning was spent on the school run, taking Claire first for eight o'clock and then taking Tony at nine o'clock and collecting the children at lunchtime each day, as they stopped for lunch at different times, and Claire returned for another hour and a half each afternoon. It was all very time consuming.

When Chris and Trisha came back for their school holidays it was impossible to ferry all the children about, so we bought two Solex bicycles for them. These are French bikes halfway between a push bike and a small motor bike, with a small engine on the front wheel that could be engaged to help up hills – although actually it was deployed most of the time! Thus the teenagers could be free to join their friends on various local expeditions. I was especially pleased as this saved me acting as a taxi so often.

I would go to the market at 7 am as it was less crowded and I got the choice of the fruit and vegetables. The Bank opened at seven anyway, so our day began early.

We belonged to the Club de Clubs, where there was a

swimming pool. Tony used to frighten everyone as he would announce that he could not swim and would need help, just before jumping in off the top of the diving board, thereby causing a rush to the rescue. He appeared to have no fear!

We bought a "caravan pliante" which was a folding tent on a trailer. It was a splendid holiday home which we used to visit various beaches and tourist attractions. The base was a 6' x 9' Trailer that opened up to form a kitchen, and the two halves of the lid formed two double beds. We all had our jobs to do when setting up on arrival at a camp site, and we were very proud of ourselves when we achieved four and a half minutes from ignition off to kettle on. Our tent unfolded to 18 feet by 12 under cover including the "auvent" in which we had created separate rooms for Patricia and Christopher. Claire and Tony slept "east to west" across one of the large double bunks formed by one of the lids, while John and I slept on the other. Wherever we went we were known as the "Palace" and we used to draw quite an audience. We spent most weekends in it and even took it on the continent and drove ourselves through Spain and France to England for John's leave.

Some friends of ours had a tiny little television set. On the day of the moon landing in July 1969 they were away, but we had the key to their house. All four of us watched together as Neil Armstrong walked on the moon. It was early in the morning, I recall, but well worth the effort.

Pru Cookhurle came in order to set up a Cheshire Home in Morocco. She stayed with us for about a month before finding a place to start a home for handicapped children in Marrakesh, two hours drive up the road. She also found a lady to run it.

Group Captain Leonard Cheshire came out to stay with us and officially open the Home. He told us he had been in the plane that had dropped the atomic bomb on Hiroshima which brought the end of World War II. The loss of life and damage it caused inspired him to dedicate the rest of his life to helping people where he could. This Home in Marrakesh was part of this pledge. He was a delightful guest and asked for scrambled egg for supper.

The home was for handicapped children and I became their "Auntie in Casablanca," as they would come to Casablanca Hospital for operations. I would meet the older ones off the train, visit them in hospital and bring them socks and toys and other little things. But I had difficulty in talking to them as many of them were Berber children and I could not speak Berber. Arabic was difficult enough and their French was a mixture of French, Arabic and Berber.

We were also members of the Churchill Club, which was the heart of the British community. It was the nearest thing to a pub and was a wonderful meeting place for all ex pats. We had dances, whist drives, amateur dramatic productions, bridge evenings and many children's birthday parties there. Christopher once won a beauty competition after being made up by Trisha and her friends. The judges had been chosen as they were strangers to the community. Unfortunately the people who knew who Chris was would not allow it to stand, as they thought it was too embarrassing for the girls.

We used to go skiing at Oukimadine, high in the Atlas Mountains, where the Churchill Club had a chalet. The bunks were three stacks high and were ranged round the large room which afforded little privacy. We did not stay there and preferred to stay in the more conventional chalet. Many weekends were enjoyed there during the winter.

Stephen, my brother, came to visit once with a friend. He borrowed the Old Lady and drove up to Marrakesh, where he unfortunately ate something and spent time feeling "indisposed". His impressions of Marrakesh were somewhat coloured by this experience. We, however, were very rarely "indisposed" in all our time in the Middle East. I think we became immune simply by living there.

Winnie Russell descended on us. We had met her before when she came through Teheran on of one of her jaunts. –we received a phone call one afternoon from a complete stranger, who said he had been asked to ring us by Winnie, whom he had met on the ferry from Spain, to tell us that she was expected to arrive at Casablanca station at 5.45 pm. Please would we meet her. We were going to a cocktail party, but we went to meet her, delivered her home and left her to be settled in by the servants.

Winnie was a lady who lived in Scotland in same village as my parents. She was of a good age and was not averse to using her friends and acquaintances to enable her to see the world.

She had little money but always paid her way in kind. This could be a mixed blessing at times! She was not a lady accustomed to doing nothing, so she persuaded me to allow her to re-cover my dining chairs and in this way to earn her keep. This did not bode too well as John soon began to ask me when she was leaving!

Eventually we found Winnie a job with the Cheshire home in Marrakesh doing the job she had been trained for, occupational therapy. After a while she moved on to the Save the Children's Home in Fez, where she worked for some time before she returned to the UK and found a little house in The Tory, Bradford-on-Avon. But, I am sad to say, she later went into a home and did not recognise us when we went to visit her.

We were invited to Christmas with the Barber family, where we had our first oysters. The Barbers had lived in Casablanca for a long time and were probably the leading expat family. There were five children in the family, so inevitably our children became good friends as they were much of an age.

One holiday we decided to park the caravan-pliante at the beach some distance from Casablanca and allow the teenagers to stay there. Word got around, and about ten or twelve youngsters joined in. There was a café at the beach and a sweet water tap. We left Trisha, Christopher and the three older Barber children in charge. As there was a typhoid warning I decided to ferry drinking water to them all, as we could not trust the water there. I also ferried picnic food to them all but I omitted to add additional cutlery and china, with the result that when they decided to have ravioli, they cooked it in the pan then set it on the table and just shared the six forks we had in the caravan. Similarly they shared the six eggcups and teaspoons when they had boiled eggs for breakfast. Not ideal from the hygienic point of view, but all seemed well and they all were allowed to go another time.

There was nearly a terrible accident, which I did not hear about at the time. Tony was knocked over by a wave and fortunately hit one of the boys' legs. The undertow was very strong there and it was lucky Tony was grabbed in time. Trisha managed to calm him down, so all was well.

My brother Stephen and I decided to send my parents on a cruise to celebrate their ruby wedding anniversary, and we all chose a boat which stopped for a couple of nights in Casablanca. We were very excited about this, and so were the children. We rushed down to meet the boat when it arrived and were duly shown over it.

We had invited a few friends in for lunch to meet them. They had brought all sorts of things for Claire and Tony including a large Spacehopper on which we were all keen to have a go. Sadly Frank Barber fell awkwardly on his turn, and broke his collar bone. After we had taken him to hospital we took my parents for a drive round the town to visit all our favourite haunts.

The next day I left Gampy in the garden and took Granjo to the souk to look for a few souvenirs. On our return Gampy was somewhat disgruntled, as Fedela had brought in two

Jehovah's Witnesses who had called at the door. I knew that my father had little time for these people but it had taken some time to politely get rid of them. We had never had a visit from these people before and never saw them again. It was strange they had chosen that day, the only day he had in Casablanca, of all days to call.

Gampy expressed a desire to go for a ride on the teenagers' Solex bicycles, which he much enjoyed. We invited more people in for dinner that night and took them back to the ship the next day. It was lovely to see them and for my Dad to have at least visited us once

Claire was learning about money at school. She decided to become a little entrepreneur all on her own. She had been making paper lanterns at school, so she set up a table outside the gate and proceeded to sell these lanterns at 1 dirham each. She sold a few to kindly neighbours before we knew about it. My brother was staying with us and proceeded to play with her by adding and removing dirhams from her purse when she wasn't looking, then asking her how much she had made, as he had forgotten. She always came up with a different amount. She won in the end as she took her purse away when she had 9 dirhams in it. I suspect she smelled a rat! !

On occasion British Navy ships would dock at Casablanca and the community were asked by the Consul to entertain the officers and men in some way. We went to cocktail parties on the boats sometimes too. It was about this time that we invited several sailors to come for lunch and to have a swim at the

Club. I think that both the sailors and the children enjoyed these outings. I remember Tony causing amusement by saying "Look how fast these shoes can run with me on them!" and demonstrating enthusiastically.

The time came when John was told to go on leave and prepare to become Chief Inspector in the British Bank of Kuwait and the Middle East.

Sadly we sold the Old Lady and the caravan-pliante and the children sold their Solexes and said goodbye to all our friends and left for UK.

Chapter Twenty

KUWAIT

Just before we were due to leave the UK for Kuwait, Tony was given a hamster. On the instructions of BOAC I proceeded to get a health certificate for it. I took the animal to the vet in Romsey and dared him to laugh at me when I made my request. He held it in his hand and looked it in the face and said that the eyes were good and bright and asked me what sex it was. I told him that I did not know but that its name was Sarah. Ah, he said, then wrote a note declaring that to the best of his knowledge Sarah Hamster was in good health. He then told me that it was nearly impossible to sex a little hamster, so my guess was as good as any.

We took off for Kuwait, complete with our hamster in its cage. Our arrival at Kuwait Airport caused quite a stir as Hammy proceeded to pedal madly round in the wheel in his cage. In spite of hamsters being indigenous to desert countries the customs men had not seen one before. Perhaps this was because they are nocturnal and only rarely seen. Hammy seemed to be celebrating coming back to his or her ancestral home.

Our new home was a pleasant villa in a row of similar houses. Kuwait was quite a modern town with mainly large blocks of flats and several rows of villas. As in Doha, the sheikhs lived in large houses with large well-stocked gardens. The roads were wide, well maintained and fairly busy. There were lots of interesting buildings round the town of which the huge water tower on the beach stretching high over the port, shaped like huge golf tee, was probably the most spectacular. Alongside this tiled spire, there hung a huge globe containing a revolving restaurant. The whole area had the appearance of wealth. The shops were stocked with every conceivable luxury item from electrical goods to clothes and ornamental china from all over the world. This was a far cry from the very early oil days of these desert Emirates to which we had first been introduced some 19 years ago.

Our house was near the Hilton Hotel, where many important people stayed, including the boxer Mohammed Ali, whose autograph Tony got on his own mini boxing gloves.

There was a large British community and the social life was considerable. Officially there was no alcohol permitted, but I think it was the hardest drinking community we had found in the Middle East. There was a cocktail party most weeks and dinner parties too. I suspect that, provided you did not call attention to yourself, the Kuwaitis were less strict than their Wahabi Saudi neighbours. Bottles of whisky were available at £15 to £20 a bottle, but then I suppose the sellers ran a big risk of being caught. Most bottles were imported, so I understand, by hanging them under the bellies of goats and camels. I don't think many customs men would dare to look there!

Tony went to the English school, which was popular and well attended. I taught in the Kindergarten and gave French oral classes there for two days per week. While I was teaching there Claire, who was at school in the UK, had fallen off a horse and had broken her arm and was in traction in hospital. As she was likely to be there for some time I flew home to be with her. The poor child was on a fracture board, as the break was too high on the arm to be put in plaster or a splint. Tony remained in Kuwait with John and was cared for by friends.

Most people spent their free time at the beach at the swimming club. The water was pleasantly warm and usually calm, so we were able to meet friends there and have picnics. There was a sailing club, but it was at Ahmadi, the KPC (Kuwait Petroleum Company), about an hour's drive up the coast. John bought a plastic Yak sailing boat which he could teach the children to sail. This he did by wading out as deep as he could and then letting the children row out as far as the painter would allow, then put the sail up and sail round him at the end of the rope and turn into the wind each time he called out "LEO". This was not the easiest way to teach them, but at least they did not sail away into the Gulf. There was no safety boat.

One of Tony's friends acquired a mini motorbike and Tony, aged seven, learned to ride it. Then John decided to buy one for Tony too. We all had fun riding it in the desert and eventually we took it home to the UK.

My friend Betty Gunter and I decided we would run a Ladies' Meeting Point at the Hilton Hotel. We found that there were several young mothers coming into Kuwait who were finding it hard to meet people as there was no club or other place to foregather. This proved to be very popular and made life more pleasant for everyone, as the community passed on the word and it steadily grew.

The previous year Trish had got married, to Toby. Then one night at 2 am we received a telephone call from Toby to say that we had become grandparents, of Rebecca. Needless to say we were very proud and had a great time boasting about this news. The only trouble John could see was he had to admit he was sleeping with a Granny! I couldn't wait to get home to see the new addition to the family.

There were a lot of Japanese working in Kuwait and they had built a golf course in the desert with "browns" instead of greens. Players would carry a square of plastic grass round with them and place their ball on it before hitting it. This was very necessary, as the ground was so stony. They also had red balls, as these were easier to see than the customary white ones. Monthly competitions began very early in the morning and ended up at someone's house for a curry lunch, which made a very pleasant day out. Most of the players took their turn and these lunches became popular international occasions. We were very proud when John won a cup on several occasions.

When Tony turned eight he went to school in England. We had found Walhampton prep School some ten years earlier for

Christopher and he had been very happy there, so we sent Tony there too. By this time John was sufficiently senior to be sent on annual leave, so we were not too bereft when he went. We saw the children out in Kuwait for two holidays a year and always arranged for our leave over the third.

We were making plans for John's retirement when he received a letter to ask him if he would like to defer it for three months and go to do a special job in Hong Kong. He had not seen the Far East since he had been in the Japanese Occupation Force just after the war, so we very pleased to accept.

We flew to Hong Kong and landed at Kai Tak airport. This was a strip of land jutting out into Victoria Harbour and was reached by flying in between blocks of flats, with washing hanging out level with the plane's wings. If one dared to look, one could almost see the people looking out of their windows. I found it quite scary the first time we did it. Later on they knocked down a mountain on Lantau Island and built the airport out there.

The original three months turned into three more years, so we spent it out there, living in luxury flats and having lovely weekends on yachts, or in holiday villas on the islands or in Macao. The children came out for wonderful holidays. All in all, it was a far better deal than our Saudi Arabian days. We had come a long way since then and seen many changes.

We also arranged to fly home, with Tony and Claire, during the summer holidays via the Seychelles and Kenya, where we had a wonderful ten-day safari. On another occasion we took them to America, where we visited Hawaii and Disneyland and Magic Mountain theme park. Then on to Las Vegas, Grand Canyon and Niagara Falls. We ended our holiday by visiting New York. All a fitting end to 30 years of life with the Bank; longer for John.

When John retired in 1980 we moved to Romsey in Hampshire. It was the end of an interesting career and the beginning of a happy retirement. I still treasure my many memories of those years in the heat and dust of the Middle East, raising a family and learning how life is lived in those fascinating countries. And in the end, I did learn to boil an egg.